College Reading

Book

2

College Reading

Book

2

Fourth Edition

Janet Maker-Inmon
Los Angeles Trade-Technical College

Minnette Lenier
Los Angeles Pierce College

Wadsworth Publishing Company
Belmont, California

A Division of Wadsworth, Inc.

English Editor: Angela Gantner
Editorial Assistant: Lisa Ensign
Production: Cece Munson, The Cooper Company
Designer: John Odam
Print Buyer: Randy Hurst
Copy Editor: Toni Haskell
Illustrator: John Odam
Cover Photo: Ron Sherman, Uniphoto
Compositor: Thompson Type, San Diego, CA
Printer: Vail-Ballou Press, Kirkwood, NY

*This book is printed on acid-free paper that meets
Environmental Protection Agency standards
for recycled paper.*

3 4 5 6 7 8 9 10 — 96 95 94 93 92

Library of Congress Cataloging-in-Publication Data

College reading. Book 2 / [compiled by] Janet
Maker-Inmon, Minnette Lenier. -- 4th ed.
    p.   cm.
  ISBN 0-534-17082-X
  1. College readers. 2. Reading (Higher education)
I. Maker-Inmon, Janet. II. Lenier, Minnette.
PE1122.C572 1992
428.6 — dc20   91-29341
                              CIP

Credits continue on page 469.

Contents

Contents by Skills

LOCATING KEY CONCEPTS

Main Ideas and Support

Words That Signal Key Concepts

Underlining Key Concepts

USING THE LIBRARY

SKIMMING AND SCANNING

READING CRITICALLY

Inferences

Author's Purpose

Argument and Support

Judging Support

READING FOR STUDY

SQ3R

Outlining

Study Mapping

To the Instructor

College Reading: Book 2 was written for students who need directed practice to develop college reading skills. The fourth edition stresses the coverage of reading fundamentals and skills practice and places emphasis on critical reading and textbook reading. The new edition is divided into three sections. Each section begins with instruction in reading skills followed by ten nonfiction articles of increasing difficulty. Articles are then followed by exercises reinforcing the skills taught in that section. The first section, Reading Fundamentals, gives the reader a thorough introduction to vocabulary skills — using the dictionary, word parts and etymology, using context clues, multiple meanings of words, and word memory. The section also covers basic comprehension skills — main ideas and support, words that signal key concepts, underlining key concepts, and using the library. The second section, Advanced Reading Skills, teaches critical reading and reading efficiency. The third section, Reading for Study, uses readings from college textbooks to teach SQ3R, outlining, study mapping, and summarizing.

Each reading selection is preceded by a Vocabulary Preview and instructions for surveying before reading. The articles can also be timed so that you may work on rate. The ten comprehension questions that follow each article are divided into three categories: subject and main idea, details, and inferences. Following the questions is an exercise that uses the article's vocabulary words in the context of sentences. Finally, there are two or more Skills Exercises. A box accompanying most exercises refers students to the page where that skill is explained.

To help students pinpoint their weak areas, there are several charts at the back of the book. The Rate Chart allows students to compute the number of words they can read per minute. The Comprehension Chart is for recording responses to each article's comprehension questions. The Progress Chart tracks comprehension and rate. These charts help you to identify students who need individual attention and to group students with similar abilities.

Answers to exercises are available in the *Instructor's Resource Manual*. The manual also contains a timed pretest and posttest, using two articles of the same readability level as those found in Unit II. Because the articles in the book progress in difficulty, the improvement in student reading rate and comprehension may not be so evident on the Progress Chart as it is on the pretest and posttest. The manual also contains readability statistics, perception exercises, and supplementary activities for vocabulary improvement. Pages are 8½″ × 11″ and are perforated for easy reproduction.

Instructors who wish their students to have the answers can order individual *complimentary answer booklets* from the publisher.

College Reading: Book 2 has two tables of contents: one arranged by article and one arranged by skill. If you decide to stay with a particular skill rather than use our spiral sequence, you can refer to the skills table of contents.

Because *College Reading: Book 2* reflects the variety of materials encountered in the college environment, it lends itself to a number of courses. It can be used in homogeneous developmental courses that emphasize comprehension and basic skills or in heterogeneous classes that include students who need more advanced training in rate. The Rate Chart, the materials for skimming and scanning, and the additional materials in the *Instructor's Resource Manual* can be emphasized with students who need extended practice in power and efficiency.

Acknowledgments

For their assistance in preparation of the fourth edition we wish to thank Claudia Gumbiner, Steve Lenier, Ilene McBride, Kathleen Tucker, Cece Munson, production coordinator, and those individuals who carefully reviewed the content of this book: Carol H. Bader, Middle Tennessee State University; Mary Ann DeArmond, San Antonio College; Jane B. Johnson, Bakersfield College; Carolyn M. Lewis, West Valley College; Betty O'Brien, West Valley College; and Nora Woodard, Valencia Community College. We also thank the many students who helped us test the book. We wish to extend a special thanks to Angie Gantner, English Editor at Wadsworth, who was always a source of pertinent suggestions and invaluable information.

To the Student Reader

According to a study reported in this book, "college students spend 8 percent of their time writing, 20 percent reading, 22 percent speaking, and 50 percent of their time listening."* The purpose of *College Reading: Book 2* is to help you spend your reading time as efficiently as possible.

To help you accomplish this goal, we have assembled a variety of reading materials that are interesting, informative, and practical. Articles were chosen from newspapers, magazines, popular books, and textbooks. Several of the articles deal with essential college skills, such as vocabulary improvement, public speaking, writing, study techniques, library use, memory improvement, and listening.

The book is divided into three sections. The first section, Reading Fundamentals, teaches basic skills in vocabulary and comprehension. The second section, Advanced Reading Skills, teaches critical reading and reading efficiency. The third section, Reading for Study, teaches SQ3R, outlining, study mapping, and summarizing.

Each of the thirty articles in Units I, II, and III begins with a Vocabulary Preview, which introduces all the difficult words in the article. Next, you are given directions for surveying the article. Understanding the vocabulary and surveying the article in advance will increase your reading speed and comprehension. There are spaces immediately before and after each article to record your reading time; you can enter your speed on the chart in the back of the book.

After you have read the article, you will answer ten comprehension questions. Two questions test your knowledge of the subject and the main idea, four questions test your memory of details, and four test your understanding of inferences. In the back of the book is a Comprehension Chart for recording your scores. With this chart you will be able to determine in which of the three areas your strengths and weaknesses lie, so you can give special attention to the areas in which you need the most practice.

---

* Rudolph F. Verderber, "Listening to Speeches," excerpted from *The Challenge of Effective Speaking* (Belmont, Calif.: Wadsworth Publishing Company, 1979), page 16.

Following the comprehension questions is an exercise called Vocabulary in Context. It tests your ability to use the words that were introduced in the Vocabulary Preview.

The final element accompanying each article is two or more Skills Exercises to reinforce the skills discussed in the instruction section. Your instructor will give you the answers to the exercises. When you find that you have made an error, you should go back to the article to try to understand why you were wrong. If you can't figure it out, refer to the pages in the instruction section where the skill was discussed. If this review doesn't clarify your mistake, it is important that you ask your instructor to explain it to you. You can learn more from wrong answers, if you use them correctly, than from right ones.

College Reading

Book

2

UNIT I

READING FUNDAMENTALS

If you are an average full-time college student, you read between eight and ten textbooks per year, or 5000 pages — not counting any other reading you do for work or for pleasure. Handling this load efficiently and getting high grades is the challenge you have to meet. Improving your reading efficiency is simply a matter of developing a few skills: improving vocabulary, locating key concepts, reading for study, making inferences, reading critically, and increasing reading flexibility. In Unit I you will work on vocabulary skills and the comprehension skills of identifying the subject, main idea, and supporting details.

IMPROVING VOCABULARY

One common reason for poor reading speed and comprehension is a poor vocabulary. If you don't understand many of the words in a chapter or article, you will not be able to grasp important concepts without taking the time to look up the words. You can increase your vocabulary by using context clues and the dictionary, and you can remember words through some of the techniques explained below.

Context Clues

You learned most of the words you know by hearing or seeing them in a particular context. When you find a new word in your reading, take a moment to see whether you can figure out its meaning from the sentence or the paragraph that it's in.

In the following four sentences, you can figure out the meanings of the difficult words by using four types of context clues: definition clues, contrast clues, example clues, and experience clues. Circle the letter of the definition that comes closest to the meaning of the underlined word.

1. It's usually hard to <u>differentiate</u>, or tell the difference between, identical twins.
   a. confuse
   b. distinguish
   c. talk to
   d. ignore

The answer is b. The context clue used in this sentence is a **definition clue**. The phrase *or tell the difference* defines the word *differentiate*.

2. Anywhere from limited to <u>extensive</u> damage can be caused by a hurricane.
   a. major
   b. minor
   c. unusual
   d. new

The answer is a. The context clue used in this case is a **contrast clue**. Extensive damage is contrasted with limited damage.

3. Examples of holidays unique to the <u>heritage</u> of the United States are the Fourth of July and Thanksgiving.
   a. tradition
   b. future
   c. problems
   d. economics

The answer is a. The context clue used is an **example clue**. The sentence gives examples of holidays unique to the heritage of the United States.

4. Most students are <u>elated</u> when final exams are over.
   a. depressed
   b. anxious
   c. angry
   d. joyous

The answer is d. The context clue used is an **experience clue**. Anyone who has ever taken final exams knows that students are happy when they are over.

Dictionary

Sometimes the context does not provide a clue to meaning, or sometimes you cannot understand the ideas being presented without finding out what a word means. In such cases, you will have to use a dictionary. Most people know how to look words up, but very few know how to make the most out of the information that a good dictionary provides.

A dictionary entry has five major parts.

1. main entry
2. pronunciation
3. part or parts of speech
4. etymology (word history)
5. definitions

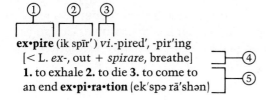

ex•pire (ik spīr′) *vi.*-pired′, -pir′ing
[< L. *ex-*, out + *spirare*, breathe]
1. to exhale **2.** to die **3.** to come to
an end **ex•pi•ra•tion** (ek′spə rā′shən)

When you look up a word in the dictionary, the first thing you see is
the **main entry**. The main entry word is divided into syllables, and the
syllables are separated by dots.

The **pronunciation** appears in parentheses after the main entry. You
can figure out how to pronounce words by using the brief pronunciation guide, which is usually located at the bottom of every other page. A
full explanation of pronunciation is usually at the beginning of a dictionary. Here is a brief pronunciation guide from *Webster's New World
Dictionary:*

> fat, āpe, cär; ten, ēven; is, bīte; gō, hôrn, tōōl, look; oil, out; up, fur; chin, she;
> thin, *then*; zh, leisure; ŋ, ring; ə for *a* in *ago;* ' as in *able* (ā′b′l)

It is sometimes necessary to use the pronunciation guide because
you can't always tell how to pronounce a word from its spelling. There
are twenty-six letters in English representing about forty-four sounds,
depending on one's dialect. For example, the letter *a* is pronounced differently in the words *cat* (kat), *father* (fä′ther), *admit* (əd mit′), *all* (ôl),
and *late* (lāt).

One sound that is common in English is the **schwa sound**. It is
written ə and is pronounced "uh." It occurs in unstressed syllables. A
stressed syllable is pronounced in a louder voice than an unstressed
syllable. For example, in the word *admit* (əd mit′), the stress is on the
second syllable. The schwa sound can be spelled with any vowel letter,
but it is always pronounced the same way.

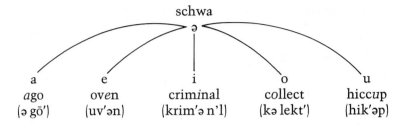

schwa

ə

a	e	i	o	u
ago	*oven*	crim*i*nal	collect	hicc*up*
(ə gō′)	(uv′ən)	(krim′ə n′l)	(kə lekt′)	(hik′əp)

When you look up a word in the dictionary, you should always take the time to figure out its pronunciation. If you can pronounce a word to yourself, you are more likely to remember it. For example, let's go back to the word *expire*. The pronunciation is presented in the dictionary as ik spīr′.

First syllable (ik):   i   appears in the guide as the vowel sound in *is*

    k   does not appear in the guide, because it can be pronounced only one way

    The syllable *ik* rhymes with *sick*.

Second syllable (spīr):   s   does not appear in the guide because it has only one pronunciation

    p   does not appear in the guide because it has only one pronunciation

    ī   appears in the guide as the vowel sound in *bite*

    r   does not appear in the guide because it has only one pronunciation

    The syllable *spīr* rhymes with *fire*.

The accent mark on the second syllable (spīr′) means that the second syllable is stressed.

For practice in using the dictionary pronunciation guide, translate the following movie titles into English spelling. (The answers to these three questions appear on page 471.)

fat, āpe, cär; ten, ēven; is, bīte; gō, hôrn, tool, look; oil, out; up, fur; chin, she; thin, *then*; zh, leisure; ŋ, ring; ə for *a* in *ago;* ′ as in *able* (ā′b′l)

1. rād′ᵿrz   uv   *thə*   lôst   ärk

2. *thə*   af′ri kən   kwēn

3. *thə*   brīd   uv   fraŋ′kən stīn′

The **part of speech** appears after the pronunciation in a dictionary entry. Here are a few of the abbreviations you will see in dictionary entries:

n. = noun:	a word that names a person, a place, or a thing
v. = verb:	a word that shows an action or a state of being
vt. or *tr. v.* = transitive verb:	an action word that affects a person or thing: "Jim dropped the pencil." A transitive verb requires a direct object to complete its meaning.
vi. = intransitive verb:	an action word that does not affect a person or thing: "The apple fell to the ground."

If you know parts of speech, you can use words correctly in a sentence. For practice, circle the letter before the correct part of speech of the underlined words in the following sentences. Use the dictionary if you need help. (The answers are on page 471.)

1. The man was a work <u>addict</u> who often spent twelve hours a day at the office.
   a. *v.*,   ə dikt′
   b. *n.*,   ad′ikt

2. People living under a cruel dictator will often try to <u>rebel</u>.
   a. *n.*,   reb″l
   b. *v.*,   ri bel′

3. Going to school at night to get a degree can be a difficult <u>project</u>.
   a. *n.*,   präj′ekt
   b. *v.*,   prə jekt′

The **etymology**, or origin of the word, appears in brackets after the part of speech.

> **ex•pire** (ik spīr′) *vi.*-pired′, -pir′ing [< L. *ex-*, out + *spirare*, breathe] **1.** to exhale **2.** to die **3.** to come to an end

The etymology for *expire* says that the word comes from the Latin word parts *ex* (meaning "out") and *spirare* (meaning "to breathe"). The symbol < (meaning "comes from") and the letter *L.* (the abbreviation for *Latin*) are defined in the front of the dictionary, along with other symbols and abbreviations.

Taking the time to read the etymology is important in vocabulary building. For example, if you know that *spir* means "to breathe," you will have an important clue to an entire word family:

Word	Meaning
expire	end, die (breathe out)
conspiracy	plot (breathe together)
respiration	act of breathing (breathe back)
aspire	to be ambitious (breathe to)
spirit	soul (breath)
inspire	motivate (breathe in)
esprit de corps	group spirit (breath of body)
perspire	sweat (breathe through)
transpire	happen (breathe across)
sprightly	lively (full of breath)
spire	tapering point (breath)

Word parts are so important in vocabulary development that a separate section of this book is devoted to discussing them.

Definitions form the next part of a dictionary entry. Many words have more than one definition. You must choose the one that best fits the context in which the word is used. For example, the following entry shows that the word *expire* has three definitions:

> **ex•pire** (ik spīr´) *vi.*-pired´, -pir´ing [< L. *ex-*, out + *spirare*, breathe] **1.** to exhale **2.** to die **3.** to come to an end

In the sentence "He confessed to the crime before he expired," definition 2 is the one that is meant.

The following words also have more than one meaning. Read each sentence, and identify the dictionary meaning that best describes how the underlined word is used. Write the number of the definition in the space provided. Be sure to choose the definition that matches the part of speech written under the blank. (The answers appear on page 471.)

_____ 1. You can <u>express</u> shades of meaning that aren't even
v.   possible in other languages.

ex•press (ik spres') *vt.* [< L. *ex*, out + *premere*, to press] **1.**
to squeeze out (juice, etc.) **2.** to put into words, state **3.** to
reveal, show **4.** to signify or symbolize **5.** to send by express — *adj.* **1.** expressed, stated, explicit **2.** exact **3.** specific **4.** fast and direct [an *express* bus, highway, etc.] **5.**
related to express — *adv.* by express — *n.* **1.** an express
train, bus, etc. **2.** *a)* service for transporting things rapidly
b) the things sent by express

_____ 2. John is in the sophomore <u>class</u>.
n.

class (klas) *n.* [< L. *classis*] **1.** a number of people or things
grouped together because of likeness; kind; sort **2.** social
or economic rank [the working *class*] **3.** *a)* a group of students taught together *b)* a group graduating together **4.**
grade or quality **5.** [Slang] excellence, as of style — *vt.* to
classify — *vi.* to be classified

_____ 3. I'll have to hurry to <u>catch</u> the train.
vt.

catch (kach) *vt.* caught, catch'ing [< L. *capere*, take] **1.** to
seize and hold, capture **2.** to take by a trap **3.** to deceive **4.**
to surprise **5.** to get to in time [to *catch* a bus] **6.** to lay hold
of; grab [*catch* a ball] **7.** to become affected with [he *caught*
a cold] **8.** to understand **9.** to get entangled **10.** [Colloq.] to
see, hear, etc. — *vi.* **1.** to become held, fastened, etc. **2.** to
take hold, as fire **3.** to keep hold, as a lock — *n.* **1.** a catching
2. a thing that catches **3.** something caught **4.** one worth
catching as a spouse **5.** a snatch or fragment **6.** a break in
the voice **7.** [Colloq.] a tricky qualification, to catch at, to
seize desperately

Whenever you read a definition in the dictionary, you should do two
things to make sure you really understand it. First, put the definition
into your own words. Second, make up a sentence using the word. Practice by defining the word *expire* and using it in a sentence. (The answers
appear on page 471.)

Definition: _____

Sentence: _____

Before each reading selection in this book, there is a preview of difficult words that appear in the article. Use the pronunciation guide at the bottom of each vocabulary preview to figure out how to pronounce the words. Read the definitions before you read each article. Then you will be more likely to know what the words mean when you see them.

Word Parts

You have seen how the dictionary etymology of the word *expire* helped you discover its meaning. The etymology also helped you discover the meaning of a whole group of words based on *spire*. Another way to understand thousands of new words is to gain a knowledge of basic word parts.

There are three types of word parts: prefixes, roots, and suffixes. **Prefixes** are syllables added at the beginning of words to change their meaning. For example, the word *mispronounce* means "pronounce wrong," because the meaning of *mis* is "wrong." **Roots** form the bases of words. *Spir*, meaning "to breathe," is a root used with different prefixes to form many words. **Suffixes** are syllables added at the end of words to change their meaning or their part of speech. An example of a suffix that changes a word's meaning is the suffix *less*, which means "without." *Useless* means "without use." An example of a suffix that changes a word's part of speech is the suffix *ize*. Adding the suffix *ize* to the noun *ideal* changes it to the verb *idealize*.

For practice, write the correct word part from the following list in each blank of the numbered exercises. Make sure that the words match their definitions. Use the underlined words as clues. (The answers appear on page 471.)

Prefixes

con = together
pro = forth, forward
re = back
de = away
sub = under

Roots

fus = pour, melt
tract = draw, pull
mit = send
vok = call, speak

Suffixes

or = someone who or something that
ion = state of

Word

1. pro _ _ _ ion
2. re _ _ _ e
3. con _ _ _ _ _

Definition

state of <u>pouring</u> forth
to <u>call</u> back
to shrink or <u>draw</u> together

4. detract ___ ___   <u>someone who</u> belittles or draws from you

5. ___ ___ ___ voke   to call <u>forth</u>

6. con ___ ___ ___ ion   state of disorder (<u>melting</u> together)

7. re ___ ___ ___   to <u>send</u> (back)

8. ___ ___ voke   to cancel or call <u>back</u>

9. sub ___ ___ ___ ___   to take away (<u>pull</u> from under)

10. ___ ___ ___ mit   yield (send <u>under</u>)

Word Memory

You will learn hundreds of new words in your college classes, but you may have a problem remembering them all. Pronouncing the word, checking the etymology, putting the definition in your own words, and using the word in a sentence are all aids to memory. In addition, there are two more ways to remember words: using word association and using flashcards.

Word association means linking the new word with one you already know. For example, to remember that *striations* refers to thin lines or grooves, you could associate it with the word *stripes*. Or to remember that *inexplicable* means "not able to be explained," you could remember the phrase *not explainable*.

For practice with word association, make up a word or phrase that you could use to remember each of the following words. (Some possible word associations appear on page 471.)

1. commentary (käm'ən ter'ē): series of explanatory remarks

   _____

2. transfixed (trans fikst'): motionless

   _____

3. aghast (ə gast'): feeling great horror or dismay

   _____

4. ad lib (ad'lib'): to make up and perform without any preparation

   _____

5. insight (in'sīt): clear understanding of the nature of things

   _____

Another way to memorize a word is to put it on a **flashcard**. Write the word and its pronunciation on one side of the card, and write the definition and a sentence using the word on the other side. Your cards should look like these sample cards.

Front

non sequitur
(nän sek' wi tar)

Back

an inference that
does not follow from
the premises

His speech was full
of non sequiturs.

You can test yourself by looking at the front of the card and trying to give the definition. When you are sure you can remember a word, you can retire the card. Carry ten to twenty cards with you so that you can use spare moments (such as when you are standing in line or eating lunch by yourself) to memorize vocabulary. That way you won't have so much work to do the night before an exam.

LOCATING THE SUBJECT, MAIN IDEA, AND SUPPORTING DETAILS IN PARAGRAPHS

To understand the structure of a paragraph, you have to find the subject, the main idea, and supporting details.

Subject

A good paragraph is a group of sentences that explain one central idea, called the subject, or topic, of the paragraph. You can find the subject of a paragraph by asking yourself who or what the whole paragraph is about. Read the following paragraph, and then circle the letter that identifies its subject:

> Newfoundland is Canada's newest province and its oldest. It is the newest because it was the last to join the Dominion, in 1949. But it is also the oldest in that it was the first to be discovered. Scientists have found the remains of a Viking camp almost 1,000 years old on the province's northern shore. Even modern Europeans discovered Newfoundland before they discovered the rest of Canada. John Cabot discovered the southern portion of the province only 5 years after Columbus landed in the West Indies and discovered America. Sir Humphrey Gilbert claimed Newfoundland for England in 1583.

The subject of the paragraph is

   a. Newfoundland's age.
   b. Newfoundland.
   c. Vikings in Newfoundland.
   d. provinces of Canada.

The answer is a. Choices b and d are too broad, and choice c is too narrow to cover the entire paragraph.

Now read the following paragraph, and circle the letter that identifies its subject:

> Computers will never be able to play the perfect game of chess. A chess player has about thirty moves to choose from on each turn, and the opponent has about thirty possible responses to each of these moves. Therefore, there are about 1,000 variations to consider for each complete move. Because each complete move allows another 1,000 potential moves, a computer would have to consider 10^{75} (1 and 75 zeros) moves to play a short twenty-five move game. Even if a computer could calculate a million moves each second, it would require 10^{69} seconds to complete the game. Since the beginning of our solar system 4.5 billion years ago, only 10^{18} seconds have elapsed.

The subject of the paragraph is

   a. chess.
   b. computers and chess.
   c. chess strategies.
   d. time involved in chess games.

The answer is b. Answers a and d are too broad, and c is off the subject.

Main Idea

Every paragraph should have a main idea, or a central point. The main idea of a paragraph is usually a complete sentence. To find the main idea, ask yourself what the subject is and what the author is saying about the subject.

Now look again at the paragraph about Newfoundland. Circle the letter that identifies its main idea:

   a. Newfoundland is a province in Canada.
   b. Newfoundland is the newest and oldest province in Canada.
   c. Newfoundland was discovered by Vikings.
   d. Newfoundland was discovered before other Canadian provinces.

The answer is b. Choice a is too broad, and choices c and d are too narrow.

Look again at the paragraph about chess and computers. Which of the following is its main idea?

a. A good chess game takes a very long time.
b. Playing chess requires a great deal of strategy.
c. Computers will never be able to play chess perfectly.
d. Computers cannot equal the human brain at chess.

The answer is c. Choices a and b don't deal with computers, and d is not implied in the paragraph.

Supporting Details

A good paragraph has details that support the main idea. The supporting details explain, clarify, or justify the main idea. Supporting details can be reasons, facts, examples, or testimony.

In the paragraph about Newfoundland, the main idea is supported by **facts** — things that have actually happened or that are true. Facts can include numbers, scientific laws, historical information, and so forth. The paragraph about Newfoundland is supported by historical facts.

In the paragraph about chess and computers, the main idea is supported by **reasons.** The author explains why computers will never be able to play perfect chess games.

Sometimes an author uses one or more **examples,** or samples, to support the main idea. In the following paragraph, underline the main idea:

> Yellowstone National Park has unusual natural attractions. It has a massive cliff of black volcanic glass. It also has geysers that release 15,000 gallons of hot water into the air hour after hour. Finally, it has bubbling mudpots and boiling springs that sometimes reach 150°F.

You should have underlined the first sentence. This main idea is supported by sentences about the cliff, the geysers, and the mudpots and boiling springs, which are all examples of unusual natural attractions.

To give **testimony** as support for the main idea means to give opinions or findings of people other than the author. Underline the main idea of the following paragraph:

> According to the *Guinness Book of World Records*, people with the highest IQs are often ordinary. They do not generally have remarkable intuition or freedom from prejudice. They often have rather ordinary jobs, and they do not necessarily excel in the academic world. They are said to have these shortcomings because they are often irritated by the repetition of what to them is obvious.

You should have underlined the part of the first sentence that follows the comma. The *Guinness Book of World Records* is cited in the first part of the sentence as authority to support the main idea.

Finding Main Ideas

In the paragraphs above, the main idea is located in the first sentence. Main ideas are usually, but not always, found in the first sentence of paragraphs. One way to locate the main idea is to look for such **signal words** as *therefore, thus, in other words,* and *most important.*

See if you can locate the main idea and signal words in the following paragraph:

> The main idea can fall in several places within the paragraph. For example, it can, and usually does, begin the paragraph. The author clearly states her most important idea and then spends the rest of the paragraph clarifying, expanding, proving, or explaining it.

The main idea is in the first sentence, and *for example* signals a supporting detail.

Now locate the main idea and signal words in this next paragraph:

> An author could also begin a paragraph by giving examples of an idea. Or she might choose to describe a scene or a historical event. At other times, the writer might begin by using a quotation from another person. In this case, the author begins with supporting details and then moves to a general conclusion. In other words, she puts the main idea at the end of the paragraph.

The main idea is in the last sentence, signaled by *in other words.* Signal words indicating supporting details in this paragraph are *also, or, at other times,* and *in this case.*

Locate the main idea and signal words in the next paragraph:

> The author who chooses to begin a paragraph with examples might not always place the main idea at the end. The main idea could be found toward the middle of the paragraph. In this case, the author follows the main idea with more supporting details. How much support precedes or follows the main idea depends on the author's purpose.

In this example, the main idea is in the second sentence. *In this case* signals a detail.

Now use what you have learned to locate the main idea and signal words in the next paragraph:

> The Amazon River is the widest river in the world, with one-fifth of all the fresh water on earth moving through its mouth. In length it is second only to the Nile, and if stretched across the United States, it would reach from New York to Los Angeles. In addition, the Amazon covers the largest area of any river. Therefore, it can be argued that the Amazon is the mightiest river on Earth.

The main idea is in the last sentence, signaled by *therefore.* The other sentences are supporting details. One of them is preceded by the signal words *in addition.*

Implied Main Idea

In the preceding paragraphs the main idea is stated somewhere in the paragraph. In some paragraphs, however, the main idea is implied rather than stated. You have to read between the lines to infer (reason out) the main idea. To do this, look at the supporting details and try to think of a statement that they all point to. This statement is the implied main idea. Read the following paragraph, and the circle the letter that identifies the implied main idea:

> Osiris, Egyptian god of the underworld, was often portrayed in mummy wrappings. Isis, frequently represented with a cow's head or horns, was the nature goddess. Ra was the sun god, whose symbol was the pyramid. Amon was often represented as a ram or with a ram's head.

   a. The most important Egyptian god was Ra.
   b. Egyptian religion is interesting.
   c. Egyptian gods were drawn as animals.
   d. The Egyptians had several gods.

The answer is d. Choice a is not implied: The paragraph does not discuss the relative importance of the gods. Choice b may be implied, but it is not the main idea of the paragraph. Choice c is not true: The paragraph does not mention animal representations for Osiris and Ra.

Now read the next paragraph, and circle the letter that identifies the implied main idea:

> Thomas Alva Edison invented or improved on the telegraph, phonograph, stock ticker, microphone, telephone, light bulb, battery, motion picture projector, and many other things. He held more than 1,300 U.S. and foreign patents and was the first American director of a research laboratory for inventors. His various companies later combined to become General Electric.

   a. Edison may have been the greatest American inventor.
   b. Edison was a leader of American industry.
   c. Edison may have been the greatest genius that ever lived.
   d. Edison discovered electricity.

The answer is a. Choices b and c may or may not be true, but the paragraph doesn't go that far. Choice d isn't true.

Here's another paragraph for you to practice on:

> The first horselike creature lived 700 million years ago and was only about 11 inches high. It had four toes on each forefoot and three on each hind foot. By 45 million years ago the creature had doubled in size and had three toes on all four feet. By 10 million years ago it had doubled in size again, and its feet had a single toe forming a hoof. The true horse, *Equus*, appeared in North America about a million years ago. It migrated to Asia and later became extinct in America. It was finally reintroduced by European settlers.

a. The modern horse should double in size in another million years.
b. The modern horse gradually evolved.
c. The modern horse is the same size as the prehistoric one.
d. The modern horse has been around for 70 million years.

The answer is b. Choices c and d are contradicted in the paragraph, and choice a is not implied.

1

How to Improve Your Vocabulary

VOCABULARY PREVIEW

addict (ad′ikt): one unable to give up a habit, such as using drugs

differentiate (dif′ə ren′shē āt′): to make unlike; to show the difference between

context (kän′tekst): parts just before and after a word or passage that influence its meaning

extensive (ik sten′siv): having a great or far-reaching area or scope

heritage (her′ə tij′): a tradition handed down from one's ancestors or the past

origin (ôr′ə jin): beginning; source; root

emancipate (i man′sə pāt′): to free from confinement

corroborate (kə räb′ə rāt′): to support or confirm

literal (lit′ər əl): following the exact words of the original

elated (i lāt′id, ē lāt′id): raised the spirits of; made very proud or happy

fat, āpe, cär; ten, ēven; is, bīte; gō, hôrn, tool, look; oil, out; up, fur; chin, she; thin, then; zh, leisure; ŋ, ring; ə for a in ago; ' as in able (ā′b'l)

SURVEY

Survey the following article by reading the author's name, the title, and the headings. This should take no longer than fifteen seconds. After your survey, answer the following questions without looking back at the article. (The answers appear on page 471.)

1. How many ways can you improve your vocabulary? _____

2. Does this article discuss prefixes? _____

3. Does the article discuss suffixes? _____

4. Does this article discuss using the dictionary? _____

In this article, Tony Randall — who is on the *American Heritage Dictionary* Usage Panel and who loves words almost as much as acting — tells how he has acquired his enormous vocabulary.

Now read the article. Write your starting time here: _____

1

How to Improve Your Vocabulary

Tony Randall

WORDS CAN MAKE US LAUGH, cry, go to war, fall in love. Rudyard Kipling called words the most powerful drug of mankind. If they are, I'm a hopeless addict — and I hope to get you hooked, too!

Whether you're still in school or you head up a corporation, the better command you have of words, the better chance you have of saying exactly what you mean, of understanding what others mean — and of getting what you want in the world.

English is the richest language — with the largest vocabulary on earth. Over 1,000,000 words!

You can express shades of meaning that aren't even *possible* in other languages. (For example, you can differentiate between "sky" and "heaven." The French, Italians and Spanish cannot.)

Yet, the average adult has a vocabulary of only 30,000 to 60,000 words. Imagine what we're missing!

Here are five pointers that help me learn — and remember — whole *families* of words at a time.

They may not *look* easy — and won't be at first. But if you stick with them you'll find they *work*!

What's the first thing to do when you see a word you don't know?

1. TRY TO GUESS THE MEANING OF THE WORD FROM THE WAY IT'S USED

You can often get at least *part* of a word's meaning — just from how it's used in a sentence.

That's why it's so important to read as much as you can — different *kinds* of things: magazines, books, newspapers you don't normally read. The more you *expose* yourself to new words, the more words you'll pick up *just by seeing how they're used.*

For instance, say you run across the word "manacle":

"The manacles had been on John's wrists for 30 years. Only one person had a key — his wife."

19

You have a good *idea* of what "manacles" are — just from the context of the sentence.

But let's find out *exactly* what the word means and where it comes from. The only way to do this, and to build an extensive vocabulary *fast*, is to go to the dictionary. (How lucky, you *can* — Shakespeare *couldn't*. There *wasn't* an English dictionary in his day!)

So you go to the dictionary. (NOTE: Don't let dictionary abbreviations put you off. The front tells you what they mean, and even has a guide to pronunciation.)

2. LOOK IT UP

Here's the definition for "manacle" in *The American Heritage Dictionary of the English Language*.

> **man-a-cle** (man'ə kəl) *n.* Usually plural. **1.** A device for confining the hands, usually consisting of two metal rings that are fastened about the wrists and joined by a metal chain; a handcuff. **2.** Anything that confines or restrains. — *tr. v.* **manacled,-cling,-cles. 1.** To restrain with manacles. **2.** To confine or restrain as if with manacles; shackle; fetter. [Middle English *manicle*, from Old French, from Latin *manicula*, little hand, handle, diminutive of *manus*, hand.]

The first definition fits here: A device for confining the hands, usually consisting of two metal rings that are fastened about the wrists and joined by a metal chain; a handcuff.

Well, that's what you *thought* it meant. But what's the idea *behind* the word? What are its *roots*? To really understand a word, you need to know.

Here's where the detective work — and the *fun* — begins.

3. DIG THE MEANING OUT BY THE ROOTS

The root is the basic part of the word — its heritage, its origin. (Most of our roots come from Latin and Greek words at least 2,000 years old — which come from even earlier Indo-European tongues!)

Learning the roots: 1) Helps us *remember* words. 2) Gives us a deeper understanding of the words we *already* know. And 3) allows us to pick up whole families of *new* words at a time. That's why learning the root is the *most important part of going to the dictionary*.

Notice the root of "manacle" is *manus* (Latin) meaning "hand."

Well, that makes sense. Now, other words with this root, <u>man</u>, start to make sense, too.

Take manual — something done "by hand" (manual labor) or a "handbook." And manage — to "handle" something (as a manager). When you emancipate someone, you're taking him "from the hands of" someone else.

When you manufacture something, you "make it by hand" (in its original meaning).

And when you finish your first novel, your publisher will see your — originally "handwritten" — manuscript.

Imagine! A whole new world of words opens up — just from one simple root!

The root gives the *basic* clue to the meaning of a word. But there's another important clue that runs a close second — the *prefix*.

4. GET THE POWERFUL PREFIXES UNDER YOUR BELT

A prefix is the part that's sometimes attached to the front of a word. Like — well, *prefix*! There aren't many — less than 100 major prefixes — and you'll learn them in no time at all just by becoming more aware of the meanings of words you already know. Here are a few. (Some of the "How-to" vocabulary-building books will give you the others.)

Prefix				
Latin	Greek	Meaning	Examples	Literal Sense
com, con, co, col, cor	sym, syn, syl	with, very, together	conform sympathy	"form with" "feeling with"
in, im, il, ir	a, an	not, without	innocent amorphous	"not wicked" "without form"
contra, counter	anti, ant	against, opposite	contravene antidote	"come against" "give against"

Now, see how the *prefix* (along with the context) helps you get the meaning of the italicized words:

• "If you're going to be my witness, your story must *corroborate* my story." (The literal meaning of *corroborate* is "strength together.")

• "You told me one thing — now you tell me another. Don't *contradict* yourself." (The literal meaning of *contradict* is "say against.")

• "Oh, that snake's not poisonous. It's a completely *innocuous* little garden snake." (The literal meaning of *innocuous* is "not harmful.")

Now, you've got some new words. What are you going to do with them?

5. PUT YOUR NEW WORDS TO WORK AT ONCE

Use them several times the first day you learn them. Say them out loud! Write them in sentences.

Should you "use" them on *friends*? Careful — you don't want them to think you're a stuffed shirt. (It depends on the situation. You *know* when a word sounds natural — and when it sounds stuffy.)

How about your *enemies*? You have my blessing. Ask one of them if he's read that article on pneumonoultramicroscopicsilicovolcanoconiosis. (You really can find it in the dictionary.) Now, you're one up on him.

So what do you do to improve your vocabulary?

Remember: 1) Try to guess the meaning of the word from the way it's used. 2) Look it up. 3) Dig the meaning out by the roots. 4) Get the powerful prefixes under your belt. 5) Put your new words to work at once.

That's all there is to it — you're off on your treasure hunt.

Now, do you see why I love words so much?

Aristophanes said, "By words, the mind is excited and the spirit elated." It's as true today as it was when he said it in Athens — *2,400 years ago!*

I hope you're now like me — hooked on words forever.

1050 words

Write your ending time here: _____

Subtract your starting time: _____

Total time: _____

Check the Rate Chart in the back of the book to find out how many words per minute you have read, and then record your score on the Progress Chart.

1

How to Improve Your Vocabulary

COMPREHENSION CHECK
Circle the letter before the best answer to each question below. Don't
look back at the article.

Subject and Main Idea
1. The subject of the article is
   a. the usefulness of the dictionary in building vocabulary.
   b. the importance of vocabulary.
   c. ways to increase your vocabulary.
   d. how to be a language detective.

2. The main idea is that
   a. everyone ought to improve his or her vocabulary.
   b. English has a larger vocabulary than any other language.
   c. there are five ways to improve your vocabulary.
   d. it's not hard to improve your vocabulary.

Details
3. English
   a. is not based on any other language.
   b. is at least 2000 years old.
   c. has more words than any other language.
   d. cannot differentiate shades of meaning like most European
      languages.

4. The first thing most people do when they see an unfamiliar word
   is to
   a. look up the meaning in the dictionary.
   b. look for the roots.
   c. look for the prefixes.
   d. try to figure out the word's meaning from its context.

5. Randall says you become a word detective when
   a. the word has more than one meaning.
   b. you can look up the meaning in the dictionary.
   c. you begin to trace a word's origin.
   d. you use the word's context to find the meaning.

6. There are
   a. more than 100 major prefixes.
   b. about 100,000 words in the English language.
   c. about half a million words in the average adult's vocabulary.
   d. fewer than 100 major prefixes.

Inferences

7. Randall was probably asked to write this article because he
   a. is an actor.
   b. is recognized as an expert in word usage.
   c. was a college professor.
   d. is a college graduate.

8. Word memory is improved by
   a. learning the roots.
   b. remembering the context in which the word was used.
   c. using the words in speaking and writing.
   d. all of the above.

9. According to the article,
   a. dictionaries have existed since before Shakespeare's time.
   b. you can learn new words without using the dictionary.
   c. the most important part of using the dictionary is learning the pronunciation of words.
   d. Aristophanes spoke English.

10. The author feels that
    a. people with large vocabularies are more successful in life.
    b. guessing the meaning of an unknown word is a bad habit.
    c. the average adult who speaks English knows most of the words in the language.
    d. a word's prefixes and roots will translate into the same definition as in the dictionary.

QUESTIONS FOR ANALYSIS AND APPLICATION

1. What are the advantages of having a large vocabulary?

2. Which of the methods that Randall discusses do you think people use most often? Why do they use it?

VOCABULARY IN CONTEXT
Fill-in

Write the best word from this list in the blank in each sentence below:

addicting	differentiate	context	extensive	heritage
origin	emancipating	corroborated	literal	elated

1. The base of the Great Pyramid in Egypt could hold ten football

   fields because it is so _____ .

2. The _____ of the word *assassin* came
   from the drug hashish, which one extreme religious group in Persia
   always smoked before terrorizing and killing its victims.

3. For years, criminals have escaped conviction for crimes
   they have committed because other people have falsely

   _____ their alibis.

4. Until recently, it was not realized that Valium, the most widely
   prescribed drug in the United States, was psychologically and

   sometimes physically _____ .

5. The _____ of a sentence will tell you
   which meaning a person is using when he or she says "That's
   baloney."

6. Abraham Lincoln is credited with _____
   the slaves in 1863, but actually he freed the slaves only in those
   states that had left the Union and over which he had no control.

7. Nose prints, not paw prints, are used by breeders and trainers to

   _____ prize dogs because, like human
   fingerprints, nose prints are all different.

8. Before writing *Roots*, Alex Haley spent years researching his

   African _____ .

9. People are usually _____ when they
   receive a promotion or pay raise at work.

10. The _____ meaning of the individual
    words do not help define an expression like "Drop in any time."

SKILLS EXERCISE: MAIN IDEAS AND SUPPORT

For explanation
see pp. 10–15

A. Read the following paragraph to find the main idea.

> A prefix is the part that's sometimes attached to the front of a word. Like —
> well, *prefix*! There aren't many — fewer than 100 major prefixes — and
> you'll learn them in no time at all just by becoming more aware of the
> meanings of words you already know. Here are a few. (Some of the "How-
> to" vocabulary-building books will give you the others.)

Prefix				
Latin	Greek	Meaning	Examples	Literal Sense
com, con, co, col, cor	sym, syn, syl	with, very, together	conform sympathy	"form with" "feeling with"
in, im, il, ir	a, an	not, without	innocent amorphous	"not wicked" "without form"
contra, counter	anti, ant	against, opposite	contravene antidote	"come against" "give against"

The main idea of this paragraph is that _to define_ *better* _a prefit_

B. The following are main ideas from this article. List the supporting ideas that the author gave. You may look back at the article.

　1. Use your words immediately.

　　a. _Say aloud_

　　b. _& frequency, writing in sentences_

　2. You need a command of words for three reasons.

　　a. _Saying exactly what to want to say_

　　b. _understand_

　　c. _____

C. In the next two examples, the supporting ideas are given. Fill in the main idea.

　1. _learning Roots_

　　a. Helps us remember the word.
　　b. Gives us a deeper understanding of the meaning.
　　c. Helps us to learn whole new families of words.

　2. _therefore we should strave to improve_

　　a. English is the richest language with the largest vocabulary on earth.
　　b. It has over 1,000,000 words.
　　c. Yet, the average adult has a vocabulary of only 30,000 to 60,000 words.

SKILLS EXERCISE:
USING THE DICTIONARY

For explanation
see pp. 2–8

A. Here are the dictionary entries (from *Webster's New World Dictionary, Pocket Edition*) for five words used in the article. Above each entry is the sentence that the word was used in. In the blank before the sentence, put the number of the definition that fits the way the word is used. The abbreviation under each blank tells you which part of speech the word is, so you can more easily find the proper definition.

_____ 1. "Here are five <u>pointers</u> that help me learn — and
   n.   remember — whole families of words at a time."

point'er *n.* **1.** a long, tapered rod for pointing to things **2.** an indicator on a meter, etc. **3.** a large, lean hunting dog with a smooth coat **4.** [Colloq.] a helpful hint or suggestion

_____ 2. "The more you <u>expose</u> yourself to new words, the
   v.   more words you'll pick up *just by seeing how they're used.*"

ex•pose (ik spōz') *vt.*-posed',-pos'-ing [see EXPOUND] **1.** to lay open **2.** to reveal; exhibit; make known **3.** *Photography* to subject (a sensitized film or plate) to actinic rays

_____ 3. "A <u>device</u> for confining the hands, usually consisting
   n.   of two metal rings that are fastened about the wrists and joined by a metal chain; a handcuff."

de•vice (di vīs') *n.* [see DEVISE] **1.** a thing devised; plan, scheme, or trick **2.** a mechanical contrivance **3.** an ornamental design, esp. on a coat of arms — **leave to one's own devices** to allow to do as one wishes

_____ 4. "Take manual — something done 'by hand' (<u>manual</u>
   adj.   labor) . . ."

man•u•al (man'yoo wəl) *adj.* [< L. *manus*, a hand] **1.** made or worked by hand [*manual* typewriter] **2.** involving skill or hard work with the hands — *n.* **1.** a handy book for use as a guide, reference, etc. **2.** prescribed drill in the handling of a weapon

——————— 5. ". . . the better <u>command</u> you have of words, the bet-
n.   ter chance you have of saying exactly what you mean,
of understanding what others mean — and of getting
what you want in the world."

com•mand (kə mand') *vt.* [<L. *com-*, intens. + *mandare*,
entrust] **1.** to give an order to; direct **2.** to have authority
over; control **3.** to have for use [to *command* a fortune]
4. to deserve and get [to *command* respect] **5.** to control
(a position); overlook — *vi.* to have authority — *n.* **1.** order;
direction **2.** controlling power or position **3.** mastery **4.** a
military or naval force, or district, under a specified
authority

B. For practice with the pronunciation guide, do the exercises below.

fat, āpe, cär; ten, ēven; is, bīte; gō, hôrn, tōōl, look; oil, out; up, fur; chin, she;
thin, *th*en; zh, leisure; ŋ, ring; ə for *a* in *ago;* ' as in *able* (ā'b'l)

1. Translate these famous book titles into English spelling.

a. *th*ə sun ôl'sō rīz'əz — Ernest Hemingway

———————————————————————————

b. ə tāl uv tōō sit'ēz — Charles Dickens

———————————————————————————

c. prīd and prej'ə dis — Jane Austen

———————————————————————————

d. *th*ə good urth — Pearl Buck

———————————————————————————

e. *th*ə tīm mə shēn' — H. G. Wells

———————————————————————————

2. Say each word below out loud and listen for the sounds. Then
circle the words that contain the sound of schwa (ə).

differentiate   context   origin   literal   elate

3. Say each word below out loud and listen for the sounds. Then
circle the words that contain long vowel sounds (ā, ē, ī, ō, ū).

addict   extensive   heritage   emancipate   corroborate

2

Unlock Your Own Creativity

VOCABULARY PREVIEW

invariably (in ver′ē əb′lē):   without variation; constantly

obsolete (äb′sə lēt′):   no longer in use; out of date

opting (äp′tiŋ):   choosing

trivial (triv′ē əl):   commonplace, insignificant, unimportant

entrée (än′trā):   the main course of a meal

germinate (jʉr′mə nāt′):   to start developing; sprout, as from a seed

metaphors (met′ə fôrz′):   figures of speech in which one thing is spoken of as if it were another

realm (relm):   an area of rule, as a kingdom or region

colleagues (käl′ēgz):   fellow workers

additive (ad′ə tiv):   something extra that is added to a product

ambiguity (am bə gyo͞o′ə tē):   lack of clearness; the quality of having more than one possible meaning

self-esteem (self ə stēm′):   self-respect; belief in oneself

---

fat, āpe, cär; ten, ēven; is, bīte; gō, hôrn, to͞ol, look; oil, out; up, fʉr; chin, she; thin, *then*; zh, leisure; ŋ, ring; ə for *a* in *ago;* ′ as in *able* (ā′b'l)

SURVEY

Survey the following article by reading the author's name, the title, the first sentence of each paragraph, and the eight italicized headings. This should take no longer than one minute. After your survey, answer the following questions without looking back at the article. (The answers appear on page 471.)

1. Write as many of the eight blocks to creativity as you can remember.

   a. _____

   b. _____

   c. _____

   d. _____

   e. _____

   f. _____

   g. _____

   h. _____

2. Do you think this article will deal with creating beautiful paintings?

   _____

3. Do you think you will learn ways to be more creative in solving everyday problems? _____

Now read the article. Write your starting time here. _____

2

Unlock Your Own Creativity

Roger von Oech

I F I HELD UP A SHEET OF WHITE PAPER and put a black dot on it with my pen, what would you see? I've used this demonstration on thousands of adults in the seminars I run, and invariably I get the same answer: "A black dot." When I tried it on a kindergarten class, a forest of hands shot up. "A Mexican hat," piped one kid. "Naw, that's a burnt hamburger," said another. "A squashed bug," observed a third.

When young, we're naturally creative because we let our minds run free. But as we're taught to follow the rules, our thinking narrows. For much of life this can be a blessing: it wouldn't do to create a new way home from work if it meant driving down the wrong side of the freeway.

But in many areas of our lives, creativity can be a matter of survival. Things are changing too fast to get along simply with old ideas. When I was working for IBM ten years ago, half of what any technical engineer had learned became obsolete in only three years; it happens even sooner now. And what about our home lives? With, for instance, more and more women opting for careers and independence, couples have to be more creative about their relationships to avoid conflicts.

Fortunately creativity isn't all that mysterious. One important creative trait was well-defined by Nobel Prize-winning physician Albert Szent-Györgyi when he said, "Discovery consists of seeing what everybody has seen and thinking what nobody has thought."

How do we start "thinking what nobody has thought"? Usually it takes a whack on the head, like Newton supposedly had when an apple striking his skull awakened him to the laws of gravity. Whacks can range from something as major as losing a job to something as trivial as wanting an unusual entrée for a dinner party. We're more likely to respond creatively — which is to say, come up with a new idea — if we've already been chipping away at the "mental locks" that close our minds.

What are these locks? As I said in my book *A Whack on the Side of the Head*, for the most part they are our uncritical acceptance of eight common statements:

1. *"Find the right answer."* Almost from the first day of school, we're taught that there's one right answer to every problem. But many important issues are open-ended. Take the question "What do I do now that I've lost my job?" The obvious right answer is: "Look for another job." There is also a second right answer: "Go back to school and learn a new trade." Or a third: "Start your own business."

The mere act of looking for a second answer will often produce the new idea you need. As French philosopher Emile Chartier said: "Nothing is more dangerous than an idea when it is the only one we have."

2. *"That's not logical."* Hard, logical thinking can be death to a new idea because it eliminates alternatives that seem contradictory. New ideas germinate faster in the loose soil of soft thinking, which finds similarities and connections among different things or situations.

In my workshops, I ask people to create metaphors to unlock their thoughts. A manager had been thinking logically about what was wrong with his company, but couldn't get a grip on it until he came up with this metaphor: "Our company is a galley ship without a drummer. We've got some people rowing at full beat, some at one-half beat, and some deadbeats." This man made himself the missing "drummer," with the result that the operation smoothed out.

3. *"Follow the rules."* To get an idea, you often have to break rules that no longer make sense. My friend Nolan Bushnell, the founder of

Atari Inc. and inventor of the first video game, is a dedicated rule breaker. Once Bushnell was trying to make pinball games more fun. For a long time he followed the rule that the playing field had to be 26 inches wide. Only when he threw away that rule and made the field 30 inches was he able to increase the game's possibilities.

4. *"Be practical."* To grow, ideas initially need the wide realm of the possible, rather than the narrow one of the practical. You can enter this realm by asking, "What if . . .?"

An engineer in a chemical company startled his colleagues by asking, "What if we put gunpowder in our house paint? When it starts peeling in a few years, we just put a match to it and blow it off." The house might blow up with such a paint, but this engineer was talking to "idea" men who brushed aside the impracticality and started thinking. Eventually they came up with the idea of an additive that could later be activated and cause paint to be easily stripped off walls. The company is now developing the process.

5. *"Don't be foolish."* One of the best ways of unleashing creativity was demonstrated in an Israeli high school. Before they were given a standard creativity test, 141 tenth-graders were treated to a recording of a popular comedian. Those who heard it did significantly better than the control group, which was not so entertained. Humor can show us the ambiguity of situations, revealing a second and often startling answer.

Being foolish is a form of play. If necessity is the mother of invention, play is its father. When faced with a problem, let yourself play, risk being foolish. And write down the ideas that then come to you.

6. *"Don't make mistakes."* If you're piloting a jetliner, you'd better keep this lock on your mind. When looking for new ideas, however, you need the attitude of Carl Yastrzemski. In 1979, after the Boston Red Sox star collected his 3000th hit, a reporter asked, "Hey, Yaz, aren't you afraid all this attention will go to your head?"

"Well," Yastrzemski said, "in my career I've been up to bat over ten thousand times. That means I've been unsuccessful over seven thousand times. That fact alone keeps me from getting a swelled head."

Success and failure, he knew, are part of the same process. And mistakes can simply be stepping stones in the creative process. As IBM founder Thomas J. Watson once said, "The way to succeed is to double your failure rate."

7. *"That's not my area."* Fresh ideas almost invariably come from outside one's field of specialization. I tell people to become hunters. The successful hunter ranges widely, keeps a sharp eye out, and knows his prey when he sees it.

A friend of mine worked in a lab experimenting with a new solar material, gallium arsenide. Her job was to make precision cuts in the material with a high-speed wafer saw. Every time she did so, the material cracked. At home, she was watching her husband make wooden cabinets and noticed that, when he wanted to make precision cuts on certain types of wood, he *reduced* his saw's speed. She tried that on the gallium arsenide and it worked.

Creative people have to be generalists, interested in everything and aware that what they learn in one field might prove useful in another. We're all generalists at home — chefs, decorators, teachers, gardeners, handymen — and home is where to start being creative. The average homemaker is confronted daily with more creative opportunities than the middle manager in a company sees in a month.

8. *"I'm not creative."* Most of us retain the idea that creativity is only for artists and inventors. And when we put ourselves down as not creative, we set in motion a self-fulfilling prophecy. A person who thinks he's not creative in his everyday life won't try a creative solution to an important problem.

A major oil company brought in a team of psychologists to find out why some people in its research and development department were more creative than others. After three months of study, the psychologists came up with this difference: the creative people *thought* they were creative and the less creative people didn't think they were.

Self-esteem is essential to creativity because any new idea makes you a pioneer. Once you put an idea into action, you're out there alone taking risks of failure and ridicule.

As management consultant Roy Blitzer has said, "The only person who *likes* change is a wet baby." But we need change — the type of change that comes only through the creative thinking of all the people, not just the geniuses.

1450 words

Write your ending time here: _____

Subtract your starting time: _____

Total time: _____

Check the Rate Chart in the back of the book to find how many words per minute you have read, and then record your score on the Progress Chart.

2

Unlock Your Own Creativity

COMPREHENSION CHECK
Circle the letter before the best answer to each of the following questions. Don't look back at the article.

Subject and Main Idea
1. The subject is
   a. doing creative things for a living.
   b. what being creative means.
   c. how to become more creative.
   d. how to analyze creative things.

2. The main idea is that
   a. creative people are more interesting than others.
   b. everyone is creative.
   c. you can develop your creativity.
   d. people are not creative enough in their daily lives.

Details
3. Creativity is lost in part by
   a. the loss of memory capacity as we grow older.
   b. the natural maturation process.
   c. becoming too serious as adults.
   d. being taught to follow rules.

4. Creativity aids in
   a. our survival in the business world.
   b. the relationships between couples.
   c. finding new answers to old problems.
   d. all of the above.

5. Which of the following is one of the author's "mental locks"?
   a. finding too many answers to a problem.
   b. saying it's outside your field.
   c. breaking all the rules.
   d. finding an answer too quickly.

6. Which of the following methods does the author use in his seminars to help his clients unlock creative abilities?
   a. creating poems.
   b. writing.
   c. creating metaphors.
   d. making a list of goals.

Inferences

7. The author implies that creativity is
   a. inborn and cannot be developed.
   b. found only in children.
   c. lost during the educational process.
   d. found more in women than in men.

8. When the author says "usually it takes a whack on the head" to unlock creativity, he means that creativity is
   a. often the result of a physical accident.
   b. often triggered by some kind of surprising experience.
   c. not a normal function of the brain.
   d. all of the above.

9. The author feels that creative people
   a. like to watch sports more than other people do.
   b. are more willing to take risks than others.
   c. never use logical thinking to solve problems.
   d. are more likely to be accident prone.

10. When the author says "new ideas germinate faster in the loose soil of soft thinking," he means that
    a. logical thinkers make more mistakes.
    b. creative thinkers like planting things outdoors.
    c. creative thinkers cannot make decisions.
    d. creative thinkers are more flexible in their thoughts.

QUESTIONS FOR ANALYSIS AND APPLICATION

1. Analyze your own creativity by listing the ways in which you are and are not creative.

2. Which of the "mental locks" that von Oech lists do the most to block your creativity, and how do you think you can unlock it?

VOCABULARY IN CONTEXT
Multiple Choice
Circle the letter before the best definition of each underlined word.

1. <u>Invariably</u>, when you have two or three items to buy in the super-
   market and you are in a hurry, you get into a checkout line in
   which everyone is cashing a check.
   a. always   b. sometimes   c. never   d. usually

2. A typewriter is almost <u>obsolete</u> in the modern office now that
   most secretaries use word processors.
   a. necessary   b. out of date   c. common   d. interesting

3. <u>Opting</u> to go to work full time and school full time means you will
   be really working two full-time jobs.
   a. trying   b. being required   c. choosing   d. hoping

4. Remembering <u>trivial</u> facts that others never knew became one of
   the most popular games in 1986 and 1987.
   a. important   b. necessary   c. interesting
   d. unimportant

5. Health-conscious people often decide to limit the number of times
   per week they have beef as an <u>entrée</u> with a meal.
   a. a dessert   b. a drink   c. a main course
   d. an appetizer

6. Having a $1 million-a-year income is beyond the <u>realm</u> of most
   people's ability.
   a. scope   b. hope   c. idea   d. wish

7. One of the <u>ambiguities</u> of the English language is a sentence such
   as "Visiting relatives can be boring." The word *visiting* can be a
   verb or an adjective, and each use gives the sentence a different
   meaning.
   a. clear meanings   b. confusions   c. uses   d. facts

Fill-in

Write the best word from this list in the blank in each of the following sentences:

additives   germinate   metaphor   colleagues   self-esteem

8. Your business _____ can become good friends or your worst enemies.

9. Your _____ can be reflected in the way you dress and talk.

10. Seeds should _____ indoors in very cold weather so that the young shoots won't freeze.

11. "He's a bear before he drinks his coffee in the morning" is a

    _____ .

12. The amount and kind of food _____, such as chemical colorings, are carefully regulated by the federal government.

SKILLS EXERCISE:
MAIN IDEAS AND SUPPORT

For explanation see pp. 10–15

Almost from the first day of school, we're taught that there's one right answer to every problem. But many important issues are open-ended. Take the question "What do I do now that I've lost my job?" The obvious right answer is: "Look for another job." There is also a second right answer: "Go back to school and learn a new trade." Or a third: "Start your own business."

A. The main idea of this paragraph is that _____

_____

B. The following is a main idea from this article. List the supporting ideas that the author gave. You may look back at the article.

   1. "Mental locks" are our uncritical acceptance of eight common statements.

      a. _____

      b. That's not logical.

      c. _____

      d. _____

      e. _____

      f. Don't make mistakes.

      g. _____

      h. _____

C. In the next two examples, the supporting ideas are given. Fill in the main idea.

   1. _____
      a. Adults see a black dot.
      b. Kindergartners see "a Mexican hat, a burnt hamburger, a squashed bug."

   2. _____
      a. Things are changing too fast to get along simply with old ideas.
      b. We must be creative at work because things we have learned become obsolete.
      c. In our homes, with more and more women opting for careers and independence, couples have to be more creative about their relationships to avoid conflicts.

**SKILLS EXERCISE:
USING THE DICTIONARY/WORD PARTS**

For explanation
see pp. 2–9

A. For practice in finding the correct meaning of a word in the dictionary, select the correct meaning of the following three words from the article. Above each entry is a sentence using the word. In the blank before the sentence, put the number of the definition that fits the way the word is used. The abbreviation under each blank tells you which part of speech the word is, so you can more easily find the proper definition.

_____ 1. When an audience wants to show an actor how much
n.   they enjoyed his performance, they will give him a big <u>hand</u> and perhaps a standing ovation.

hand (hand) *n.* [<OE.] **1.** the part of the arm below the wrist, used for grasping **2.** a side or direction [at my right *hand*] **3.** possession or care [the land is in my *hands*] **4.** control [to strengthen one's *hand*] **5.** an active part [take a *hand* in the work] **6.** a promise to marry **7.** skill **8.** one having a special skill **9.** manner of doing something **10.** handwriting **11.** applause **12.** help [to lend a *hand*] **13.** a hired worker [a farm *hand*] **14.** a source [to get news at first *hand*] **15.** anything like a hand, as a pointer on a clock **16.** the breadth of a hand **17.** *Card Games a)* the cards held by a player at one time *b)* a round of play — *adj.* of, for, or controlled by the hand — *vt.*

_____ 2. Being the <u>head</u> of a large corporation such as IBM
n.   means that you not only have to run the company but also represent that company at community affairs.

head (hed) *n.* [<OE. *heafod*] **1.** the part of the body containing the brain, and the jaws, eyes, ears, nose, and mouth **2.** the mind; intelligence **3.** *pl.* **head** a unit of counting [ten *head* of cattle] **4.** the main side of a coin **5.** the uppermost part or thing; top **6.** the topic or title of a section, chapter, etc. **7.** the foremost or projecting part; front **8.** the part designed for holding, striking, etc. [the *head* of a nail] **9.** the membrane across the end of a drum, etc. **10.** the source of a river, etc. **11.** froth, as on beer **12.** the pressure in an enclosed fluid, as steam **13.** a position of leadership or honor **14.** a leader, ruler, etc. — *adj.* **1.** most important; principal **2.** at the top or front **3.** striking against the front [*head* current] — *vt.* **1.** to be the chief of; command **2.** to lead; precede **3.** to cause to go in a specified direction — *vi.* to set out; travel [to *head* eastward]

_____ 3. There is usually only one <u>right</u> answer to objective
adj.   questions on a test.

right (rit) *adj.* [< OE. *riht,* straight] **1.** with a straight or
perpendicular line **2.** upright; virtuous **3.** correct **4.** fitting;
suitable **5.** designating the side meant to be seen **6.** mentally or physically sound **7.** *a)* designating or of that side
toward the east when one faces north *b)* designating or of
the corresponding side of something *c)* closer to the right
side of one facing the thing mentioned — *n.* **1.** what is right,
just, etc. **2.** a power, privilege, etc. belonging to one by law,
nature, etc. **3.** the right side **4.** the right hand **5.** [*often* R-]
Politics a conservative or reactionary position, party, etc.
(often with *the*) — *adv.* **1.** straight; directly [go *right* home]
2. properly; fittingly **3.** completely **4.** exactly [*right* here]
5. according to law, justice, etc. **6.** correctly **7.** on or toward
the right side **8.** very; in certain titles [the *right* honor-
able] — *vt.* **1.** to put upright **2.** to correct **3.** to put in order

B. For practice with the pronunciation guide, translate the names of
these famous comedians into English spelling.

fat, āpe, cär; ten, ēven; is, bīte; gō, hôrn, tōōl, look; oil, out; up, fʉr; chin, she;
thin, *th*en; zh, leisure; ŋ, ring; ə for *a* in *ago;* ' as in *able* (ā'b'l)

1. kar'əl   bʉr net'

_____

2. rich'ərd   prī'ər

_____

3. gōl'dē   hôn

_____

4. bil   käz'bē

_____

5. che'vē   chās

_____

6. ed'ē   mər'fē

_____

C. By looking at a word's etymology in the dictionary, you can find the meaning of its prefixes. Here are ten words from the article that contain common prefixes. The prefixes, their meanings, and other words that can help you remember the meanings are also provided.

Word	Prefix	Meaning of Prefix	Another Word
independence	in, im	not	incapable
respond	re	back	return
uncritical	un	not	unstable
eliminates	e, ex	out	edit
contradictory	contra	against	contrary
connections	con, com	with, together	conform
mistake	mis	wrong, not	misbehave
similarities	sim, sym, syn, syl	same, together	simultaneous
ambiguity	ambi, amphi	both	amphibian
prophecy	pro	before, forward	project

Using these prefixes, match the following difficult words to their definitions.

_____ 1. indelible

_____ 2. resilient

_____ 3. unconditional

_____ 4. emit

_____ 5. contrapuntal

_____ 6. concentric

_____ 7. misnomer

_____ 8. symbiosis

_____ 9. ambidextrous

_____ 10. prognosis

a. send out; let out

b. without conditions

c. cannot be erased

d. having a common center with another

e. forecast, especially of outcome of a disease

f. the living together in close union of two dissimilar organisms

g. able to use both hands

h. against the beat (the point of rhythm)

i. wrong name

j. able to bounce back

3

How to Write Clearly

VOCABULARY PREVIEW

inspired (in spīrd'):   motivated by creative urges

objective (əb jek'tiv):   concerned with the realities of the thing dealt with; without bias or prejudice

detract (di trakt'):   to take away

fundamental (fun'də men't'l):   of or forming a foundation or basis; basic; essential

ironically (ī rän'i k'lē):   having a meaning contrary to what is expressed or what is expected

sequence (sē'kwəns):   coming of one thing after another; order

delete (di lēt'):   to take out; to cross out

jargon (jär'gən):   specialized vocabulary of those in the same line of work, way of life, etc., which outsiders cannot understand

mortality (môr tal'ə tē):   1. death rate 2. death

endeavoring (in dev'ər iŋ):   trying (to do something)

condensing (kən dens'iŋ):   1. making more compact 2. expressing in fewer words

anecdotes (an'ik dōts'):   short, entertaining accounts of some event

belabor (bi lā'bər):   to develop in too great detail

fat, āpe, cär; ten, ēven; is, bīte; gō, hôrn, tōol, look; oil, out; up, fʉr; chin, she; thin, *then*; zh, leisure; ŋ, ring; ə for *a* in *ago;* ' as in *able* (ā'b'l)

SURVEY
Survey the following article by reading the author's name, the title, the headings, and the sentences indicated by the dots at the end of the article. This should not take more than thirty seconds. After your survey, answer the following questions without looking back at the article. (The answers appear on page 471.)

1. Is this about writing fiction or nonfiction?

2. How many guidelines are presented?

3. Does this article discuss editing your material?

Edward T. Thompson was editor-in-chief of *Reader's Digest*. Here he shares some of the things he learned in the nineteen years he worked at *Reader's Digest*, a magazine famous for making complicated subjects understandable to millions of readers.

Now read the article. Write your starting time here: _____

3

How to Write Clearly

Edward T. Thompson

I F YOU ARE AFRAID to write, don't be.

    If you think you've got to string together big fancy words and high-flying phrases, forget it.

    To write well, unless you aspire to be a professional poet or novelist, you only need to get your ideas across simply and clearly.

    It's not easy. But it *is* easier than you might imagine.

There are only three basic requirements:

First, you must *want* to write clearly. And I believe you really do, if you've stayed this far with me.

Second, you must be willing to *work hard*. Thinking means work — and that's what it takes to do anything well.

Third, you must know and follow some *basic guidelines*.

If, while you're writing for clarity, some lovely, dramatic or inspired phrases or sentences come to you, fine. Put them in.

But then with cold, objective eyes and mind ask yourself: "Do they detract from clarity?" If they do, grit your teeth and cut the frills.

FOLLOW SOME BASIC GUIDELINES

I can't give you a complete list of "dos and don'ts" for every writing problem you'll ever face.

But I can give you some fundamental guidelines that cover the most common problems.

1. Outline What You Want to Say

I know that sounds grade-schoolish. But you can't write clearly until, *before you start*, you know where you will stop.

Ironically, that's even a problem in writing an outline (i.e., knowing the ending before you begin).

So try this method:

- On 3″ × 5″ cards, write — one point to a card — all the points you need to make.
- Divide the cards into piles — one pile for each group of points *closely related* to each other. (If you were describing an automobile, you'd put all the points about mileage in one pile, all the points about safety in another, and so on.)
- Arrange your piles of points in a sequence. Which are most important and should be given first or saved for last? Which must you present before others in order to make the others understandable?
- Now, *within* each pile, do the same thing — arrange the *points* in logical, understandable order.

There you have your outline, needing only an introduction and conclusion.

This is a practical way to outline. It's also flexible. You can add, delete or change the location of points easily.

2. Start Where Your Readers Are

How much do they know about the subject? Don't write to a level higher than your readers' knowledge of it.

CAUTION: Forget that old — and wrong — advice about writing to a 12-year-old mentality. That's insulting. But do remember that your prime purpose is to *explain* something, not prove that you're smarter than your readers.

3. Avoid Jargon
Don't use words, expressions, phrases known only to people with specific knowledge or interests.

Example: A scientist, using scientific jargon, wrote, "The biota exhibited a one hundred percent mortality response." He could have written: "All the fish died."

4. Use Familiar Combinations of Words
A speech writer for President Franklin D. Roosevelt wrote, "We are endeavoring to construct a more inclusive society." F.D.R. changed it to, "We're going to make a country in which no one is left out."

CAUTION: By familiar combinations of words, I do *not* mean incorrect grammar. *That* can be *un*clear. Example: John's father says he can't go out Friday. (Who can't go out? John or his father?)

5. Use "First-Degree" Words
These words immediately bring an image to your mind. Other words must be "translated" through the first-degree word before you see the image. Those are second/third-degree words.

First-Degree Words	Second/Third-Degree Words
face	visage, countenance
stay	abide, remain, reside
book	volume, tome, publication

First-degree words are usually the most precise words, too.

6. Stick to the Point
Your outline — which was more work in the beginning — now saves you work. Because now you can ask about any sentence you write: "Does it relate to a point in the outline? If it doesn't, should I add it to the outline? If not, I'm getting off the track." Then, full steam ahead — on the main line.

7. Be as Brief as Possible
Whatever you write, shortening — *condensing* — almost always makes it tighter, straighter, easier to read and understand.

Condensing, as *Reader's Digest* does it, is in large part artistry. But it involves techniques that anyone can learn and use.

- *Present your points in logical ABC order*: Here again, your outline should save you work because, if you did it right, your points already stand in logical ABC order — A makes B understandable, B makes C understandable and so on. To write in a straight line is to say something clearly in the fewest possible words.
- *Don't waste words telling people what they already know*: Notice how we edited this: "Have you ever wondered how banks rate you as a credit risk? ~~You know, of course, that it's some combination of facts about your income, your job, and so on. But actually,~~ Many banks have a scoring system. . . ."
- *Cut out excess evidence and unnecessary anecdotes*: Usually, one fact or example (at most, two) will support a point. More just belabor it. And while writing about something may remind you of a good story, ask yourself: "Does it *really help* to tell the story, or does it slow me down?"

(Many people think *Reader's Digest* articles are filled with anecdotes. Actually, we use them sparingly and usually for one of two reasons: either the subject is so dry it needs some "humanity" to give it life; or the subject is so hard to grasp, it needs anecdotes to help readers understand. If the subject is both lively and easy to grasp, we move right along.)

- *Look for the most common word wasters*: windy phrases.
- *Look for passive verbs you can make active*: Invariably, this produces a shorter sentence. "The cherry tree *was* chopped down by George Washington." (Passive verb and nine words.) "George Washington *chopped* down the cherry tree." (Active verb and seven words.)
- *Look for positive/negative sections from which you can cut the negative*: See how we did it here: "The answer ~~does not rest with carelessness or incompetence. It lies largely in~~ having enough people to do the job."

Finally, to write more clearly by saying it in fewer words: when you've finished, stop.

1000 words

Write your ending time here: _____

Subtract your starting time: _____

Total time: _____

Check the Rate Chart in the back of the book to find out how many words per minute you have read, and then record your score on the Progress Chart.

3

How to Write Clearly

COMPREHENSION CHECK
Circle the letter before the best answer to each question below. Don't look back at the article.

Subject and Main Idea
1. The subject of this article is
   a. writing.
   b. writing clearly.
   c. choosing a topic.
   d. writing for *Reader's Digest* magazine.

2. The main idea is that
   a. you shouldn't be afraid to write.
   b. writing clearly is possible if you fulfill the three basic requirements.
   c. you must work hard to be a good writer.
   d. wanting to write is not enough to make you a good writer.

Details
3. The first thing you do in preparing an outline is to
   a. arrange the points in a logical order.
   b. put your ideas on 3-inch × 5-inch cards.
   c. divide the cards into piles.
   d. do none of the above.

4. All of the following will make your writing briefer and clearer *except*
   a. using an outline.
   b. using one or two examples.
   c. editing a positive/negative section so it is only positive.
   d. using passive verbs.

5. When writing, you should
   a. make your point as clearly as possible.
   b. use as much support for your ideas as you can.
   c. impress your readers with your vocabulary.
   d. use jargon to add color.

49

6. Thompson says that a clear writer avoids
   a. familiar word combinations, because they are boring.
   b. jargon, because it is confusing.
   c. first-degree words, because they make writing too choppy.
   d. dramatic words, because they are unnecessary.

Inferences

7. Clear writers
   a. no longer need to outline after they turn professional.
   b. never write more than a page.
   c. are made, not born.
   d. never need to use more than one example to prove a point.

8. Thompson feels that
   a. you should try to impress your audience.
   b. the most effective words are the ones that form an image in the reader's mind.
   c. most people are naturally clear writers.
   d. grammar is not important.

9. The purpose of outlining is to
   a. provide an organizational pattern for what you are about to write.
   b. help the writer stick to a point.
   c. allow the writer to differentiate main ideas and support.
   d. do all of the above.

10. Thompson implies that
    a. of all his guidelines, the most important is outlining.
    b. interesting examples are always helpful.
    c. in order to be clear, the writer must use a large vocabulary.
    d. well-organized writing needs no editing.

QUESTIONS FOR ANALYSIS AND APPLICATION

1. Was this explanation of how to write helpful to you or not? Explain your answer.

2. Below is a sample paragraph of wordy writing. Condense and rewrite it.

> Guilt is without any possible doubt or question in anyone's mind one of the most painfully hurtful and one of the most useless emotions anyone can possibly experience in the entire universe. This is without a doubt especially true of guilt that you don't happen to be in any way responsible for, even if someone else tries to make you feel guilty about it. This unearned guilt, which most of us have experienced at one time or another for one reason or another because we are human, saps all of our energy to the point where we may be so exhausted that all we can do or want to do is sleep all day long and not get any work of any kind done, makes us feel as if we aren't worth anything at all to anybody else in the world and especially not to ourselves, and of course, if you really think about it for a little while, doesn't even accomplish anything that might in any shape or form help us feel better about ourselves or the situation in the future.

VOCABULARY IN CONTEXT
Multiple Choice
Circle the letter before the best definition of each underlined word or phrase.

1. Fashion experts say that accessories such as shoes and jewelry should not <u>detract from</u> clothes.
    a. draw attention to   b. add cost to   c. complement
    d. draw attention from

2. It was once thought that one <u>fundamental</u> difference between the Neanderthal, a prehistoric human, and ourselves was that we had a larger brain; however, the opposite is true.
    a. basic   b. small   c. unimportant   d. area of

3. Censors <u>delete</u> scenes from movies shown on television that they think younger family members should not see.
    a. include   b. take out   c. expand   d. recognize

4. Even at birth, the <u>mortality rate</u> of males is higher than for females; 30 to 50 percent more males are conceived, but only 5 to 6 percent more males are born.
    a. size   b. number   c. death rate   d. birth rate

5. Doctors are <u>endeavoring to</u> discover why teenagers are 50 percent more likely to catch colds than people over fifty are.
    a. failing to   b. attempting to   c. succeeding at
    d. refusing to

6. The Reader's Digest company is famous for <u>condensing</u> longer novels and selling several of these in one regular-size book.
    a. increasing   b. shortening   c. changing   d. rewriting

Fill-in
Write the best word from this list in the blank in each sentence below:

inspired   objective   ironically   sequence   jargon

anecdotes   belabor

7. People who _____ a point tend to make you impatient.

8. Because most people memorize the alphabet in forward

    _____, they have great difficulty saying it backwards.

9. *BLT* is restaurant _____ for a bacon, lettuce, and tomato sandwich.

10. It is difficult to be _____ about the faults of the other person when you are in love; this is one reason why over 60 percent of the marriages in the United States fail.

11. Claude Monet was _____ to paint more than 300 pictures of the lily pads in his garden.

12. People who tell funny _____ are usually popular at parties.

13. _____, although many people think that chop suey is a Chinese dish, it was created by a restaurant owner in San Francisco as a way of serving leftovers.

SKILLS EXERCISE: MAIN IDEAS AND SUPPORT

For explanation see pp. 10–15

A. Read the following paragraph, and then circle the letter that identifies the implied main idea. Finally, identify the type of support used: facts, reasons, examples, testimony.

> A speech writer for President Franklin D. Roosevelt wrote, "We are endeavoring to construct a more inclusive society." F.D.R. changed it to "We're going to make a country in which no one is left out."

The implied main idea is that Franklin Delano Roosevelt
a. was a good president.
b. used speech writers.
c. believed that simple language was most effective.
d. liked to impress people with his vocabulary.

Type of support: _____

B. The following are main ideas from this article. List the supporting ideas that the author gave. You may look back at the article.

1. There are three basic requirements for writing clearly.

a. _____

b. _____

c. _____

2. There are six ways to condense your writing.

    a. _____

    b. _____

    c. _____

    d. _____

    e. _____

    f. _____

C. In the next two examples, the supporting ideas are given. Fill in the main idea.

    1. _____
       a. Write one point per 3 × 5 card.
       b. Divide cards into piles according to closely related points.
       c. Arrange piles in the order they are to be used.
       d. Arrange points in sequence in each pile.

    2. _____
       a. Outline what you want to say.
       b. Start where your readers are.
       c. Avoid jargon.
       d. Use familiar combinations of words.
       e. Use "first-degree" words.
       f. Stick to the point.
       g. Be as brief as possible.

SKILLS EXERCISE:
WORDS THAT SIGNAL KEY CONCEPTS

Authors offer their readers several kinds of clues to what is important in an article. First, they might use different kinds of type — *italics*, CAPITALS, and **boldface**. Second, they might use numbers, letters, and Roman numerals to call attention to ideas. Finally, they might use **signal words** to help readers find the important information. These three devices help indicate how the article is organized; therefore, you should usually locate them before you start underlining. Because the three kinds of type stand out, you do not have to mark them, but you should circle numbers, letters, and Roman numerals and underline important signal words when you mark an article from a textbook.

Signal words can indicate five things: emphasis, addition, example, change of direction, and conclusion. Here are examples of each kind of signal word:

Emphasis
most important
remember that
caution
the main idea
especially important
actually
here again
above all
note that

Addition
first (second . . .)
one (two . . .)
for one thing
and
also
in addition
moreover
next
another
then

Example
for example
for instance
to illustrate
such as

Change of Direction
but
on the other hand
however
in contrast
ironically
yet
even though
otherwise
on the contrary
still

Conclusion
in conclusion
in summary
therefore
thus
last of all
finally
as a result
hence

This article uses signal words from all the above categories. Search the article for an example of each kind, and write it in the appropriate space below.

1. Emphasis: _____

2. Addition: _____

3. Example: _____

4. Change of direction: _____

5. Conclusion: _____

SKILLS EXERCISE:
WORD PARTS

For explanation
see pp. 8–9

Below are eight words from the article and their dictionary etymologies, which are provided so that you can see the prefix and root of each word. Another word using the root is also given to help you remember what the root means.

Word	Etymology	Another Word
ob<u>jec</u>tive	[< L. *ob-*, to, toward + *jacere*, to throw + *ive*, like, relating to]	reject
de<u>tract</u>	[< L. *de-*, from + *trahere*, to draw]	tractor
<u>mor</u>tality	[< L. *mors*, death + *al*, like, relating to + *ity*, state or quality]	mortuary
<u>human</u>ity	[< L. *humanus*, person + *ity*, state or quality]	human
be<u>labor</u>	[< OE. *be-*, by + < L. *laborare*, to work]	labor
in<u>vari</u>ably	[*in-*, not + < ME. < M Fr. < LL. *variabilis*, change + *-ly*, < ME. < OE.]	varied
ex<u>cess</u>	[< L. *ex-*, out + *cessus*, cease]	success
re<u>side</u>	[< *re-*, back + *sedere*, to sit]	president

Now, using these roots as clues, match the difficult words below to their definitions.

_____ 1. eject

_____ 2. intractable

_____ 3. mortify

_____ 4. posthumous

_____ 5. collaborate

_____ 6. variegated

_____ 7. incessant

_____ 8. residue

a. never ceasing

b. to work together

c. stubborn (not able to be drawn along)

d. to make ashamed (make you wish you were dead)

e. to throw out

f. after a person's death

g. having varied colors; particolored

h. that which remains (sits) after part is taken away

4

The Many Miracles of Mark Hicks

VOCABULARY PREVIEW

portfolios (pôrt fō'lē ōz'):   selections of representative works, as of artists

quadriplegic (kwäd'rə plē'jik):   one who is totally paralyzed from the neck down

intrigued (in trēgd'):   interested

severed (sev'ərd):   cut in two

disarming (dis är'miŋ):   removing suspicion, fear, or hostility

impassioned (im pash'ənd):   filled with strong feeling

documentary (däk'yə men'tə rē):   a motion picture or a television show that presents factual material in a dramatic way

excruciating (iks krōō'shē āt'iŋ):   intensely painful

transpose (trans pōz'):   to transfer or shift the position of

lithographs (lith'ə grafs'):   prints made by a method that uses the repulsion between grease and water

wry (rī):   humorous in a twisted or sarcastic way

aspirated (as'pə rāt'id):   sucked or drawn in, as by inhaling

prestigious (pres tij'əs):   having the power to impress as the result of having success or wealth

integrity (in teg'rə tē):   the quality or state of being of high moral principle; uprightness, honesty, and sincerity

bantered (ban'tərd):   joked or teased good-naturedly

fat, āpe, cär; ten, ēven; is, bīte; gō, hôrn, tōōl, look; oil, out; up, fʉr; chin, she; thin, *then*; zh, leisure; ŋ, ring; ə for *a* in *ago;* ' as in *able* (ā'b'l)

SURVEY

Survey the following article by reading the title, the author's name, and the first and last paragraph. This should take no longer than one minute. After your survey, answer the following questions without looking back at the article. (The answers appear on page 471.)

1. What does the author, Jan Stussy, do for a living? _____

2. What is Mark Hicks's handicap? _____

3. What skill makes Mark special? _____

4. What award did the film win? _____

5. Why couldn't Mark Hicks be at the award ceremony? _____

6. What is the main idea of the article? _____

Now read the article. Write your starting time here: _____

4

The Many Miracles of Mark Hicks

Jan Stussy

EIGHT YEARS AGO, I was reviewing the art portfolios of applying students in my studio classroom on the campus of the University of California at Los Angeles. My secretary approached me with a special request from a quadriplegic student who wished to join my class in life drawing. "He draws by holding the pencil in his teeth," she said.

"That's crazy!" I replied. "It's tough enough to learn with skilled hands, but to try to draw with your mouth is . . . impossible. My answer is *No!*"

When I turned back to the portfolios of the waiting students— accepting some and rejecting others on the merits of their ability as draftsmen—my secretary added another student's portfolio to the pile.

The work was above average in skill, and the drawings intrigued me. "Yes," I said, "I'll accept this student."

Before I could say another word, the quadriplegic flashed past me in his wheelchair, turned and stopped — facing the suddenly quiet class and a red-faced professor.

I tried not to look at him as I explained to the class (but mostly to him) that the work was going to be very hard for all of them (*especially* him) and now was the time to withdraw if anyone (*anyone!*) had second thoughts. Two students left, but those serious eyes from the wheelchair didn't even blink. I dismissed the class and asked the young man to remain.

In a soft, quiet voice, 23-year-old Mark Hicks told me that when he was 12 he fell from a tree house in his back yard in Manhattan Beach, Calif. "It was nobody's fault," he said calmly. "I just fell." The accident severed his spinal column, causing permanent paralysis from the neck down.

Mark had drawn before his accident. Slowly, he began to sketch again (and later taught himself to paint with oils) by holding the tools clenched in his teeth. He developed very strong jaw muscles. "If all my muscles were as strong as my jaws," he remarked with disarming good humor, "I could lift up this building."

Perfecting his drawing was, for Mark, like learning to fly. Through it, he could escape from his body into the make-believe world of his mind. He worked with a tutor at home to complete high school, then went to a junior college to major in art and to develop his skill as a draftsman.

Mark did not think of himself as pitiful, so he was not embarrassed. He simply was what he was. He accepted his limitations and worked beyond his capacities, setting an example and inspiring other students. True, I was his teacher — but in a larger sense, he was mine.

His impact on me and the class was so dramatic and useful that I resolved to capture him on film. I wanted to show other people how courage and spirit can achieve great things in spite of all odds. I had never made a film, but if Mark could draw, I could make a movie.

In September 1973 I wrote an impassioned letter to my dean telling him how I wanted to make a short documentary so others could share what we found in Mark. The dean was so moved that he sent a check for $6000 from funds earmarked for special projects. It was the first of many improbable miracles.

Mark knew a student, John Joseph, in the U.C.L.A. cinema department, who wanted to make a film for his senior project. We joined forces.

Four other talented students soon joined us. We rented cameras, tripods, sound equipment and lights, and shot Mark as he lived his life. No real story, no firm plot. We filmed his father getting him out of bed, sitting him in his chair and brushing his teeth. We followed his mother cooking food and feeding it to him. We shot his attendant putting him into his van and driving him to school. We photographed him in my life-drawing class, going to exhibits, parties and back to the hospital.

The high point of the movie came about when my gallery director — unaware that Mark made his pictures with his teeth — saw his paintings and offered to give Mark a one-man exhibition. We followed Mark's van to San Francisco and documented the opening of his show, the reception party and the highly successful exhibit. Mark sat among his pictures enjoying one of the happiest moments of his life. "I reached my goal," he said. "And I did it sitting down."

At that point we ran out of money and film. In our enthusiasm, we had spent the entire $6000 and had shot 64 rolls of expensive color film. Not a dime was left to develop it. It was excruciating to have that huge stack of film and not be able to see what we had done. It was, said Mark, "like being pregnant, forever."

Hat in hand and trembling nervously, I called on Paul Flaherty, chief executive at the Technicolor laboratory. When I told him about Mark and the film project, he offered to develop and print 15 rolls as a charitable gesture. So, I sent 30. If the miracle was going to work, we might just as well go for 30.

About a month later, Flaherty called: "That film is very, very good. Can I meet Mark?"

We wheeled Mark in the next day. After 35 minutes of conversation, Flaherty promised to develop the remaining 34 rolls — again for free. The miracles were holding.

But we were still broke. We had editing to do and sound tapes to transpose and music to score and inserts and titles to make and a final print to get. We needed more money. I wrote a letter describing our project and offering one of Mark's lithographs for a $200 donation, or a set of one of his and one of mine for $500. I mailed it to everyone I ever knew. The money began to roll in, and we went back to work.

When it came time for a title, we recalled a wry observation Mark made in the movie and chose *Gravity Is My Enemy*. (It was perhaps the only enemy he ever had.)

Then the money problem struck again. The rough cut was finished but we needed a major miracle to get the final and expensive print and negative made. We had begged and borrowed from everyone. It looked like the miracles had finally run out.

At that dark moment, Mark died.

He had aspirated some food into his lung while swallowing and was unable to cough it up. It could have happened a dozen times before. But it didn't happen until he had finished his film and seen a rough cut.

Mark was gone, but we had come this far because of him and we could not stop now. We had to show others what he had been. About three weeks after Mark's funeral, I took our scratchy work print to Ray Wagner, then a vice president of M-G-M. Halfway through he turned on the lights and, with tears running down his face, told me he would make a free final print. Mark's miracles were still operating.

We sent the finished film to the prestigious San Francisco Film Festival. To our surprise it took first place in the documentary-films competition, winning the Golden Gate Award, the top festival prize. This made it automatically eligible to be nominated for an Academy Award — and to our astonishment, it *was*. Yet another miracle!

Although we knew we hadn't a chance of winning the Oscar, it was well worth the price of our rented tuxedos for John Joseph and me to attend the glamorous Academy Awards. As I sat through the opening presentations my mind drifted back to Mark and how much I wished he could be sharing the nomination with us. Despite the realities, I really wanted that Oscar — for Mark and U.C.L.A. and for everyone who had made the film possible. Most of all, I wanted it to prove to other students who want to make movies that if you do it with feeling and integrity . . . you can win.

My mouth was dry as the moment approached for the presentation in our category. Time passed in slow motion as Kirk Douglas and Raquel Welch bantered before opening the envelopes. Then I heard Raquel say: "And the winner is — *Gravity* . . ."

I have no recollection of walking up that long aisle of applauding movie stars and reaching the podium. I meant to thank everyone, but I froze.

Then, as in a dream, I heard myself saying, "Just finishing our film was a miracle — and this award is another. But the greatest miracle of all was Mark Hicks. He showed us how to live life as a hero. It's Mark's film and his award. He can't be here tonight; he has left his wheelchair and is running free somewhere in God's Heaven." Then, I took the golden Oscar, held it over my head and concluded: "Mark, *this* is for you."

1450 words

Write your ending time here: _____

Subtract your starting time: _____

Total time: _____

Check the Rate Chart in the back of the book to find out how many words per minute you have read, and then record your score on the Progress Chart.

4

The Many Miracles of Mark Hicks

COMPREHENSION CHECK
Circle the letter before the best answer to each of the following questions. Don't look back at the article.

Subject and Main Idea
1. The subject of the article is
   a. handicapped people.
   b. the remarkable Mark Hicks.
   c. the making of a movie.
   d. winning an Oscar.

2. The main idea is that
   a. handicapped people can succeed.
   b. making a movie is difficult.
   c. Mark Hicks and the movie were remarkable.
   d. winning an Oscar is not easy.

Details
3. John Joseph was
   a. another art instructor.
   b. Mark's attendant.
   c. a cinema student at UCLA.
   d. the person who presented the academy award.

4. Mark had injured himself
   a. in an auto accident.
   b. by falling from a tree.
   c. during an art class.
   d. while making a film.

5. At first, the art teacher thought that Mark
   a. should take the class to improve his drawings.
   b. did not like him very much.
   c. couldn't draw very well.
   d. would not be able to pass the class.

6. The person who wrote the story for the movie was
   a. the art instructor.
   b. Mark.
   c. John Joseph, a cinema student.
   d. nobody; there was no real story or plot.

Inferences
7. You can infer from the article that
   a. an Academy Award can be won by an amateur.
   b. Mark did not know many people.
   c. Mark became rich as an artist.
   d. Mark's parents blamed themselves for the accident.

8. You can infer from the article that Mark
   a. was a good filmmaker.
   b. was an angry young man.
   c. felt good about himself.
   d. was a person who gave up easily.

9. The gallery director probably
   a. could tell that Mark was handicapped by the drawings.
   b. would not have let Mark show his paintings if he had known that Mark was handicapped.
   c. was surprised to find out that Mark was handicapped.
   d. took the paintings because he felt sorry for Mark.

10. The film about Mark
   a. was sad for the people who made it.
   b. cost Mark his life.
   c. was much more expensive than the art teacher thought it would be.
   d. looked amateurish.

QUESTIONS FOR ANALYSIS AND APPLICATION
1. The author says, "True, I was his teacher, but in a larger sense he was mine." What did the art teacher learn from Mark?

2. Describe what you think Mark Hicks's parents were like.

VOCABULARY IN CONTEXT
Multiple Choice
Circle the letter before the best definition of each underlined word.

1. The children were <u>intrigued</u> by watching the baby chicks hatch.
   a. interested   b. offended   c. sick   d. scared

2. It is now possible to sew a <u>severed</u> finger back on.
   a. cut off   b. joined   c. grown   d. uncovered

3. The union leader's <u>impassioned</u> speech moved the members to go on strike.
   a. short   b. inspiring   c. cool   d. awkward

4. Dancers often go on stage with <u>excruciating</u> pain in their legs.
   a. minor   b. stimulating   c. agonizing   d. justified

5. <u>Aspirating</u> smoke can make us cough.
   a. inhaling   b. exhaling   c. seeing   d. avoiding

6. The judge's <u>integrity</u> was unquestioned.
   a. untruthfulness   b. stupidity   c. honesty
   d. hopefulness

7. The Nobel Peace Prize is one of the most <u>prestigious</u> awards a
   person can win.
   a. unimportant   b. inflated   c. familiar   d. impressive

8. His <u>wry</u> remark was meant to be funny, but it hurt her feelings.
   a. stupid   b. intelligent   c. sarcastic   d. brief

Fill-in

Write the best word from the following list in the blank in each
sentence.

portfolios   **quadriplegics**   **disarming**   **documentary**

transposed   **banter**   **lithographic**

9. There is a lot of good-natured _____ at
   a class reunion.

10. The musician _____ the song into an
    easier key for him to sing.

11. Actors carry _____ of pictures to show
    producers the various types of characters they can portray.

12. The doctor's _____ manner put her
    patient at ease.

13. _____ have great difficulty doing the
    simple tasks we take for granted.

14. A great deal of research should be done before making a
    _____ film.

15. After a certain number of prints, _____
    plates are destroyed so that no unauthorized prints can be made.

**SKILLS EXERCISE:
MAIN IDEAS AND SUPPORT**

For explanation see pp. 10–15

A. Read the following paragraph, and then circle the letter that identifies the implied main idea. Finally, identify the type of support used: facts, reasons, examples, or testimony.

   I tried not to look at him as I explained to the class (but mostly to him) that the work was going to be very hard for all of them (*especially* him) and now was the time to withdraw if anyone (*anyone!*) had second thoughts. Two students left, but those serious eyes from the wheelchair didn't even blink. I dismissed the class and asked the young man to remain.

   1. The implied main idea is that

      a. the art teacher was prejudiced against handicapped people.
      b. the art teacher thought Mark couldn't do the work, but Mark thought he could.
      c. Mark wanted to leave the class but was afraid to.
      d. the art teacher wasn't going to allow Mark into the class under any circumstances.

   Type of support: _____

B. The following is a main idea from this article. List the supporting ideas that the author gave. You may look back at the article.

   1. Expenses for "Gravity Is My Enemy" were paid by contributions from several sources.

      a. _____
      b. _____
      c. _____
      d. _____

C. In the next two examples, the supporting ideas are given. Fill in the implied main idea.

   1. _____

      a. His father got him out of bed, put him in his chair, and brushed his teeth.
      b. His mother cooked his food and fed it to him.
      c. His attendant put him in his van and drove him to school.

2. _____

    a. He learned to draw with his teeth.

    b. He entered UCLA.

    c. He took a life drawing class without needing extra attention from the teacher.

    d. He didn't leave the class after learning how difficult it would be.

SKILLS EXERCISE: USING THE DICTIONARY/WORD PARTS

For explanation see pp. 2–9

A. For practice in finding the correct meaning of a word in the dictionary, select the correct meaning of the following seven words from the article. Above each entry is a sentence using the word. In the blank before the sentence, put the number of the definition that fits the way the word is used. The abbreviation under each blank tells you which part of speech the word is, so you can more easily find the proper definition.

_____ 1. When I turned <u>back</u> to the portfolios of the waiting stu-
adv.   dents — accepting some and rejecting others on the mer-
    its of their ability as draftsmen — my secretary added
    another student's portfolio to the pile.

    back (bak) *n.* [< OE. *bæk*] **1.** the rear part of the body from the nape of the neck to the end of the spine **2.** the backbone **3.** a part that supports or fits the back **4.** the rear part or reverse of anything **5.** *Sports* a player or position behind the front line — *adj.* **1.** at the rear **2.** remote **3.** of or for the past *[back* pay] **4.** backward — *adv.* **1.** at, to, or toward the rear **2.** to or toward a former condition, time, activity, etc. **3.** in reserve or concealment **4.** in return or requital *[pay him *back]* — *vt.* **1.** to move backward **2.** to support **3.** to bet on **4.** to provide or be a back for

_____ 2. Before I could say another word, the quadriplegic <u>flashed</u>
v.   past me in his wheelchair, turned and stopped — facing
    the suddenly quiet class and a red-faced professor.

    flash (flash) *vt.* [ME. *flashen*, to splash] **1.** to send out a sudden, brief light **2.** to sparkle **3.** to come or pass suddenly **4.** to send (news, etc.) swiftly — *n.* **1.** a sudden, brief light **2.** a brief moment **3.** a sudden, brief display **4.** a brief news item sent by radio, etc. **5.** a gaudy display — *adj.* happening swiftly or suddenly — **flash'er** *n.*

_____ 3. It's Mark's <u>film</u> and his award.

n.

film (film) *n.* [OE. *filmen*] **1.** a fine, thin skin, coating, etc. **2.** a flexible cellulose material covered with a substance sensitive to light and used in photography **3.** a haze or blur **4.** a motion picture — *vt., vi.* **1.** to cover or be covered as with a film **2.** to photograph or make a motion picture (of)

_____ 4. He developed very <u>strong</u> jaw muscles.

adj.

strong (strôŋ) *adj.* [OE. *strang*] **1.** *a)* physically powerful *b)* healthy; sound **2.** morally or intellectually powerful [a *strong* will] **3.** firm; durable [a *strong* fort] **4.** powerful in wealth, numbers, etc. **5.** of a specified number [troops 50,000 *strong*] **6.** having a powerful effect **7.** intense in degree or quality [*strong* coffee, a *strong* light, *strong* colors, etc.]

_____ 5. He <u>developed</u> very strong jaw muscles.

v.

de•vel•op (di vel'əp) *vt.* [< Fr. *dé-* apart + OFr. *voloper*, to wrap] **1.** to make fuller, bigger, better, etc. **2.** to show or work out by degrees; disclose **3.** *Photog.* to put (a film, etc.) in chemical solutions to make the picture visible **4.** to come into being or activity; occur or happen

_____ 6. He <u>simply</u> was what he was.

adv.

sim•ply (sim'plē) *adv.* **1.** in a simple way **2.** merely [*simply* trying] **3.** completely [*simply* overwhelmed]

_____ 7. The dean was so <u>moved</u> that he sent a check for

v. $6,000. . . .

move (mo͞ov) *vt.* moved, mov'ing [<L. *movere*] **1.** to change the place or position of **2.** to set or keep in motion **3.** to cause (*to do, say,* etc.) **4.** to arouse the emotions, etc. of **5.** to propose formally, as in a meeting **6.** to change one's residence **7.** to make progress **8.** to take action **9.** to make a formal application (*for*) **10.** to evacuate: said of the bowels **11.** *Commerce* to be sold: said of goods — *n.* **1.** act of moving **2.** an action toward some goal **3.** *Chess, Checkers,* etc. the act of moving a piece, or one's turn to move

B. For practice with the pronunciation guide, translate these holidays into English spelling.

fat, āpe, cär; ten, ēven; is, bīte; gō, hôrn, tōōl, look; oil, out; up, fᵘr; chin, she; thin, *then*; zh, leisure; ŋ, ring; ə for *a* in *ago;* ' as in *able* (ā'b'l)

1. sānt pa'triks dā

_____

2. val'ən tīnz'dā

_____

3. thə fôrth'əv joo lī'

_____

4. mə môr'ē əl dā

_____

5. nōō'yirz ēv

_____

6. fä'thərz dā

_____

C. By looking at a word's etymology in the dictionary, you can find the meaning of its roots. Here are six words from the article that contain common roots. The roots, their meanings, and other words that can help you remember the meanings are also provided.

Word	Root	Meaning of Root	Another Word
1. quadriplegic	quad	four	quadrangle
2. request	ques	to ask or to seek	question
3. resolve	solv	to explain	solve
4. impassioned	pass	feeling	passion
5. photographed	photo	of or produced by light	photocopy
6. transpose	pos	put or place	pose

Using these roots, match the following difficult words to their definitions:

1. quadrennial

2. inquest

3. absolve

4. impassive

5. photic

6. juxtapose

a. to free from guilt (explain why someone is not guilty)

b. to put side by side

c. showing or having no feelings

d. having to do with the effect of light upon, or the production of light by, organisms

e. occurring once every four years

f. an official inquiry, usually to seek out the cause of a sudden and unexpected death

5

Superstitions:
Just Whistling in the Dark

SURVEY

Survey the following article by reading the author's name, the title, and the headings. This should take no longer than fifteen seconds. After your survey, answer the following questions without looking back at the article. (The answers appear on page 471.)

1. List five of the superstitions that are discussed.

_____

_____

_____

_____

_____

2. Is Friday the thirteenth discussed? _____

3. Are any superstitions about animals discussed? _____

Now read the article. Write your starting time here: _____

5

Superstitions:
Just Whistling in the Dark

Don Boxmeyer

WHY DO YOU SUPPOSE the boss is so grumpy?

"Dunno. Maybe he got up on the wrong side of the bed."

"He'd probably feel better if you got him a cup of coffee."

"Right. Knock on wood."

One of these fellows is superstitious. He probably goes out of his way to avoid meeting black cats. He doesn't walk under ladders, step on sidewalk cracks or open umbrellas indoors, and he worries a lot if he breaks a mirror.

That makes him a trifle silly and just like almost everybody else.

A superstition is a belief based wholly on fear and not in harmony with any known law of science. How do you know the number 13 is unlucky? You just know it. How do you know that spilling salt is unlucky? It just is.

Irrational? Yes and no.

Superstitions, wrote Rabbi D. R. Brasch in his book, "How Did It Begin?" have reasons, backgrounds and practical explanations. They belonged to the social life of both the civilized and the savage.

Here are some examples.

THE UNLUCKY NUMBER 13

In some European countries, you can't live in house No. 13. It does not exist. No. 12 is followed by No. 12½ and then No. 14. Many office buildings in this country skip the 13th floor. Some airlines and sports arenas omit 13 as a seat number. A true triskaidekaphobiac would not start a journey on the 13th of any month (on Friday the 13th he stays right in bed with the covers pulled way up over his head), will not buy or use 13 of anything, will not wear a number 13 on a uniform or eat with 12 others.

Why? Historically, 13 represents the number of men present at the Last Supper. Greek philosophers and mathematicians scorned the number 13 as being "imperfect," and in Norse mythology, 12 gods were present when the evil spirit Loki busted a party at a good address in Valhalla and killed Balder, a very popular god.

WALKING UNDER LADDERS

This superstition has a practical application. You could get a bucket of paint on the head. But custom says if you walk under a ladder, the wrath of the gods will be on you in any case and what you ought to do is quickly cross your fingers and make a wish.

Historians have rationalized that the ladder, leaning against a wall, forms a triangle signifying the Holy Trinity. To pass through such sacred space is a punishable offense. It's flat dangerous to play with such supernatural forces; a bucket of paint on the head is nothing compared to what could be in store.

GETTING OUT OF BED ON THE WRONG SIDE

It is written that to get out of bed on the left side is to subject your day to misfortune and misery. You are supposed to rise from the right and place your right foot on the floor first. If you err, go back to bed until you can do it correctly. This superstition has to do with the ancient belief that right was right and left was wrong.

SPILLING SALT

If this happens to you, you're supposed to take a pinch of salt and toss it over your left shoulder into the face of the devil.

This superstition is rooted in the ancient and biblical importance of salt. Salt purifies; hence it became the symbol of incorruptibility. Salt on the table became the emblem of justice, and to upset it became a forewarning of injustice.

In a famous Last Supper painting by Leonardo da Vinci, the faces of Jesus and the Apostles vividly show consternation and grief. Why? Historians say because someone just dumped the salt shaker over.

Who did it? Judas, of course. But there is no confirmation of this episode; Brasch said da Vinci merely used the old superstition to dramatize his painting.

BREAKING A MIRROR

This is good for seven years of bad luck or it could cause a death in the family. If a mirror breaks, legend instructs you to get the pieces out of the house posthaste and bury them in the ground.

Before the invention of mirrors, man gazed at his reflection in pools, ponds and lakes. If the image was distorted, disaster was sure to strike. (Sometimes a sneaky enemy would ruin his foe's day by pitching a pebble into the water.)

Gradually water gave way to shiny metal and then glass, but man still was convinced any injury to the reflection would be visited upon the real thing, just as he thought that by piercing the eyes of an enemy in a picture would cause the enemy to go blind. And the seven years? It is thought that the figure stems from Roman belief that a man's body physically rejuvenated itself every seven years and he became, in effect, a new man.

MEETING A BLACK CAT

Custom dictates that if your path is crossed by a black cat, you're really going to be in for it unless you return home immediately.

To the Egyptians, the cat was a god and anyone who killed one was punished. Come the Middle Ages, however, and the cat was linked to witches and Satan. Everyone knows what happens when you cross the devil.

WHISTLING

This is a professional superstition; newsmen are not supposed to whistle in the newsroom, and actors do not whistle in the dressing room. It probably goes back to the sailor's deep aversion to whistling except at very special times.

In the days of sail, seamen believed it was possible to call up a storm by the accidental use of magic — like duplicating the noise of wind in the rigging. Whistling on board was to invite bad luck, except when the ship was becalmed, and then only by an expert who would know in which precise direction to send the whistle as an order for wind.

1000 words

Write your ending time here: ⸺⸺⸺⸺⸺⸺⸺⸺

Subtract your starting time: ⸺⸺⸺⸺⸺⸺⸺⸺

Total time: ⸺⸺⸺⸺⸺⸺⸺⸺

Check the Rate Chart in the back of the book to find how many words per minute you have read, and then record your score on the Progress Chart.

5

Superstitions:
Just Whistling in the Dark

COMPREHENSION CHECK
Circle the letter before the best answer to each question below. Don't look back at the article.

Subject and Main Idea
1. The subject of this article is
   a. unusual superstitions.
   b. the history of superstitions.
   c. people's fears.
   d. triskaidekaphobia.

2. The main idea is that
   a. only silly people are superstitious.
   b. everyone is superstitious.
   c. superstitions come from uncivilized cultures.
   d. superstitions have historical explanations.

Details
3. The author thinks people who believe in superstitions are
   a. abnormal.
   b. logical.
   c. a bit silly.
   d. correct.

4. A triskaidekaphobiac
   a. stays home on Friday the thirteenth.
   b. believes the number thirteen has religious value.
   c. thinks the number thirteen is lucky.
   d. thinks numbers determine destiny.

5. Superstitions
   a. do not affect most people's thinking.
   b. are based on scientific fact.
   c. only involve things that are seen.
   d. come from many countries.

6. If you break a mirror, you are supposed to
    a. stay indoors that day.
    b. bury the pieces.
    c. throw the pieces into a river, ocean, or lake.
    d. throw a piece over your shoulder.

Inferences

7. From the article, we can conclude that superstitions
    a. are no longer believed.
    b. have been believed in every period of time.
    c. come from Europe.
    d. keep people from doing evil things.

8. The author seems to believe that
    a. superstitions are religious in origin.
    b. superstitions have no place in modern society.
    c. superstitious people do silly things.
    d. superstitious people are dangerous to society.

9. Superstitions
    a. didn't influence ancient people.
    b. were used by the church to control people.
    c. aren't believed by educated people.
    d. are found all over the world.

10. The author probably is
    a. superstitious.
    b. an astrologer.
    c. a detective.
    d. a religious leader.

QUESTIONS FOR ANALYSIS AND APPLICATION

1. Why do you think most people are superstitious?

2. Give some examples of how fear of the number 13 changes people's behavior.

VOCABULARY IN CONTEXT
Fill-in

Write the best word from this list in the blank in each sentence below:

irrational   philosopher   Norse   wrath   rationalize

incorruptibility   consternation   episodes   distort

aversion

1. Some people have such a strong _____
   to cabbage that even the smell of it cooking makes them sick.

2. Thursday was named after the _____
   god Thor, the god of thunder.

3. Most _____ of television programs are re-
   corded on videotape for later broadcast rather than presented live.

4. During the Middle Ages, beliefs about witchcraft were so

   _____ that cows, insects, and birds were
   convicted of being witches and put to death.

5. You must make someone very angry to incur his or her

   _____ .

6. Mirrors in carnival fun houses are shaped to

   _____ people's reflections.

7. Scandals such as Watergate have shaken our faith in the

   _____ of our political leaders.

8. People _____ continued smoking by
   pointing to healthy elderly people who have smoked all of their
   lives.

9. Eighteenth-century patients at St. Bartholomew's hospital must

   have felt _____ at being asked to pay
   their funeral expenses when they were admitted.

10. Socrates, probably the best known Greek

    _____ , never wrote down his own teach-
    ings; we know what he said because a student, Plato, took notes.

SKILLS EXERCISE: MAIN IDEAS AND SUPPORT

For explanation see pp. 10–15

A. Read the following paragraph, and then circle the letter that identifies the implied main idea. Finally, identify the type of support
   used: facts, reasons, examples, testimony.

   One of these fellows is superstitious. He probably goes out of his way to
   avoid meeting black cats. He doesn't walk under ladders, step on sidewalk
   cracks or open umbrellas indoors, and he worries a lot if he breaks a mirror.

The implied main idea is that

a. superstitious people try to avoid anything that will bring them bad luck.
b. most people are superstitious.
c. superstitious people won't go out of the house.
d. superstitions are funny.

Type of support: _____

B. The following are main ideas from this article. List the supporting ideas that the author gave. You may look back at the article.

1. Cats have often been objects of superstition.

   a. _____

   b. _____

2. Superstitions are often based on religious beliefs.

   a. _____

   b. _____

3. Superstitions come from many cultures.

   a. _____

   b. _____

   c. _____

   d. _____

   e. _____

C. In the next three examples, the supporting ideas are given. Fill in the main idea.

1. _____

   a. Newsmen
   b. Actors
   c. Sailors

2. _____

   a. Symbol of incorruptibility
   b. Emblem of justice

3. _____

   a. Number of men at the Last Supper
   b. Greek philosophers
   c. Norse mythology

SKILLS EXERCISE:
USING CONTEXT CLUES/WORD PARTS

For explanation see pp. 1–2; 8–9

A. To practice using context clues to determine the meaning of words, circle the letter of the best definition for each underlined word below. The words are shown here in the context in which they appear in the article.

1. ". . . In Norse <u>mythology</u>, 12 gods were present when the evil spirit Loki busted a party at a good address in Valhalla and killed Balder, a very popular god."

   a. history   b. legends   c. world   d. geography

2. ". . . In Norse mythology, 12 gods were present when the evil spirit Loki busted a party at a good address in <u>Valhalla</u> and killed Balder, a very popular god."

   a. heaven   b. the ocean   c. hell   d. history

3. "To pass through such sacred space is a punishable offense. It's flat dangerous to play with such <u>supernatural</u> forces; a bucket of paint on the head is nothing compared to what could be in store."

   a. deadly   b. godlike   c. funny   d. scientific

4. "You are supposed to rise from the right and place your right foot on the floor first. If you <u>err</u>, go back to bed until you can do it correctly."

   a. do it correctly   b. trip   c. make a mistake
   d. fall asleep

5. "Salt purifies; <u>hence</u> it became the symbol of incorruptibility."

   a. therefore   b. because   c. when   d. also

6. "But there is no <u>confirmation</u> of this episode; Brasch said da Vinci merely used the old superstition to dramatize his painting."

   a. story   b. song   c. proof   d. painting

7. "If a mirror breaks, legend instructs you to get the pieces out of the house <u>posthaste</u> and bury them in the ground."

   a. secretly   b. quickly   c. slowly   d. eventually

8. "It is thought that the figure stems from Roman belief that a man's body physically <u>rejuvenated</u> itself every seven years and he became, in effect, a new man."

   a. aged   b. killed   c. saw   d. renewed

B. Here are some common word parts that will help you with this exercise:

Prefixes	**Roots**	**Suffixes**
in, im, ir = not	*tort* = twist	*ate* = become
dis = not, apart, very	*phil* = love	*ology* = study of
re = again, back	*sophos* = wise	*ible* = able to be
super = over, beyond	*juven* = young	*er* = one who
a = away	*myth* = legend	*al* = like, of
com, con, cor =	*rupt* = break, spoil	*tion, ion* = act of,
together, very, with	*vert, vers* = turn	state of
	firm = strong	
	rat = think	

Using these word parts as hints, match the following words to their definitions.

_____ 1. irrational

_____ 2. philosopher

_____ 3. mythology

_____ 4. supernatural

_____ 5. incorruptible

_____ 6. confirmation

_____ 7. distort

_____ 8. rejuvenate

_____ 9. aversion

a. can't be broken down or morally destroyed

b. beyond the natural or ordinary

c. twist

d. feeling of wanting to turn away because of dislike

e. act of proving or making something stronger

f. using illogical thinking

g. a person who studies because of a love of wisdom

h. study of legends

i. to make young again

6

Saved

SURVEY

Survey the following article by reading the author's name, the title, and the first sentence of each paragraph. This should take about one minute. Then answer the following questions without looking back at the article.

1. Why did Malcolm X want to improve his reading? _____

2. How far did Malcolm X go in school? _____

3. What did Malcolm X study first? _____

4. Where did Malcolm X do most of his reading? _____

Now read the article. Write your starting time here: _____

6

Saved

Malcolm X

I BECAME INCREASINGLY frustrated at not being able to express what I wanted to convey in letters that I wrote, especially those to Mr. Elijah Muhammad. In the street, I had been the most articulate hustler out there — I had commanded attention when I said something. But now, trying to write simple English, I not only wasn't articulate, I wasn't even functional. How would I sound writing in slang, the way I would *say* it, something such as, "Look, daddy, let me pull your coat about a cat, Elijah Muhammad — "

Many who today hear me somewhere in person, or on television, or those who read something I've said, will think I went to school far beyond the eighth grade. This impression is due entirely to my prison studies.

It had really begun back in the Charlestown Prison, when Bimbi first made me feel envy of his stock of knowledge. Bimbi had always taken charge of any conversation he was in, and I had tried to emulate him. But every book I picked up had few sentences which didn't contain anywhere from one to nearly all of the words that might as well have been in Chinese. When I just skipped those words, of course, I really ended up with little idea of what the book said. So I had come to the Norfolk Prison Colony still going through only book-reading motions. Pretty soon, I would have quit even these motions, unless I had received the motivation that I did.

I saw that the best thing I could do was get hold of a dictionary — to study, to learn some words. I was lucky enough to reason also that I should try to improve my penmanship. It was sad. I couldn't even write in a straight line. It was both ideas together that moved me to request a dictionary along with some tablets and pencils from the Norfolk Prison Colony school.

I spent two days just riffling uncertainly through the dictionary's pages. I'd never realized so many words existed! I didn't know *which* words I needed to learn. Finally, just to start some kind of action, I began copying.

In my slow, painstaking, ragged handwriting, I copied into my tablet everything printed on that first page, down to the punctuation marks.

I believe it took me a day. Then, aloud, I read back, to myself, everything I'd written on the tablet. Over and over, aloud, to myself, I read my own handwriting.

I woke up the next morning, thinking about those words — immensely proud to realize that not only had I written so much at one time, but I'd written words that I never knew were in the world. Moreover, with a little effort, I also could remember what many of these words meant. I reviewed the words whose meanings I didn't remember. Funny thing, from the dictionary first page right now, that "aardvark" springs to my mind. The dictionary had a picture of it, a long-tailed, long-eared, burrowing African mammal, which lives off termites caught by sticking out its tongue as an anteater does for ants.

I was so fascinated that I went on — I copied the dictionary's next page. And the same experience came when I studied that. With every succeeding page, I also learned of people and places and events from history. Actually the dictionary is like a miniature encyclopedia. Finally the dictionary's A section had filled a whole tablet — and I went on into the B's. That was the way I started copying what eventually became the entire dictionary. It went a lot faster after so much practice helped me to pick up handwriting speed. Between what I wrote in my tablet, and writing letters, during the rest of my time in prison I would guess I wrote a million words.

I suppose it was inevitable that as my word-base broadened, I could for the first time pick up a book and read and now begin to understand what the book was saying. Anyone who has read a great deal can imagine the new world that opened. Let me tell you something: from then until I left that prison, in every free moment I had, if I was not reading in the library, I was reading on my bunk. You couldn't have gotten me out of books with a wedge. Between Mr. Muhammad's teachings, my correspondence, my visitors — usually Ella and Reginald — and my reading of books, months passed without my even thinking about being imprisoned. In fact, up to then, I never had been so truly free in my life.

The Norfolk Prison Colony's library was in the school building. A variety of classes was taught there by instructors who came from such places as Harvard and Boston universities. The weekly debates between inmate teams were also held in the school building. You would be astonished to know how worked up convict debaters and audiences would get over subjects like "Should Babies Be Fed Milk?"

Available on the prison library's shelves were books on just about every general subject. Much of the big private collection that Parkhurst had willed to the prison was still in crates and boxes in the back of the library — thousands of old books. Some of them looked ancient: covers faded, old-time parchment-looking binding. Parkhurst, I've mentioned, seemed to have been principally interested in history and religion. He had the money and the special interest to have a lot of books that you wouldn't have in general circulation. Any college library would have been lucky to get that collection.

As you can imagine, especially in a prison where there was heavy emphasis on rehabilitation, an inmate was smiled upon if he demonstrated an unusually intense interest in books. There was a sizable number of well-read inmates, especially the popular debaters. Some were said by many to be practically walking encyclopedias. They were almost celebrities. No university would ask any student to devour literature as I did when this new world opened to me, of being able to read and *understand*.

I read more in my room than in the library itself. An inmate who was known to read a lot could check out more than the permitted maximum number of books. I preferred reading in the total isolation of my own room.

When I had progressed to really serious reading, every night at about ten P.M. I would be outraged with the "lights out." It always seemed to catch me right in the middle of something engrossing.

Fortunately, right outside my door was a corridor light that cast a glow into my room. The glow was enough to read by, once my eyes adjusted to it. So when "lights out" came, I would sit on the floor where I could continue reading in that glow.

At one-hour intervals the night guards paced past every room. Each time I heard the approaching footsteps, I jumped into bed and feigned sleep. And as soon as the guard passed, I got back out of bed onto the floor area of that light-glow, where I would read for another fifty-eight minutes — until the guard approached again. That went on until three or four every morning. Three or four hours of sleep a night was enough for me. Often in the years in the streets I had slept less than that. . . .

I have often reflected upon the new vistas that reading opened to me. I knew right there in prison that reading had changed forever the course of my life. As I see it today, the ability to read awoke inside me some long dormant craving to be mentally alive. I certainly wasn't seeking any degree, the way a college confers a status symbol upon its students. My homemade education gave me, with every additional book that I read, a little bit more sensitivity to the deafness, dumbness, and blindness that was afflicting the black race in America. Not long ago, an English writer telephoned me from London, asking questions. One was, "What's your alma mater?" I told him, "Books." You will never catch me with a free fifteen minutes in which I'm not studying something I feel might be able to help the black man.

900 words

Write your ending time here: _____

Subtract your starting time: _____

Total time: _____

Check the Rate Chart in the back of the book to find how many words per minute you have read, and then record your score on the Progress Chart.

6

Saved

COMPREHENSION CHECK
Circle the letter before the best answer to each of the following questions. Don't look back at the article.

Subject and Main Idea
1. The subject of the article is
   - a. the education of Malcolm X.
   - b. Black Muslims.
   - c. the life of Malcolm X.
   - d. the importance of reading.

2. The main idea of the article is that
   - a. Malcolm X became an important leader.
   - b. Malcolm X was a street hustler.
   - c. Malcolm X educated himself in prison.
   - d. Prisoners are more intelligent than most people think.

Details
3. Malcolm X read to
   - a. gain status and power.
   - b. become wealthy.
   - c. become a great speaker.
   - d. help black people.

4. Malcolm X completed
   - a. high school.
   - b. college.
   - c. eighth grade.
   - d. junior college.

5. An aardvark is
   - a. a termite.
   - b. an African bird.
   - c. a burrowing mammal.
   - d. an armadillo.

6. Malcolm X read in semi-darkness because
   a. he didn't pay his electric bill.
   b. the prison guards were cruel.
   c. there was no window in his room.
   d. he read after "lights out."

Inferences

7. Malcolm X began reading books after
   a. completing high school.
   b. improving his vocabulary.
   c. getting out of prison.
   d. finishing second grade.

8. Malcolm X copied the dictionary because
   a. he didn't know a better method of vocabulary improvement.
   b. there are no better methods of vocabulary improvement.
   c. he didn't have any other books.
   d. he was bored.

9. Malcolm X's story shows that
   a. illiterate people are stupid.
   b. illiterate people are inarticulate.
   c. prison helps people reform.
   d. illiterate people can learn.

10. The administration at Norfolk Prison Colony
    a. encouraged prisoners to improve themselves.
    b. forced prisoners to work constantly.
    c. kept prisoners isolated.
    d. allowed prisoners to read whenever they wished.

QUESTIONS FOR ANALYSIS AND APPLICATION

1. Malcolm X taught himself to read by copying the dictionary. If you had the same reading problem he had, what other methods could you use?

2. Malcolm X eventually became a well-known leader of black people. What characteristics can you see in the article that suggest his potential for leadership?

VOCABULARY IN CONTEXT
Multiple Choice
Circle the letter before the best definition of each underlined word.

1. Because of the multiple definitions of words, it is sometimes difficult to convey exactly what we mean.
   a. infer   b. communicate   c. transfer   d. defer

2. Many politicians are so articulate that their speaking ability alone
   gets them elected to office.
   a. smooth and clear   b. sloppy and trivial   c. halting
   d. fast and disoriented

3. Susan had always admired her successful uncle, and when she
   grew up she tried to emulate him.
   a. undermine or destroy   b. imprison   c. win by force
   d. equal or surpass

4. The immense portions served at the restaurant were impossible
   to eat.
   a. small   b. trivial   c. enormous   d. tasty

5. He feigned illness to avoid work.
   a. ascertained   b. attempted   c. achieved   d. faked

6. The invention of the printing press opened new vistas for the common person.
   a. vocations   b. views or outlooks   c. incentives
   d. motivations

7. The seed, planted in the fall, lay dormant until the spring rains.
   a. dying   b. inactive   c. exposed   d. active

8. Many universities confer over 2000 degrees a year.
   a. revoke   b. give   c. will   d. remit

9. The most common disease, afflicting over 53 percent of the people
   in the United States, is tooth decay.
   a. involving   b. causing joy to   c. causing suffering to
   d. caught by

10. Until recently, most top business executives claimed Ivy League
    colleges as alma maters.
    a. schools graduated from   b. places visited
    c. schools where they wanted to go
    d. places their mothers came from

Fill-in
Write the best word from the following list in the blank in each sentence.

engrossing   inevitable   riffling   rehabilitation

hustlers   isolation   functional   motivation   circulation

devours

11. People who favor the death penalty usually don't believe in the

_____ of criminals.

12. Two-dollar bills are no longer in general _____.

13. My daughter loves fairy tales so much that she _____
     the Disney videos of *Snow White, Cinderella,* and *Sleeping
     Beauty.*

14. Con artists are _____ who take advan-
     tage of people.

15. Success in school depends on _____ as
     well as on ability.

16. You can get a general idea of a book by _____
     through its pages.

17. Death and taxes are said to be the only two things that are

_____.

18. In order to be _____ in society, you need
     to know basic mathematics.

19. For those who like them, crossword puzzles are

_____.

20. Solitary confinement is considered a severe punishment because

people suffer from _____.

SKILLS EXERCISE:
MAIN IDEAS AND SUPPORT

For explanation see pp. 10–15

A. Read the following paragraph, and then circle the letter that identifies the implied main idea.

> I woke up the next morning, thinking about those words — immensely proud to realize that not only had I written so much at one time, but I'd written words that I never knew were in the world. Moreover, with a little effort, I also could remember what many of these words meant. I reviewed the words whose meanings I didn't remember. Funny thing, from the dictionary first page right now, that "aardvark" springs to my mind. The dictionary had a picture of it, a long-tailed, long-eared, burrowing African mammal, which lives off termites caught by sticking out its tongue as an anteater does for ants.

1. The implied main idea is that
   a. copying the dictionary didn't do any good.
   b. an aardvark is an African mammal.
   c. copying the dictionary was effective.
   d. Malcolm X was able to remember what he read.

B. The following is a main idea from the article. List the supporting details that the author gave. You may look back at the article.

Malcolm X had had repeated trouble with the law.

   a. _____

   b. _____

C. In the next two examples, the supporting ideas are given. Fill in the main idea.

1. _____
   a. He needed to write letters.
   b. He envied another prisoner's stock of knowledge.
   c. He wanted to gather information that would help black people.

2. _____
   a. They had a library.
   b. They had classes.
   c. Inmates participated in debates.
   d. They had a good collection of books.
   e. Inmates who read a lot could check out a lot of books.
   f. They had spare time for study.

SKILLS EXERCISE:
USING THE DICTIONARY/WORD PARTS

For explanation see pp. 2–9

A. For practice in finding the correct meaning of a word in the dictionary, select the correct meaning of the following six words from the article. Above each entry is a sentence using the word. In the blank before the sentence, put the number of the definition that fits the way the word is used. The abbreviation under each blank tells you which parts of speech the word is, so you can more easily find the proper definition.

_____ 1. I became increasingly frustrated at not being able to ex-
n.   press what I wanted to convey in <u>letters</u> that I wrote, es-
                pecially those to Mr. Elijah Muhammad.

let•ter (let'ər) *n.* [<L. *littera*] **1.** any character of the alphabet **2.** a written or printed message, usually sent by mail **3.** [*pl.*] *a*) literature *b*) learning; knowledge **4.** literal meaning — *vt.* to mark with letters

_____ 2. When I just <u>skipped</u> those words, of course, I really ended
v.   up with little idea of what the book said.

skip (skip) *vi., vt.* **skipped, skip'ping** [ME. *skippen*] **1.** to leap lightly (over) **2.** to ricochet or bounce **3.** to pass from one point to another, omitting or ignoring (what lies between) **4.** [Colloq.] to leave (town, etc.) hurriedly — *n.* a skipping; specif., a gait alternating light hops on each foot

_____ 3. I couldn't even write in a straight <u>line</u>.
n.

line (līn) *n.* [< L. *linea*, lit., linen thread] **1.** a cord, rope, wire, etc. **2.** any wire, pipe, etc., or system of these, conducting fluid, electricity, etc. **3.** a thin, threadlike mark **4.** a border or boundary **5.** a limit **6.** outline; contour **7.** a row of persons or things, as of printed letters across a page **8.** a succession of persons or things **9.** lineage **10.** a transportation system of buses, ships, etc. **11.** the course a moving thing takes **12.** a course of conduct, action, explanation, etc. **13.** a person's trade or occupation **14.** a stock of goods **15.** a piece of information **16.** a short letter, note, etc. **17.** a verse of poetry **18.** [*pl.*] all the speeches of a character in a play **19.** the forward combat position in warfare **20.** *Football* the players in the forward row **21.** *Math.* the path of a moving point — *vt.* **lined, lin'ing 1.** to mark with lines **2.** to form a line along

_____ 4. Between what I wrote in my tablet, and writing letters,
n.   during the <u>rest</u> of my time in prison I would guess I
          wrote a million words.

rest (rest) *n.* [OE.] **1.** sleep or repose **2.** ease or inactivity after exertion **3.** relief from anything distressing, tiring, etc. **4.** absence of motion **5.** what is left **6.** a supporting device **7.** *Music* a measured interval of silence between tones, or a symbol for this — *vi.* **1.** to get ease and refreshment by sleeping or by ceasing from work **2.** to be at ease **3.** to be or become still **4.** to be supported; lie or lean (*in, on,* etc.) **5.** to be found [the fault *rests* with him] **6.** to rely; depend — *vt.* **1.** to cause to rest **2.** to put for ease, etc. [*rest* your head here]

_____ 5. Anyone who has read a <u>great</u> deal can imagine the new
adj.   world that opened.

great (grāt) *adj.* [OE.] **1.** of much more than ordinary size, extent, etc. **2.** most important; main **3.** designating a relationship one generation removed [*great*-grandparent] **4.** [Colloq.] skillful (often with *at*) **5.** (Colloq.) excellent; fine — *n.* a distinguished person

_____ 6. Fortunately, right outside my door was a corridor light
v.   that <u>cast</u> a glow into my room.

cast (kast) *vt.* **cast, cast'ing** [<ON. *kasta*] **1.** to throw with force; fling; hurl **2.** to deposit (a ballot or vote) **3.** to direct [to *cast* one's eyes] **4.** to project [to *cast* light] **5.** to throw off or shed (a skin) **6.** to shape (molten metal, etc.) by pouring into a mold **7.** to select (an actor) for (a role or play) — *n.* **1.** a casting; throw **2.** something formed in a mold **3.** a plaster form for immobilizing a limb **4.** the set of actors in a play or movie **5.** an appearance, as of features **6.** kind; quality **7.** a tinge; shade

B. By looking at a word's etymology in the dictionary, you can find the meaning of its roots. Here are six words from the article that contain common roots. The roots, their meanings, and other words that can help you remember the meanings are also provided.

Word	Root	Meaning of Root	Another Word
1. tele<u>vis</u>ion	vis	see	vision
2. <u>dic</u>tionary	dic	to say	predict
3. pro<u>gress</u>	gress	to go, walk, or step	aggression
4. tele<u>phon</u>ed	phon	sound	phonograph
5. at<u>ten</u>tion	ten	to hold	retention
6. <u>mot</u>ions	mot	to move	locomotive

Using these roots, match the following difficult words to their definitions.

1. vis-à-vis   a. a place to walk out (exit)

2. abdicate   b. capable of spontaneous movement

3. egress   c. to say you're leaving a high position

4. cacophony   d. the length of time something is held

5. tenure   e. (to see a person) face to face

6. motile   f. harsh, jarring sound

7

Don't Tell Jaime Escalante Minorities Can't Meet (High) Standards!

VOCABULARY PREVIEW

barrio (bä′rē ō):   A chiefly Spanish-speaking community or neighborhood in a U.S. city

rigorous (rig′ər əs):   strict; severe; hard

demographic (dem′ə graf′ik):   having to do with the study of size,
growth, density, and distribution of human populations

turmoil (tʉr′moil):   commotion; uproar; confusion

cosmetology (käz′mə täl′ə jē):   the work of a beautician

culminate (kul′mə nāt′):   to reach the highest point or climax

skeptical (skep′ti k′l):   not easily convinced; doubting; questioning

commitment (kə mit′mənt):   a pledge or promise to do something

feat (fēt):   a deed of unusual daring or skill

idiosyncratic (id′ē ə siŋ kra′tik):   having to do with a personal peculiarity
or mannerism

virtually (vʉr′choo wə lē):   as if in effect, although not in actual fact or
name

podium (pō′dē əm):   an elevated platform for a lecturer or conductor

---

fat, āpe, cär; ten, ēven; is, bīte; gō, hôrn, to͞ol, look; oil, out; up, fʉr; chin, she; thin, *th*en; zh,
leisure; ŋ, ring; ə for *a* in *ago;* ′ as in *able* (ā′b′l)

SURVEY

Survey the following article by reading the title, the first sentence of each paragraph, and all of the last paragraph. This should take no longer than one minute. After your survey, and without looking back at the article, write three questions that you think will be answered by reading it.

1. _____

2. _____

3. _____

Now read the article. Write your starting time here: _____

7

Don't Tell Jaime Escalante Minorities Can't Meet (High) Standards!

David Savage

T HE SCHOOL DAY STARTS EARLY for students of Jaime Escalante, mathematics teacher at Garfield High School in east Los Angeles. By 7 a.m., students from Escalante's trigonometry and calculus classes are stopping by to ask his help on a difficult problem before they head off to their other classes. Some of the students are tenth graders taking math analysis or trigonometry. Others are working on second-year, college-level calculus.

These students work on mathematics afternoons, evenings, on weekends, and, for many, during the summer at a nearby community college. Ask one of them what they think of this demanding schedule, and the likely answer is, "It's fun."

Fun? And this unexpected reaction is just the beginning of the surprises at Garfield High School.

"He makes you want to work hard. He psyches you up to do it," says Frank Quezada, a Garfield senior. "He makes mathematics fun. But you also feel guilty if you don't do the work for him."

The "he" is Escalante — a Bolivian immigrant, who over the past decade has transformed a barrio high school known more for gangs than for good grades into the city's best training ground for young mathematicians. Nearly 100 percent of Garfield's students are Hispanic. And among the 50 high schools in Los Angeles, Garfield is the leader in the number of students who take and pass the College Board's rigorous advanced placement tests in algebra and calculus.

Escalante — whose achievements with his young charges have been recognized by the California State Board of Education, *Reader's Digest* magazine, and President Reagan — succeeds through a combination of drive, inspiration, and humor. And although his success story is unique, it raises an issue that goes beyond one school and one teacher.

That issue — the most difficult one facing California — is what education officials refer to, in a code of sorts, as the "demographic problem." What it boils down to, in more direct terms, is whether minority students can be expected to meet the more rigorous standards of recent education reforms.

By the year 2000, a majority of the state's schoolchildren will be minorities — Hispanic, black, and Asian. Already, Hispanic students make up more than half of the student population in the huge Los Angeles Unified School District, the nation's second largest school system. Whether the measure is grades, test scores, or college degrees, Hispanic and black students crowd at the bottom.

According to the California Commission on Postsecondary Education, for every 1,000 Hispanic ninth graders, only 661 will be graduated from high school. Black students fare only slightly better, with 667 ending up as high school graduates.

Distressingly few of those graduates move further up the educational ladder. Among Hispanic ninth graders, only 17 of that 1,000 will end up as university graduates. The picture for blacks is nearly the same: 16 will earn university degrees.

A clue to Hispanics' and blacks' low achievement record might lie in what Jaime Escalante found when he arrived at Garfield in 1974: Low grades, low morale, and low aspirations were the norm. Failure, however, doesn't fit into Escalante's frame of reference. A decade earlier, Escalante had been a highly successful mathematics teacher in Bolivia; his student teams had won national championships. When Escalante and his wife left the country because of political turmoil, he arrived in the United States unable to speak the language of the majority and with education credentials that were not recognized in California. His first job was as a busboy in a Pasadena coffee shop.

"My English was nothing, zero, an empty set," he recalls. After taking night classes to improve his English, he earned a high-paying job with the Burroughs Corp. as a computer analyst. A high salary, however, didn't satisfy him; his true love was teaching. Escalante took a big pay cut to go to work in the Los Angeles school district. And at Garfield, he found a school where most students took one math class and quit.

"I was ready to quit, too," he says. "All they were taking were Mickey Mouse courses — cosmetology, cooking. I tell them, 'You have a great future ahead — at McDonald's cooking hamburgers.'"

Escalante set out to raise students' sights and show them that minority students can succeed in a demanding academic program. He says he "scrapped the textbooks we were using" and ordered a high-level mathematics series. He spoke to the principal, his fellow math teachers, and even teachers in Garfield's junior high feeder schools about creating a new sequence of math courses that would culminate in a senior year of advanced calculus.

Many were skeptical, and a few resisted the idea of scrapping proficiency math courses in favor of algebra, trigonometry, and calculus. But the toughest sell was the students. What they needed, he told them, was not extraordinary mathematical ability, but *ganas* — a Spanish word that loosely translated means "drive" or "desire to succeed."

Giving his students *ganas* — that is, discipline, desire, determination, and the will to work — says Escalante, is his main task in the first two weeks of the school year.

"I have a heart-to-heart talk with students. We talk about money and about success. Everyone wants to play football, be a big star. I ask them, 'How many Garfield students have become pro football players and make big money?' They don't know the answer, but I do. Zero.

"Then I tell them the money is in computers and physics and chemistry and biology. And they want you out there. But you have to speak their language first, and the language is math."

Though his classes have 50 students or more, Escalante sits down with each tenth grader and goes over a learning contract. The students and their parents must sign the contracts, committing themselves to a program of hard work in school and at home. For most, the commitment is a stiff challenge.

But Escalante has found potential among Garfield students. In May 1982, 14 of his students achieved a top score on the College Board's advanced placement examination in calculus, an extraordinary feat for such a school. The accomplishment was noticed first, however, because the Educational Testing Service (E.T.S.) questioned the scores. Examiners had noted that the students had worked problems in a similar, idiosyncratic way.

Many in the Hispanic community suspected that E.T.S. questioned the scores only because the students came from a barrio school. E.T.S. officials denied the charge.

"We followed the same procedures in this case as in any other. The graders don't know the names or schools of the papers they are grading," says Frank Romero, director of the E.T.S. office in Los Angeles.

Escalante put the controversy to rest by rounding up his students in August and having E.T.S. officials administer the test to them again. Once again, all 12 (two had already left the city) achieved passing scores on the rigorous exam, despite having virtually no time for preparation.

"It was clear that the students did know calculus. It was a credit to Mr. Escalante," said Romero.

Since then, Escalante's program — and its reputation — have grown steadily. Last year, 102 of his seniors took the advanced placement (A.P.) calculus exam, and more than three-fourths got passing grades, an achievement that will earn them a year's worth of college credit in math. This year, he has 150 students enrolled in courses to prepare for the A.P. exams. And his success has created a farm system in the junior high schools of east Los Angeles, as teachers and students upgrade to get ready for Escalante's major league program.

Escalante's high expectations, however, tell only part of the reason for his success. The rest, as with any outstanding teacher, lies in his approach to teaching. In front of his class, Escalante is part tough taskmaster and part comedian. Each class begins with a five-minute quiz. Students pick up the quizzes on their way into the room and work the problems quietly. When Escalante sounds a bell, selected students collect the papers. The teacher has yet to say a word.

But as he moves through a set of problems in rapid-fire style, Escalante the actor emerges. Under his podium, he keeps a collection of dolls and stuffed animals, each of which has a meaning to the students. He wanders through the aisles as he talks, offering a mock karate chop to those who stumble on a question. Their eyes follow him wherever he moves. He can turn suddenly and whisper an answer that can be heard throughout the small auditorium.

"You need the skill of an actor to keep their attention," he says. "You need to show that energy to attract people. The teacher also needs the patience of a doctor to show love to the kids."

1450 words

Write your ending time here: _____

Subtract your starting time: _____

Total time: _____

Check the Rate Chart in the back of the book to find how many words per minute you have read, and then record your score on the Progress Chart.

ANSWERS TO SURVEY QUESTIONS

Without looking back at the article, write the answer to your survey questions here:

1. _____

2. _____

3. _____

SKILLS EXERCISE:
UNDERLINING KEY CONCEPTS

Before you complete the Comprehension Check, go back to the article and underline the important points. Use signal words and visual clues to help. Since the purpose of your underlining is to provide for quick review, try not to underline more than 10 percent of the material. Remember that you usually don't have to underline a complete sentence to remember the important idea or detail. Also remember to underline the important signal words, because they will quickly show you the relationship of the ideas.

When you have finished, read what you have underlined and write one complete sentence stating the main idea of this article:

_____

_____

Your answer should be similar to the correct answer for question 2 in the Comprehension Check.

7

Don't Tell Jaime Escalante Minorities Can't Meet (High) Standards!

COMPREHENSION CHECK
Circle the letter before the best answer to each question below. Don't look back at the article.

Subject and Main Idea
1. The subject of the article is
   a. Jaime Escalante's life.
   b. Jaime Escalante's teaching.
   c. the importance of believing in your students.
   d. how to develop higher standards.

2. The main idea is that
   a. Jaime Escalante gave up a high paying career to become a teacher.
   b. minority students don't believe in themselves.
   c. Jaime Escalante led his students to exceptional accomplishments.
   d. immigrants make good teachers.

Details
3. Escalante emigrated from
   a. East Los Angeles.
   b. Mexico.
   c. Bolivia.
   d. Ecuador.

4. He taught
   a. English.
   b. mathematics.
   c. both English and mathematics.
   d. only advanced calculus classes.

5. Escalante
   a. could not get any job but teaching.
   b. secured a teaching job as soon as he arrived in Los Angeles.
   c. finally got a teaching job after waiting fifteen years.
   d. had to take his teaching credentials again.

6. The students
    a. took an SAT test and failed.
    b. took an advanced calculus test but cheated.
    c. took an advanced calculus test and passed.
    d. never got to take the test because they were Hispanic.

Inferences

7. An additional 150 students signed up for Escalante's high-level math courses because
    a. he walked around campus with a sign-up list.
    b. their parents insisted.
    c. they were required to do so.
    d. the other students had been so successful.

8. Jaime Escalante's students were able to succeed because
    a. he made them more intelligent.
    b. he recognized their abilities and motivated them.
    c. he restructured the classes so they were no longer difficult.
    d. they took easier versions of the Advanced Placement exams.

9. Because of their success in the math courses
    a. the students got great jobs.
    b. all Escalante's students went to college.
    c. the students increased their belief in themselves.
    d. many of his students became student teachers.

10. From the article we can infer that Jaime Escalante
    a. has a PhD in child psychology.
    b. is a good lecturer.
    c. has children of his own.
    d. hates the American school system.

QUESTIONS FOR ANALYSIS AND APPLICATION

1. List the ways that Jaime Escalante motivated his students to excel in mathematics. What similar methods could be used to help students advance in other subjects?

2. Discuss one situation in which you were not motivated in class and why. Discuss one situation where you were motivated in class and why.

VOCABULARY IN CONTEXT
Multiple Choice
Circle the letter before the best definition of each underlined word or phrase.

1. The army places its new enlistees in a very <u>rigorous</u> physical training program.
   a. lenient   b. easy   c. strict   d. boring

2. The teacher was <u>skeptical</u> about whether or not Susan's dog had really eaten her homework.
   a. doubting   b. believing   c. frustrated   d. interested

3. When people get married they make <u>a commitment</u> to honor and respect each other.
   a. an option   b. a contract   c. a pledge   d. a choice

4. The heavy rains in Santa Cruz <u>virtually</u> stopped traffic because of mud slides.
   a. in effect   b. completely   c. usually   d. hardly

5. After Boris Becker hurt his knee earlier in the year, it was quite an unusual <u>feat</u> for him to play tennis at Wimbledon.
   a. adventure   b. disappointment   c. thrill   d. deed

6. The government of East Germany was in <u>turmoil</u> in 1989–90 as the country tried to break free from Soviet control.
   a. anxiety   b. tranquility   c. utter confusion
   d. civil war

Fill-in
Write the best word from this list in the blank in each sentence below:

culminates   podium   demographic   cosmetology

barrio   idiosyncratic

7. A great baseball team's season _____ in playing in the World Series.

8. Students who learn _____ make people more beautiful than they were before.

9. Many _____ habits become irritating to others.

10. When Jesse Jackson wants to add emphasis to his speech, he often pounds on the _____ he's standing behind.

11. There's often a strong sense of community among Mexican-American families living in the _____.

12. The amount of money given to a state by the federal government is often determined by _____ studies.

SKILLS EXERCISE:
USING CONTEXT CLUES AND ANALOGIES

For explanation
see pp. 1–2

A. Circle the letter of the best definition for each underlined word or phrase below. The underlined material is shown here in the context in which it appears in the article.

1. "And his success has created a farm system in the junior high schools of east Los Angeles, as teachers and students upgrade to get ready for Escalante's <u>major league</u> program."

   a. easier   b. higher level   c. algebra
   d. more expensive

2. "'All they were taking were <u>Mickey Mouse</u> courses — cosmetology, cooking.'"

   a. important   b. funny   c. easy   d. boring

3. "What it <u>boils down to</u> in more direct terms, is whether minority students can be expected to meet the more rigorous standards of recent education reforms."

   a. means   b. proves   c. doesn't mean   d. disproves

4. ". . . He arrived in the United States unable to speak <u>the language of the majority</u>."

   a. a second language   b. the best language   c. Spanish
   d. English

5. "Failure, however, doesn't fit into Escalante's <u>frame of reference</u>."

   a. prejudices   b. book   c. experience   d. dreams

6. "By the year 2000, a majority of the state's schoolchildren will be minorities — <u>Hispanic</u>, black, and Asian."

   a. African-American   b. American
   c. of Latin-American or Spanish origin
   d. of unknown origin

7. "By 7 a.m., students from Escalante's <u>trigonometry</u> and calculus classes are stopping by to ask his help on a difficult problem before they head off to their other classes."

   a. science class   b. basic mathematics class
   c. economics class   d. advanced mathematics class

8. "That issue — the most difficult one facing California — is what education officials refer to, in a code of sorts, as the <u>demographic</u> problem." What it boils down to, in more direct terms, is whether minority students can be expected to meet the more rigorous standards of recent education reforms."

    a. educational   b. population   c. quality of education
    d. scheduling

9. "Giving his students *ganas* — that is, discipline, desire, determination, and the will to work — says Escalante, is his main task in the first two weeks of the school year."

    a. trouble   b. skills to do well   c. desire to succeed
    d. extraordinary mathematical ability

10. "But as he moves through a set of problems in <u>rapid-fire</u> style, Escalante the actor emerges."

    a. decorative   b. boring   c. quick
    d. calm and quiet

B. A word analogy is a puzzle in which two sets of words are compared. The two words in the first set have a relationship to each other. You have to recognize the relationship in order to fill in the blank. Analogies use the mathematical symbols :, which means *is to*, and ::, which means *as*.

easy : simple : : _____ : daring deed

The example reads: *easy* is to *simple* as _____ is to *daring deed*. You must understand the relationship between *easy* and *simple*. They are synonyms; they mean the same thing. Now look at the vocabulary preview for this article. Which words fit in the blank? What is a synonym for *daring deed*? The answer is *feat*.

For each analogy below, write the word from the vocabulary preview that completes the analogy. Look back at the preview if you need help.

1. mock : fake : : _____ : strict

2. minority : majority : : _____ : peace

3. huge : tiny : : _____ : sure

4. extraordinary : average : : _____ : begin

5. aspirations : goals : : _____ : pledge

8

How to Use a Library

SURVEY
Survey the following article by reading the author's name, the title, the first paragraph, and the headings. This should take no longer than thirty seconds. After your survey, and without looking back, write three questions that you think will be answered by reading the article.

1. _____

2. _____

3. _____

James A. Michener is the Pulitzer Prize-winning author of *Tales of the South Pacific, Hawaii, Centennial, Chesapeake,* and other novels.

Now read the article. Write your starting time here: _____

8

How to Use a Library

James A. Michener

YOU'RE DRIVING YOUR CAR home from work or school. And something goes wrong. The engine stalls out at lights, holds back as you go to pass.

It needs a tune-up — and soon. Where do you go? The library.

You can take out an auto repair manual that tells step-by-step how to tune up your make and model.

Or your tennis game has fallen off. You've lost your touch at the net. Where do you go?

The library — for a few books on improving your tennis form.

"The library!" you say. "That's where my teacher sends me to do — ugh — homework."

Unfortunately, I've found that's exactly the way many people feel. If you're among them, you're denying yourself the easiest way to improve yourself, enjoy yourself and even cope with life.

It's hard for me to imagine what I would be doing today if I had not fallen in love, at the ripe old age of seven, with the Melinda Cox Library in my hometown of Doylestown, Pennsylvania. At our house, we just could not afford books. The books in that free library would change my life dramatically.

Who knows what your library can open up for you?

My first suggestion for making the most of your library is to do what I did: read and read and read. For pleasure — and for understanding.

HOW TO KICK THE TV HABIT

If it's TV that keeps you from cultivating this delicious habit, I can offer a sure remedy. Take home from the library a stack of books that might look interesting.

Pile them on the TV set. Next time you are tempted to turn on a program you really don't want to see, reach for a book instead.

Over the years, people collect a mental list of books they mean to read. If you don't have such a list, here is a suggestion. Take from the library some of the books you might have enjoyed dramatized on TV, like Remarque's *All Quiet on the Western Front*, Clavell's *Shōgun*, Tolkien's *The Hobbit*, or Victor Hugo's *Les Misérables*.

If you like what you read, you can follow up with other satisfying books by the same authors.

Some people in their reading limit themselves to current talked-about best sellers. Oh, what they miss! The library is full of yesterday's best sellers; and they still make compelling reading today. Some that I've enjoyed: A. B. Guthrie's *The Big Sky*, Carl Van Doren's *Benjamin Franklin*, Mari Sandoz's *Old Jules*, and Norman Mailer's *The Naked and the Dead*.

How do you find these or any other books you're looking for? It's easy — with the card catalog.

LEARN TO USE THE CARD CATALOG

Every time I go to the library — and I go more than once a week — I invariably make a beeline to the card catalog before anything else. It's the nucleus of any public library.

The card catalog lists every book in the library by:

1. author; 2. title; 3. subject.

Let's pick an interesting subject to look up. I have always been fascinated by astronomy.

You'll be surprised at the wealth of material you will find under "astronomy" to draw upon. And the absorbing books you didn't know existed on it.

CAUTION: Always have a pencil and paper when you use the card catalog. Once you jot down the numbers of the books you are interested in, you are ready to find them on the shelves.

LEARN TO USE THE STACKS

Libraries call the shelves "the stacks." In many smaller libraries which you'll be using, the stacks will be open for you to browse.

To me there is a special thrill in tracking down the books I want in the stacks! For invariably, I find books about which I knew nothing, and these often turn out to be the very ones I need. You will find the same thing happening to you when you start to browse in the stacks. "A learned mind is the end product of browsing."

CAUTION: If you take a book from the stacks to your work desk, do not try to return it to its proper place. That's work for the experts. If you replace it incorrectly, the next seeker won't be able to find it.

LEARN TO KNOW THE REFERENCE LIBRARIAN

Some of the brightest and best-informed men and women in America are the librarians who specialize in providing reference help.

Introduce yourself. State your problem. And be amazed at how much help you will receive.

CAUTION: Don't waste the time of this expert by asking silly questions you ought to solve yourself. Save the reference librarian for the really big ones.

LEARN TO USE THE *READER'S GUIDE TO PERIODICAL LITERATURE*

This green-bound index is one of the most useful items in any library. It indexes all the articles in the major magazines, including newspaper magazine supplements.

Thus it provides a guide to the very latest expert information on any subject that interests you.

So if you want to do a really first-class job, find out which magazines your library subscribes to, then consult the *Reader's Guide* and track down recent articles on your subject. When you use this wonderful tool effectively, you show the mark of a real scholar.

FOUR PERSONAL HINTS

Since you can take most books home, but not magazines, take full notes when using the latter.

Many libraries today provide a reprographic machine that can quickly copy pages you need from magazines and books. Ask about it.

If you are working on a project of some size which will require repeated library visits, keep a small notebook in which you record the identification numbers of the books you will be using frequently. This will save you valuable time, because you won't have to consult the card catalog or search aimlessly through the stacks each time you visit for material you seek.

Some of the very best books in any library are the reference books, which may not be taken home. Learn what topics they cover and how best to use them, for these books are wonderful repositories of human knowledge.

YOUR BUSINESS AND LEGAL ADVISOR
Your library can give you help on *any* subject. It can even be your business and legal advisor.

How many times have you scratched your head over how to get a tax rebate on your summer job? You'll find answers in tax guides at the library. Thinking of buying or renting a house? You'll find guides to that. Want to defend yourself in traffic court? Find out how in legal books at the library.

LIBRARY PROJECTS CAN BE FUN — AND REWARDING
Here are a few ideas:

1. *What are your roots?* Trace your ancestors. Many libraries specialize in genealogy.

2. *Did George Washington sleep nearby?* Or Billy the Kid? Your library's collection of local history books can put you on the trail.

3. *Cook a Polynesian feast.* Or an ancient Roman banquet. Read how in the library's cookbooks.

4. *Take up photography.* Check the library for consumer reviews of cameras before you buy. Take out books on lighting, composition, or darkroom techniques.

Or — you name it!

If you haven't detected by now my enthusiasm for libraries, let me offer two personal notes.

I'm particularly pleased that in recent years two beautiful libraries have been named after me: a small community library in Quakertown, Pennsylvania, and the huge research library located at the University of Northern Colorado in Greeley.

And I like libraries so much that I married a librarian.

1150 words

Write your ending time here: _____

Subtract your starting time: _____

Total time: _____

Check the Rate Chart in the back of the book to find out how many words per minute you have read, and then record your score on the Progress Chart.

ANSWERS TO SURVEY QUESTIONS

Without looking back at the article, write the answers to your survey questions here:

1. _____

2. _____

3. _____

SKILLS EXERCISE:
UNDERLINING KEY CONCEPTS

Before you complete the Comprehension Check, go back to the article and underline the important points; also circle the numbers, letters, and Roman numerals that indicate important headings. Use signal words and visual clues to help. Since the purpose of your underlining is to provide for quick review, try not to underline more than 10 percent of the material. Remember that you usually don't have to underline a complete sentence to remember the important idea or detail. Also remember to underline the important signal words, because they will quickly show you the relationship of the ideas.

When you have finished, read what you have underlined and write one complete sentence stating the main idea of this article:

_____

_____

Your answer should be similar to the correct answer for question 2 in the Comprehension Check.

8

How to Use a Library

Circle the letter before the best answer to each question below. Don't look back at the article.

Subject and Main Idea
1. The subject of this article is
   a. using the library.
   b. doing research.
   c. why people don't like going to the library.
   d. using a college library more effectively.

2. The main idea is that
   a. if you know how to use the library more efficiently, you will find it a tremendous help to you.
   b. all great writers, like Michener, go to the library often.
   c. people cannot be successful without learning how to use the library.
   d. there are many different tools in the library.

Details
3. Michener feels that the library is a way to
   a. cope with life.
   b. improve yourself.
   c. enjoy yourself.
   d. do all of the above.

4. Michener's family
   a. was rich enough to buy books.
   b. couldn't afford books.
   c. lived in a foreign country before coming to the United States.
   d. came from a large city.

5. If you take a book from the stacks to use in the library, Michener suggests that you
   a. check it out.
   b. return it as soon as possible to the stacks.
   c. don't try to return it to the shelves yourself.
   d. take a chair with you so that you can read it in the stacks.

6. According to Michener
   a. you can find the answers to a lot of problems in the library.
   b. using books in the library is better than taking them home.
   c. the *Reader's Guide* is the nucleus of any public library.
   d. most libraries won't let you browse in the stacks.

Inferences

7. Michener feels that most people
   a. enjoy going to the library.
   b. never go to the library.
   c. associate the library with school.
   d. don't know where the nearest library is located.

8. The *Reader's Guide*
   a. lists only a few popular magazines.
   b. cannot be taken out of the library.
   c. indexes everything in the newspaper.
   d. lists every magazine published in the United States.

9. To encourage you to use the library more, Michener suggests that you should
   a. stop watching all TV programs.
   b. spend some time every day at the library.
   c. go to the library whenever possible.
   d. go to the library whenever you have homework.

10. Michener feels that the library is a place
    a. most people want to explore.
    b. designed only for the "real scholars."
    c. that frightens most people.
    d. not used enough by people.

QUESTIONS FOR ANALYSIS AND APPLICATION

1. Michener implies that television has reduced the amount of pleasure reading that people do. Some people would disagree that television is the culprit. List some other things that could account for the change.

2. Many college students report that they don't use the library as often as they should because they feel intimidated there. What could be intimidating about your college library, and what might be done to make it less so?

VOCABULARY IN CONTEXT
Fill-in
Write the best word from this list in the blank in each sentence below:

cope   compel   nucleus   jotted   reprographic

repositories   rebate   genealogies

1. Hunger is usually enough to _____ someone to find a job.

2. Although Lincoln's Gettysburg Address is one of the most famous speeches ever presented, history tells us that Lincoln

   _____ it down on the back of an envelope.

3. The sun is the _____ of our solar system.

4. Mattresses are not safe _____ for your money.

5. To induce you to buy their product, automobile companies will

   sometimes offer a _____ .

6. People who make their living by betting on horse races

   often know the _____ of all the horses running that day.

7. Those who cannot _____ with life often find themselves on a psychiatrist's couch.

8. _____ machines can now make copies in color as well as in black and white.

SKILLS EXERCISE:
USING THE LIBRARY
You must go to a library to complete the following exercise.

Library: _____ Hours Open: _____

A. Card catalog
   1. Give the call numbers for at least two of the following books recommended by Michener:

      a. A. B. Guthrie's *The Big Sky* _____

      b. Carl Van Doren's *Benjamin Franklin* _____

      c. Mari Sandoz's *Old Jules* _____

      d. Norman Mailer's *The Naked and the Dead* _____

2. Give the author, title, and call number for one book on astronomy.

_____

_____

3. A library can use either of two systems to classify books:

Library of Congress	Dewey Decimal
LB2395	378.17
L447	02812
	L1

Which system does your library use? _____

B. General information
   1. What days and hours is the reference librarian on duty?

   _____

   2. Does your library have a reprographic machine? _____

C. _Reader's Guide to Periodic Literature_
   Use the following sample to help you complete the exercise.

①   ②
| |

COLLEGE and school journalism School newspapers have
the right to freedom of the press. A. Karp. Seventeen 35:
88 Je '76
| \ | | |
⑥   ⑦   ③   ④   ⑤

1. subject
2. title
3. author
4. magazine
5. volume
6. page
7. date

The 1991 _Reader's Guide_ listed an article on insomnia by J. Jurnovoy and S. Smith. Find the article in the _Reader's Guide_ and fill in the following information:

1. Magazine in which it appeared: _____

2. Date the article appeared: _____

3. Pages on which the article appeared: _____

SKILLS EXERCISE: MULTIPLE MEANINGS OF WORDS AND ANALOGIES

For explanation
see pp. 6–7

A. The following six words, which appear in this article, have multiple meanings. Find the number identifying the meaning used in each sentence below, and write it in the space. To make it easier for you to find the proper meanings, the part of speech has been provided.

1. **game** (gām) *n.* [OE., *gamen*] **1.** any form of play; amusement **2.** *a)* amusement or sport involving competition under rules *b)* a single contest in such a competition **3.** the number of points required for winning **4.** a scheme; plan **5.** wild birds or animals hunted for sport or food **6.** [Colloq.] a business or job, esp. one involving risk — *vi.* **gamed, gam'ing** to play cards, etc. for stakes; gamble — *adj.* **1.** designating or of wild birds or animals hunted for sport or food **2.** *a)* plucky; courageous *b)* enthusiastic; ready (*for*) **3.** [Colloq.] lame or injured [a *game* leg]

_____ a. Wild <u>game</u> such as deer and pheasant are often
n.　　　　hunted for food.

_____ b. If you are <u>game</u> to try hang gliding, I am willing to
adj.　　　try it too.

2. **touch** (tuch) *vt.* [< OFr. *tochier*] **1.** to put the hand, etc. on, so as to feel **2.** to bring (something), or come, into contact with (something else) **3.** to border on **4.** to strike lightly **5.** to give a light tint, aspect, etc. to [*touched* with pink] **6.** to stop at (a port) **7.** to handle; use **8.** to come up to; reach **9.** to compare with; equal **10.** to affect; concern **11.** to arouse sympathy, gratitude, etc. in **12.** [Slang] to seek a loan or gift of money from — *vi.* **1.** to touch a person or thing **2.** to be or come in contact **3.** to verge (*on* or *upon*) **4.** to pertain; bear (*on* or *upon*) **5.** to treat in passing (with *on* or *upon*) — *n.* **1.** a touching or being touched; specif., a light tap **2.** the sense by which physical objects are felt **3.** a special quality or skill **4.** a subtle change or addition in a painting, story, etc. **5.** a trace, tinge, etc. **6.** a slight attack [a *touch* of the flu] **7.** contact or communication [keep in *touch*] **8.** [Slang] the act of seeking or getting a gift or loan of money **9.** *Music* the manner of striking the keys of a piano, etc.

_____ a. All purples have a <u>touch</u> more of either pink
n.　　　　or blue.

_____ b. I was <u>touched</u> by the loud applause when I won
vt.　　　the award.

3. **form** (fôrm) *n.* [< L. *forma*] **1.** shape; general structure **2.** the figure of a person or animal **3.** a mold **4.** a particular mode, kind, type, etc. /ice is a *form* of water, the *forms* of poetry/ **5.** arrangement; style **6.** a way of doing something requiring skill **7.** a customary or conventional procedure; formality; ceremony **8.** a printed document with blanks to be filled in **9.** condition of mind or body **10.** a chart giving information about horses in a race **11.** a changed appearance of a word to show inflection, etc. **12.** type, etc. locked in a frame for printing — *vt.* **1.** to shape; fashion **2.** to train; instruct **3.** to develop (habits) **4.** to make up; constitute — *vi.* to be formed

_____ a. It was written in a very old <u>form</u> of language.
n.

_____ b. Sculptors <u>form</u> an object from clay, wood, metal,
vt.   or stone.

4. **sub·ject** (sub′jikt; *for v.* səb jekt′) *adj.* [< L. *sub-*, under + *jacere*, throw] **1.** under the authority or control of another **2.** having a tendency /*subject* to anger/ **3.** exposed /*subject* to censure/ **4.** contingent upon /*subject* to approval/ — *n.* **1.** one under the authority or control of another **2.** one made to undergo a treatment, experiment, etc. **3.** something dealt with in discussion, study, etc.; theme **4.** *Gram.* the word or words in a sentence about which something is said — *vt.* **1.** to bring under the authority or control of **2.** to cause to undergo something /to *subject* him to questioning/

_____ a. The contract is <u>subject</u> to review by the attorneys.
adj.

_____ b. The <u>subjects</u> had to pay taxes to the ruler of the
n.   kingdom.

5. **ma·te·ri·al** (mə tir′ē əl) *adj.* [< L. *materia*, matter] **1.** of matter; physical /a *material* object/ **2.** of the body or bodily needs, comfort, etc.; not spiritual **3.** important, essential, etc. — *n.* **1.** what a thing is, or may be made of; elements or parts **2.** cloth; fabric

_____ a. <u>Material</u> possessions are not supposed to be important to monks.
adj.

_____ b. The construction <u>materials</u> have to meet the code,
n.   or the city permit will not be granted.

6. **draw** (drô) *vt.* **drew, drawn, draw'ing** [OE. *dragan*] **1.** to make move toward one; pull **2.** to pull up, down, back, in, or out **3.** to need (a specified depth of water) to float in; said of a ship **4.** to attract **5.** to breathe in **6.** to elicit (a reply, etc.) **7.** to bring on; provoke **8.** to receive (to *draw* a salary) **9.** to withdraw (money) held in an account **10.** to write (a check or draft) **11.** to deduce **12.** to take or get (cards, etc.) **13.** to stretch **14.** to make (lines, pictures, etc.), as with a pencil—*vi.* **1.** to draw something **2.** to be drawn **3.** to come; move **4.** to shrink **5.** to allow a draft, as of smoke, to move through **6.** to make a demand (*on*) — *n.* **1.** a drawing or being drawn **2.** the result of drawing **3.** a thing drawn **4.** a tie; stalemate **5.** a thing that attracts

_____ a. <u>Draw</u> your own conclusions from the evidence.
vt.

_____ b. When children are learning to swim they need to
vt. learn to <u>draw</u> a deep breath and hold it before dunking their heads under water.

B. For each analogy below, write the word from the vocabulary preview that completes the analogy. Look back at the preview if you need help.

1. cope : ignore : : _____ : outside

2. compelling : important : : _____ : refund

3. stacks : bookshelves : : _____ : storehouses

4. catalog : file : : _____ : reproductive

5. jot : write : : _____ : heritage

9

Some Questions and Answers About Sleep and Dreams

VOCABULARY PREVIEW

extravagant (ik strav'ə gənt):   going beyond reasonable limits; excessive

REM (rem):   [r(apid) e(ye) m(ovement)] the rapid, jerky movements of the eyeballs during stages of sleep associated with dreaming

intense (in tens'):   very strong

stimuli (stim'yə lī'):   any actions or agents that cause activity in an organism, organ, and so on

deprived (di prīvd'):   kept from having

explicit (ik splis'it):   clearly stated and leaving nothing implied; distinctly expressed

spontaneous (spän tā'nē əs):   occurring without apparent cause

synthesis (sin'thə sis):   putting together parts to form a whole

coherent (kō hir'ənt):   logically connected; consistent; clearly stated

inhibit (in hib'it):   to check or repress

impairment (im per'mənt):   worsening; lessening

fat, āpe, cär; ten, ēven; is, bīte; gō, hôrn, tōōl, look; oil, out; up, fʉr; chin, she; thin, then; zh, leisure; ŋ, ring; ə for a in ago; ' as in able (ā'b'l)

SURVEY

Survey the following article by reading the author's name, the title, the headings, and the last sentence. This should take no longer than thirty seconds. After your survey, and without looking back at the article, write three questions that you think will be answered by reading it.

1. _____

2. _____

3. _____

Now read the article. Write your starting time here: _____

9

Some Questions and Answers About Sleep and Dreams

James Kalat

RE THERE DIFFERENCES BETWEEN "GOOD SLEEPERS" AND "POOR SLEEPERS"? Yes. "Good sleepers" fall asleep within 10 minutes after going to bed and seldom wake up without reason during the night. "Poor sleepers" take more than an hour to fall asleep and wake up one or more times during the night. About one fourth of all adults have some difficulty sleeping, and nearly three fourths of all psychiatric patients have difficulty sleeping. Whether sleep is good or poor has nothing to do with how long it lasts; 6 hours for one person may be more restful than 9 hours for another.

Good sleepers spend more time lying motionless. Poor sleepers change position more often and spend more time lying on their back, though we cannot conclude that lying on one's back causes poor sleep. Many overweight middle-age men sleep on their back because it is uncomfortable for them to lie on their stomach. They also have difficulty sleeping for reasons that are related to being overweight and not to sleeping position.

Is it possible to learn while asleep? Extravagant claims have been made about learning while asleep. Because the brain is relaxed and distractions are absent, the argument goes, people learn more efficiently from a tape recording while asleep than while awake.

However, learning during sleep is less effective than wakeful learning. People who listen to tape-recorded information while asleep can recall little of it when they wake up, though they may learn the information more easily *after* they wake up.

Does everyone dream? Everyone studied in the laboratory has gone through normal REM periods. Even people who claim they never dream will say, if they are awakened during an REM period, "Well, I guess I was dreaming that time," and then proceed to describe a dream. Apparently such people do have dreams; they just fail to remember them. However,

127

their dreams are usually less intense and less emotional than most people's dreams are. Perhaps they forget their dreams because their dreams are, frankly, boring.

We all dream more than we remember. When people are awakened more than 5 minutes after the end of an REM period, they seldom report a dream. When we awake in the morning, the only dream we remember is the one that has just ended. And we quickly forget that dream unless we think or talk about it.

How long do dreams last?   People once believed that dreams last only a second or so, but evidence indicates that dreams last about as long as they seem to last. William Dement and Edward Wolpert awakened people after varying periods of REM sleep and asked them to describe their dreams. A person awakened after 1 minute of REM sleep would usually tell a 1-minute story. A person awakened after 5 minutes of REM sleep would usually tell a 5-minute story — and so on, up to about 15 minutes. After more than 15 minutes of REM sleep, people would still tell only 15-minute stories, apparently forgetting the rest.

Occasionally a dream seems to last hours, even days. That is because of cuts and shifts in scenes. As in a play or a movie, a dream sometimes includes the transition, "Now it's the next day. . . ."

What do we dream about?   The content of dreams comes from many sources, sometimes including the stimuli that happen to be acting on your body at the moment. A sprinkle of water on your face may become a dream about rainfall, a leaky roof, or going swimming. A sudden loud noise may become a dream about an earthquake or a plane crash. A bright light may become a dream about flashes of lightning or a fire.

Some common motivations carry over from wakefulness into dreams. People deprived of fluids frequently dream about drinking. People who have been kept in isolation dream about talking in groups. Several experiments have tested the effects of watching movies just before going to sleep. People who have watched violent movies tend to have unusually clear, vivid, and emotional dreams, though they are not necessarily violent. After watching movies with a great deal of explicit sexual content, people who are asked about their dreams frequently say, "I, uhh . . . forget what I was dreaming about."

To a large degree, dream content reflects spontaneous activity in the brain. During REM sleep, heightened activity occurs spontaneously in the cerebral cortex, especially in the areas responsible for vision, hearing, and movement. According to the activation-synthesis theory of dreams, the brain experiences this spontaneous activity as sensations, links the sensations together, and tries to synthesize them into a coherent pattern. The product of that attempt is a dream. Because brain activity is spontaneous, the dream has a quality of "just happening." We do not decide to make a movement; the movement just happens. We do not decide to speak or to look to the left; the action just happens.

I sometimes dream that I am trying to move but I can't. Why is that?   During REM sleep, one little section of the midbrain (the *caudal locus coeruleus*) sends messages to the nerves of the spinal cord causing the large muscles that control posture to relax completely. (Finger movements, twitches, and other small movements are unaffected.) Those messages make it almost impossible for you to move your muscles during REM sleep. Is that why we dream about an inability to move? Perhaps, although we cannot be sure.

Cats with damage to this section of the midbrain have nothing to inhibit their muscle activity; they become very active during REM sleep, running, jumping, pouncing, and giving every indication of acting out a dream.

Why do I frequently dream that I am falling or flying?   During sleep your head is in a different position from the position it is in when you are awake. Either for that reason, or just spontaneously, bursts of high activity occasionally occur in the part of the cerebral cortex responsible for *vestibular sensation* (sensation arising from the tilt of the head). Such sensations may get incorporated into dreams of flying, falling, twirling, and the like.

Do we dream in color?   The very fact that people ask this question reveals why it is difficult to answer. People ask because they do not remember whether their dreams were in color. But how can an investigator determine whether people dream in color except by asking them? The best answer we have is that when people are awakened during REM sleep, when their recall is sharpest, they report color half the time or more. This does not mean that their other dreams are necessarily in black and white; it may mean only that the colors in those dreams are not bright, distinct, or memorable. Generally, dreams that occur toward the end of the night are the most visual, with the brightest colors.

What do blind people dream about?   A person who has had vision and then lost it because of damage to the eyes continues to see during dreams. But a person who has never had vision or who has lost it because of damage to the occipital cortex does not see during dreams. People with any degree of visual impairment are more likely than sighted people to dream about things that are experienced through touch — such as wood or bricks.

What does it mean when I have the same dream over and over again?   The content of such a dream is probably related to something you are concerned about or perhaps to something that worries you from time to time. People who have a single dream at least a few times a year tend to report more anxiety, depression, and stress in their waking lives than do other people.

Do dreams ever give us creative ideas?   Sometimes. Dreaming is less inhibited and restricted than wakeful thinking; it permits associations that you might abandon out of hand while awake. When you dream you accept anything as possible; you seldom stop to test reality. Some people keep a pencil and paper next to their bed so they can jot down notes when they awaken from a dream in the middle of the night. In the light of day, they reject most of their dream "insights" as nonsense, though occasionally they find something of value.

Can psychologists learn about people's thoughts and personalities from the content of their dreams?   People do dream about matters that concern them. Many psychotherapists rely on dream interpretations to learn about their clients' thoughts and problems. But be cautious about dream interpretations. Some therapists interpret dreams so imaginatively that the interpretations probably reveal more about the therapist than they do about the client. Most of their claims of dream interpretation have not been verified scientifically.

1600 words

Write your ending time here: _____

Subtract your starting time: _____

Total time: _____

Check the Rate Chart in the back of the book to find how many words per minute you have read, and then record your score on the Progress Chart.

ANSWERS TO SURVEY QUESTIONS
Without looking back at the article, write the answers to your survey questions here:

1. _____

2. _____

3. _____

SKILLS EXERCISE:
UNDERLINING KEY CONCEPTS
Before you complete the Comprehension Check, go back to the article and underline the important points. Use signal words and visual clues to help. Since the purpose of your underlining is to provide for quick review, try not to underline more than 10 percent of the material. Remember that you usually don't have to underline a complete sentence to remember the important idea or detail. Also remember to underline the important signal words, because they will quickly show you the relationship of the ideas.

When you have finished, read what you have underlined and write one complete sentence stating the main idea of this article:

_____

_____

Your answer should be similar to the correct answer for question 2 in the Comprehension Check.

9

Some Questions and Answers About Sleep and Dreams

COMPREHENSION CHECK
Circle the letter before the best answer to each question below. Don't look back at the article.

Subject and Main Idea
1. The subject of the article is
   a. interpreting dreams.
   b. curing insomnia.
   c. learning while you sleep.
   d. sleeping and dreaming.

2. The main idea is that
   a. dreams are mysterious and cannot be understood.
   b. there are explanations for why we sleep and dream.
   c. insomnia is a serious problem.
   d. there is a field of research that studies sleep and dreams.

Details
3. During sleep
   a. you can learn almost anything faster.
   b. most people do not dream.
   c. it's impossible to remember your dreams.
   d. it seems everyone has dreams.

4. Most dreams last
   a. one second or so.
   b. about as long as they seem to last while asleep.
   c. less than the amount of time we think while dreaming.
   d. the whole sleep period.

5. Dreams
   a. cannot be explained.
   b. sometimes have explainable causes.
   c. are not affected by outside situations.
   d. are always affected by outside situations.

132

6. REM
   a. occurs after you are awakened suddenly.
   b. occurs when you are dreaming.
   c. is another name for deep sleep.
   d. doesn't occur every time you sleep.

Inferences

7. From the article we can infer that
   a. there is no way to explain dreams.
   b. dream research is not very scientific.
   c. analyzing dreams is difficult.
   d. REM doesn't exist.

8. The article seems to indicate that
   a. we have many dreams during the course of a night.
   b. we remember all of our dreams.
   c. boring people never dream.
   d. dreams help us live longer.

9. The author probably
   a. remembers all of his dreams.
   b. has insomnia often.
   c. believes that dreams have a function.
   d. was a pioneer in dream research.

10. We can infer from the article that
   a. REM periods are very tiring.
   b. no one can explain anything about what we dream.
   c. depending on sleep learning to study for a test is a poor idea.
   d. listening to a tape while you're asleep is very effective for learning.

QUESTIONS FOR ANALYSIS AND APPLICATION

1. Set your alarm early for a day or two and write down your dreams. Can you explain any of them? Which ones?

2. Some people are better sleepers than others. List at least three reasons a person might not be able to sleep on a particular night.

VOCABULARY IN CONTEXT
Multiple Choice
Circle the letter before the definition of each underlined word or phrase.

1. Princess Diana rarely wears the same clothes twice, which could be described as <u>extravagant</u>.
   a. sensible   b. necessary   c. excessive   d. wise

2. Whitney Houston had an <u>intense</u> desire to be a famous singer.
   a. subdued   b. strong   c. life-long   d. foolish

3. Even though Joe had had too much to drink, he managed to use <u>coherent</u> sentences when talking to the policeman.
   a. logical   b. incomplete   c. intelligent   d. short

4. Prisoners of war are sometimes <u>deprived of</u> food and water for days at a time.
   a. given   b. kept from having   c. forced to have
   d. wanting

5. When assigning the final paper for the semester, Mr. Garcia was <u>explicit</u> about what he expected.
   a. unsure   b. clear   c. hesitant   d. confused

6. Michelle is not very outgoing around her relatives because her brother's teasing <u>inhibits</u> her.
   a. encourages   b. frightens   c. represses   d. hurts

Fill-in
Write the best word from this list in the blank in each sentence below:

REM   stimuli   spontaneous   synthesis   impairment

7. The period during sleep in which dreaming occurs is ___Rem___.

8. David's visual _____ caused him to have difficulty reading.

9. _____ people are fun because they are always ready to go at a moment's notice.

10. The _____ from electric shock cause muscles to contract.

11. When presented with facts, a historian makes a _____ of ideas in formulating a theory.

SKILLS EXERCISE:
ANALOGIES
For each analogy below, write the word from the vocabulary preview that completes the analogy. Look back at the preview if you need help.

1. deprived : denied : : _____ : unplanned

2. impairment : worsening : : _____ : repress

3. depression : sadness : : _____ : consistent

4. anxiety : nervousness : : _____ : lavish

5. cause : effect : : _____ : implied

SKILLS EXERCISE:
WORDS THAT SIGNAL KEY CONCEPTS

For explanation see p. 13

As you learned in the introduction to this unit, an author can use signal words to indicate emphasis, addition, example, change of direction, and conclusion. Indicated before each sentence below is the type of signal word to use for that sentence. Write a logical word in each blank. Try not to use any word more than once. If you need help, refer to p. 54.

(example)   1. Whether sleep is good or poor has nothing to do with how long it lasts; _____, six hours for one person may be more restful than nine hours for another.

(change of direction)   2. Good sleepers spend more time lying motionless; _____, poor sleepers change position more often and spend more time lying on their back.

(example)   3. Everyone studied in the laboratory has gone through normal REM periods. _____, even people who claim they never dream will say, "Well, I guess I was dreaming that time" if they are awakened during an REM period.

(change of direction)   4. Apparently such people do have dreams. _____, they just fail to remember them.

(addition)
5. We only remember the dream that just
ended. _____ , we
quickly forget that dream unless we think
or talk about it.

(change of direction)
6. People once believed that dreams last only a
second or so. _____ ,
evidence indicates that dreams last about as
long as they seem to last.

(example)
7. The content of dreams comes from many
sources, sometimes including the stimuli
that happen to be acting on your body at the
moment. _____ , a
sprinkle of water on your face may become
a dream about a rainfall, a leaky roof, or
going swimming.

(example)
8. Some common motivations carry over from
wakefulness into dreams. _____
thirsty people frequently dream about
drinking.

(addition)
9. Poor sleepers take more than an hour to fall
asleep. _____ ,
they wake up one or more times during
the night.

(conclusion)
10. It is uncomfortable for many middle-
aged men to sleep on their stomach.
_____ , they sleep
on their back.

10

How to Strengthen Your Memory Power

VOCABULARY PREVIEW

cosmological (käz mə lä′jə k′l):   relating to the branch of philosophy and science that deals with the study of the universe as a whole and of its form and nature as a physical system

retrieval (ri trē′v′l):   possibility of getting something back or recovering it

retention (ri ten′shən):   holding or keeping

relatively (rel′ə tiv′lē):   in relation to or compared with something else; not absolutely

distinctive (dis tiŋk′tiv):   distinguished from others; characteristic

heredity (hə red′ə tē):   passing of characteristics from parent to child by means of genes

neuropsychologist (noo′rō sī käl′ə jist):   psychologist who studies the mind and the nervous system

associative (ə sō′shē āt′iv, ə sō′shə tiv):   of, characterized by, or causing association, as of ideas

perception (pər sep′shən):   mental grasp of objects, qualities, and so on by means of the senses; awareness; comprehension

physiological (fiz′ē ə läj′i k′l):   bodily; physical

senility (si nil′ə tē):   state typical of or resulting from old age; showing the marked deterioration often accompanying old age, especially confusion or memory loss

fat, āpe, cär; ten, ēven; is, bīte; gō, hôrn, tool, look; oil, out; up, fur; chin, she; thin, *then*; zh, leisure; ŋ, ring; ə for *a* in *ago*; ′ as in *able* (ā′b′l)

SURVEY

Survey the following article by reading the author's name, the title, the first paragraph, the first sentence of the other paragraphs, and the last paragraph. This should take no longer than forty-five seconds. After your survey, and without looking back at the article, write three questions that you think will be answered by reading the article.

1. _____

2. _____

3. _____

Now read the article. Write your starting time here: _____

10

How to Strengthen Your Memory Power

Mary Russ

ONE OF ALBERT EINSTEIN'S biographers tells a story about an encounter between the physicist and a neighborhood girl that took place as he was walking through slush and snow-drifts on his way to teach a class at Princeton. After they had chatted for a while, the girl looked down at Einstein's moccasins, which were soaking wet. "Mr. Einstein, you've come out without your boots again," she said. Einstein laughed and pulled up his trousers to show his ankles. "And I forgot my socks," he confessed.

Although you probably don't have your head in the clouds of cosmological physics, you undoubtedly experience a fair share of forgetfulness: You are introduced to someone at a party and forget the name

139

before the handshake is over; you walk away from a department-store counter, leaving your umbrella tilted against it; you reach for the car keys only to discover that you have no idea where you left them.

Why is it that our memory sometimes lets us down? To understand this breakdown, it's important first to have an idea of how the whole process works. Memory is a set of mental abilities, more wide-ranging than the one word would seem to imply. It involves the registration, storage and retrieval of information.

Though there is disagreement over how memory actually works, many scientists believe that a memory causes a "trace" in the brain — not a physical mark or groove but rather a chemical change. It also is believed that the function of memory is divided into the two categories of short-term and long-term memory. Short-term has a very low retention rate, usually less than 20 seconds. Long-term memory is relatively permanent and has virtually unlimited capacity.

The nerve changes that take place in the brain are different for each type of memory. In short-term, the processing of a fact or impression involves a speedy but complex chain of events. Suppose you look up the telephone number of the local pizzeria. As you see the number, there are chemical changes on the retina of the eye. This triggers impulses in the brain that persist for a brief time and then die out as they're replaced by other patterns of activity: new facts, sights and sounds that you experience. This dying out is the reason that you forget the number practically immediately after you've dialed it and started talking.

If you don't want the pattern to fade out — if you want the fact or impression to be part of long-term memory — it must in some way be selectively maintained and reestablished as a distinctive pattern. This will happen if the impression is repeated enough or is made more vivid or important to you. For instance, you make yourself remember a good friend's telephone number by rehearsing it in your mind. As a long-term memory it is there for keeps, just waiting for the right cue to retrieve it.

Of course, some of us do a better job at remembering than others. One popular view is that certain people are simply born with better memories than others, but a number of psychologists doubt that heredity is the determining factor. Dr. Barbara Jones, a Massachusetts neuropsychologist, observes, "While heredity has something to do with it, it appears that there are certain personality styles that relate more specifically to memory. People who have more rigid personalities — who rely on routine, are well-organized, and aim toward gaining control of their lives — tend to have very good memories because they depend more on their knowledge of facts."

Is there a way to improve your memory? Can you make certain that essential information doesn't get dumped out of a short-term compartment in 20 seconds? The memory experts say yes.

"Association is the key," says Harry Lorayne, author of *The Memory Book*. You have to relate what you want to remember to something verbal or visual. Lorayne offers an example of how this works: Very few people can accurately remember the shape of foreign countries – except perhaps Italy. That's because most people have come to note that Italy is shaped like a boot. The shape of a boot is something already known and therefore hard to forget.

All human memory is associative. It involves connecting particular concepts, events, facts and principles and weaving them into systematic relation with each other. Enthusiasm, fear or anything which causes a heightening of perception can intensify this process of association. Your interest – or lack of it – in what you are seeing, hearing or learning can make all the difference.

Good organization can also assist your memory, just as an orderly street plan helps you to find your way to a particular corner in a city. Organization involves grouping items by categories and establishing a pattern to make remembering easier. For instance, if you start making a point of placing the car keys on the shelf near the door to the garage, you're not likely to lose track of them.

Failure to pay attention is frequently the real reason why we forget. We blame our memory for something that is really the fault of our concentration. At a party you may forget the names of people you met because during the introductions you were actually concentrating on the impression you were giving – and not the new names. Failure to pay attention is also the most common reason for absentmindedness – you may "forget" where you put your car keys because you were not paying a bit of attention when you put them down.

Certain physiological states can interfere with memory function. Anyone who has ever had too much to drink knows that the morning after it may be difficult to recollect what happened the night before. "People who are drunk are not processing information," says Dr. Laird Cermak, a professor and research psychologist. Since alcohol depresses the brain and the nervous system, it's particularly difficult to learn anything when you've been drinking.

There are also memory disorders that result from accidents, strokes and serious psychological stress. Following a severe head injury that produces a concussion, a person may experience a loss of memory known as amnesia. Such loss can cover periods ranging from a few minutes prior to an accident to weeks or even years before the injury. The more serious the injury, the greater the period of amnesia is likely to be. Occasionally amnesia is permanent, but usually the patient recovers most of the lost memories.

Perhaps the memory loss feared most by people is the one that begins to appear at the onset of old age. Psychologists agree that as we get older there is a very gradual loss of the ability to learn and to recall. As a person grows older, some brain cells die or are destroyed by minute injuries of various kinds. But the memory problems common among many older people should not be confused with senility, and it is dangerous to make general statements about the long-term functional changes which take place as a person ages. Professor Ian Hunter, author of *Memory*, says: "So much depends on the individual, his circumstances and interests, the sort of accomplishments he has acquired and whether he continues to use those accomplishments or not. Some people become old before their time while others continue to function at high levels of achievement into extreme old age."

Doctors are currently working on developing a drug that will help slow down or prevent memory loss due to age. Though there's no miracle pill yet, you can make your memory work better by using some of the techniques of association and organization mentioned above. Here are a few tricks to try:

One of the most famous systems for remembering a list of errands or objects is called the "link" method. According to Lorayne, it works like this: You link together the objects by associating the first to the second, the second to the third, the third to the fourth, and so on. You should make your associations as ridiculous or exaggerated as possible, so that you "see" them in your mind's eye. Let's say that one morning you want to remember to visit a sick friend at the hospital and pick up some postage stamps. Try picturing your friend lying under a giant stamp rather than a blanket. This image will be hard to forget.

Another good trick that will help you remember tasks that must be done is to make a physical change in your environment. This acts as a cue. For instance, Lorayne suggests that if you're worried about burning dinner while you watch TV, put a frying pan on the set to remind you that dinner's in the oven.

When you're introduced to lots of people at a party it can be hard to remember names. Make sure you hear the name when you're introduced. If you didn't get it, ask the person to repeat it. Then say the name over several times in your head. This repetition will help the name to stick.

1600 words

Write your ending time here: _____

Subtract your starting time: _____

Total time: _____

Check the Rate Chart in the back of the book to find out how many words per minute you have read, and then record your score on the Progress Chart.

ANSWERS TO SURVEY QUESTIONS

Without looking back at the article, write the answers to your survey questions here:

1. _____

2. _____

3. _____

SKILLS EXERCISE:
UNDERLINING KEY CONCEPTS

Before you complete the Comprehension Check, go back to the article and underline the important points. Use signal words and visual clues to help. Since the purpose of your underlining is to provide for quick review, try not to underline more than 10 percent of the material. Remember that you usually don't have to underline a complete sentence to remember the important idea or detail. Also remember to underline the important signal words, because they will quickly show you the relationship of the ideas.

When you have finished, read what you have underlined and write one complete sentence stating the main idea of this article:

_____

_____

Your answer should be similar to the correct answer for question 2 in the Comprehension Check.

10

How to Strengthen Your Memory Power

COMPREHENSION CHECK
Circle the letter before the best answer to each question below. Don't look back at the article.

Subject and Main Idea

1. The subject of the article is
   a. how memory works.
   b. the causes of forgetting.
   c. how to improve your memory.
   d. none of the above.

2. The main idea is that
   a. anyone can improve his or her memory.
   b. association is the key to memory.
   c. some people can remember better than others.
   d. there are important differences between short-term and long-term memory.

Details

3. The type of person who remembers best is
   a. brilliant.
   b. well organized.
   c. very young.
   d. a student.

4. A major reason for forgetting is
   a. low intelligence.
   b. drinking.
   c. amnesia.
   d. failure to pay attention.

5. Scientists believe that memory is
   a. electronic, like a computer.
   b. chemical.
   c. physical, like a mark or groove.
   d. all of the above.

6. Short-term memory lasts
   a. a few hours.
   b. almost forever.
   c. less than thirty seconds.
   d. about thirty minutes.

Inferences

7. From the story about Albert Einstein, you can infer that he didn't have a good memory for
   a. everyday things.
   b. anything.
   c. numbers.
   d. physics.

8. Russ implies that the best way to remember a lecture is to
   a. try to copy down everything that's said.
   b. use a tape recorder.
   c. use drugs that aid memory.
   d. repeat the key concepts over and over.

9. Russ suggests that a good way to remember material for tests would be to
   a. organize it in categories.
   b. make visual and verbal associations.
   c. repeat the facts you don't remember over and over.
   d. do all of the above.

10. Memory experts
   a. are still learning about memory.
   b. believe that the principles of memory are based on cosmological physics.
   c. believe that long-term memories fade within a few days and cannot be retrieved.
   d. have finally identified all the chemicals involved in the memory process.

QUESTIONS FOR ANALYSIS AND APPLICATION

1. Use the "link" method to remember a list of five errands. In the first column, list the errands. In the second column, describe the mental pictures you can use to remember each errand.

Errands   Mental Pictures

a. _____   _____

b. _____   _____

c. _____   _____

d. _____   _____

e. _____   _____

2. Which memory techniques would have helped the last time you forgot something important? Why?

VOCABULARY IN CONTEXT
Fill-in
Write the best word from this list in the blank in each sentence below:

cosmology   **retrieval**   **retention**   **relatively**

distinctive   **heredity**   **neuropsychologist**   **associative**

perception   **physiological**   **senility**

1. Scientists are experimenting with new "youth" drugs like

   Gerovital to prevent _____ .

2. The _____ markings on certain animals
   serve as a form of camouflage in their natural habitats.

3. If you were hearing the voices of invisible beings, you might

   go to a _____ .

4. _____ determines the color of our eyes.

5. No one has yet found a _____ cause for
   mental illness, although it has long been suspected that it is not
   completely psychological.

6. The _____ of game by some breeds of
   hunting dogs almost seems to be an inborn ability.

7. Musicians become skilled at the _____
   of small differences in sound that most of us can't hear.

8. When the interest rates go up, "hard money" investments like

   gold and silver become _____ cheaper.

9. The eye's _____ of visual images
   enables us to see a motion picture as a flowing unit rather than as a
   series of separate pictures.

10. The principle of _____ memory involves
    relating new information to what is already known.

11. Einstein's theory on the _____ of the
    spatial universe is that it curves back on itself and is, therefore,
    infinite.

SKILLS EXERCISE:
WORD MEMORY/ANALOGIES

For explanation see pp. 9–10

A. There are four major ways to memorize new words: (1) make the word meaningful by using it in context, (2) make associations between the new word and a familiar word, (3) use word parts, and (4) use flash cards.

1. *Use the word in context.* Write sentences that make clear the meanings of the following words from this article:

a. retention _____

b. relatively _____

c. distinctive _____

d. perception _____

e. concept _____

2. *Make word associations.* In the space next to each of the following words from this article, write a familiar word that can help you remember the new one.

a. heredity _____

b. associative _____

c. physiological _____

d. functional _____

3. *Use word parts.* In the space after each word part below, write in the letter of its definition. Use the dictionary if you need help. The definitions may be used more than once.

a. *cosmo* = _____   *logy*   = _____   1. state or
                                                      condition of
b. *senil* = _____   *ity*   = _____   2. again
                                                    3. mind
c. *neuro* = _____   *psycho* = _____   4. study of
                                                    5. old
    log   = _____   *ist*   = _____   6. one who
                                                    7. nerve
d. *re*   = _____   *trieve* = _____   8. find
                                                    9. universe

4. *Make flash cards.* Find ten words from previous articles in this book that you are having trouble remembering. On the front of a card, write the word and its pronunciation. On the back, write the definition in your own words and use the word in a sentence. Test yourself by looking at the front of the card and trying to restate the definition and a sentence. The average person needs seven self-testing sessions to thoroughly master a new word.

B. Write the word from the following list that best completes each analogy.

neuropsychologist   associative   perception

physiological   senility   cosmology   retrieval

retention   relatively   distinctive   heredity

1. relatively : absolutely : : _____ : ordinary

2. retrieval : recovery : : _____ : awareness

3. retention : forgetting : : _____ : immaturity

4. mind : body : : _____ : psychological

5. inheritance : training : : _____ : environment

ADVANCED READING SKILLS

If you want to read effectively, you must be able to do more than understand what is said and find the subject, the main idea, and the supporting details. You must be able to read critically and efficiently.

READING CRITICALLY
Critical reading in nonfiction is the process of making judgments about what you read and deciding what to believe and what not to believe. Critical reading enables you to size up the author's arguments and to evaluate how well he or she supports them so that you can draw your own conclusions.

Critical reading requires both literal and inferential comprehension. If you do not understand the facts and what they imply, you are not in a position to make any judgments.

Inference
When you found the implied main ideas in the preceding articles, you were using inference. Making inferences is important in daily life. For example, if you see storm clouds, you might infer that it will rain. Inference in reading is a type of informed guesswork in which you make judgments about the author's meaning. You must read "between the lines."

Sometimes you can correctly guess the author's meaning from information implied in a paragraph. But other times your inferences may not be supported by what the author has implied. Read the following paragraph, and then write *yes* before each statement that can be inferred and *no* before each statement that cannot be inferred from what the author has implied. Finally, underline the main idea in the paragraph, and identify the type of supporting details used: facts, reasons, examples, testimony.

> Words can have interesting origins. Salt, which has always been the most widely used seasoning in the world, was so important in Roman times that it was given for monthly wages to the soldiers. It was called "salt money" or, in Latin, *salarium*. This is the reason that today we use the word *salary* to mean money.

149

_____ 1. Salt was used for payment because it was worth more than gold.

_____ 2. The Romans used salt in their food.

_____ 3. The origins of some of our words can be traced to earlier languages.

_____ 4. Salt was very valuable because the Romans had to import it from the Far East.

_____ 5. Soldiers did not get enough salt in their diets.

_____ 6. Salt was very valuable in Rome.

Type of supporting details: _____

You should have written *yes* before statements 2, 3, and 6. Choice 1 is not valid because the paragraph does not compare the value of salt and gold. Choice 2 is a valid inference since it's hard to imagine other uses besides seasoning that the Romans would have for salt. Choice 3 is a valid inference because we know at least one word (*salary*) that came from an earlier language (Latin). Choice 4 cannot be inferred because the paragraph never discusses where the Romans obtained their salt. Choice 5 is not a valid inference because the paragraph never implies that the soldiers were deprived of salt. Choice 6 is a valid inference because salt was used as money. The main idea is in the first sentence, and it is supported by an example.

Now complete the following exercise in the same way. Write *yes* before the sentences that can be inferred, and write *no* before the ones that cannot be inferred. Then underline the main idea, and fill in the type of supporting details used.

If the ice in Antarctica were to melt, there would be a worldwide disaster. First, the ocean level would rise by 240 feet and flood a quarter of the world. Also, with warmer temperatures in the Antarctic, the Earth could support only a limited amount of sea life. The cold water tends to fertilize the rest of the world. Cold water is rich in oxygen; because of the temperature, it travels northward at the bottom of the ocean, increasing the oxygen content of all the water. If the temperature were altered, the water would travel at a higher level, losing more oxygen and minerals. This would alter the entire ocean environment.

_____ 1. It is important that the temperature in the Antarctic not increase.

_____ 2. Antarctic water is colder than Arctic water.

_____ 3. Antarctic water affects other oceans.

_____ 4. Sea life from Antarctica migrates to northern waters.

_____ 5. Water closer to the bottom of the ocean holds more oxygen than water at a higher level.

_yes_____ 6. Cold water is heavier than warm water.

Type of supporting details: _____facts_____

You should have written *yes* before statements 1, 3, 5, and 6. Choice 1 is a valid inference, because if the temperature increased, the world might be flooded and the ocean waters would contain less oxygen and therefore less sea life. Choice 2 is not a valid inference, because the article never compares Antarctic and Arctic temperatures. Choice 3 is a valid inference, because the paragraph says that Antarctic water fertilizes the rest of the world. Choice 4 is not a valid inference; sea life grows in northern waters because of the oxygen, not because it migrated there. Choice 5 is a valid inference; the paragraph says that water at a higher level loses more oxygen. Choice 6 is a valid inference, because cold water travels on the bottom and rises as it gets warmer. The main idea is in the first sentence. The type of supporting detail is reasons (supported by facts).

Now complete the following exercise in the same way you did the previous two.

> Scientists have been able to accurately reconstruct the scene during the eruption of Mount Vesuvius in southwestern Italy in the summer of A.D. 79. They believe that the 20,000 inhabitants in the city of Pompeii were caught unawares by the eruption. People were choked to death by the poisonous fumes. The cinders from the volcano set much of the city on fire. About 2,000 people were buried alive in the crush of volcanic ash. Now, nearly 1,800 years later, scientists have poured plaster of Paris into the hollows left in the hardened ash by the bodies. Incredibly, the scientists have been able to get such perfect casts of the victims that the terrified and pained facial expressions of the people are clear.

_____ 1. Hardened ash makes an excellent mold for statues.

_____ 2. The location of Pompeii is known.

_____ 3. Most of the people escaped the volcano.

_____ 4. There are many volcanoes in the southwestern part of Italy.

_____ 5. Mount Vesuvius had erupted many times before.

_____ 6. The people were frightened when the volcano erupted.

Type of supporting details: _____

You should have written *yes* before statements 1, 2, and 6. Choice 1 is valid because the hollows left where the bodies had been made perfect casts. Choice 2 is valid because scientists had to discover the city to find the bodies of the victims. Choice 3 is not a valid inference because we don't know how many people escaped; we only know that many people were choked by the poisonous fumes and 2,000 were buried alive. Choice 4 is not a valid inference; we only know of one volcano, Mount Vesuvius. Choice 5 is not valid since there is nothing said about how many times Mount Vesuvius had erupted in the past; it probably had not erupted frequently or the inhabitants would not have been "caught unawares by the eruption." Choice 6 is a valid inference since the people had terrified expressions on their faces, as the plaster of Paris statues revealed. The main idea is in the first sentence. It is supported by facts.

Author's Purpose

Authors can have any or all of three main purposes in mind when they write: to inform, to persuade, and to entertain. The author's purpose can often be understood from the title. For example, an article titled *Coping With Stress* is probably factual and informative. However, it could also be persuasive; for example, the author might be advocating the use of a particular diet as a method for stress reduction. It could even be entertaining, if, for example, several humorous methods of stress reduction were presented in a tongue-in-cheek tone.

Stylistic elements will also further the author's purpose. An example is use of language. No matter what the purpose, the author will strive for clear and vivid language so that the reader will understand and remember the main ideas. However, informative articles might have a serious tone, whereas entertaining articles might be more lively or humorous. Persuasive writing in particular might use words intended to sway the reader to agree with the argument. This practice is commonly seen in courtrooms, for example. If a defendant's car is involved in a collision while traveling at 25 miles per hour, the prosecutor might ask, "How fast were you going when you *crashed* into the truck?" The defense attorney might ask, "How fast were you going when you *bumped* into the truck?"

For example, in Article 7 "Don't Tell Jaime Escalante Minorities Can't Meet (High) Standards," the author describes Jaime Escalante's teaching style in such a way as to enable the reader to understand how he motivates his students with his rapid-fire delivery and exaggerated gestures and his use of dolls and stuffed animals while wandering through the aisles.

Argument and Support

When an author is trying to persuade you, his or her main ideas could be called **arguments**. The author uses details to support these arguments. You need to look critically at the details to see whether the author is leaving out any important ideas, whether he or she is exaggerating the importance of any one piece of support, whether the support is logical, and whether the author's facts are really facts or merely opinions.

Read the following paragraph, and then fill in the outline, stating the argument next to Roman numeral I and the supporting details next to letters A, B, and C. In this paragraph the argument is the same as the main idea.

> The peanut is one of the most nutritious foods in the world. Pound for pound, the peanut provides more fat than heavy cream. It has more vitamins, minerals, and protein than beef liver and more calories than sugar.

I. _____ peanut   most   nutrition   foods _____

   A. _____ more fat _____
   B. _____ minerals _____
   C. _____

Next to Roman numeral I you should have written "The peanut is one of the most nutritious foods in the world." The supporting statements are as follows: A "Provides more fat than heavy cream," B "Has more vitamins, minerals, and protein than beef liver," C "Has more calories than sugar."

Now, outline the argument and support for the following paragraph. Again, the argument is the same as the main idea.

> Being left-handed can be a real hardship. First, even the word is negative. The Latin word for *left* is *sinister*. The French word is *gauche*. Even in English, the word has negative connotations. You receive a left-handed compliment. You are *left* out. Everyone else is *right*. Second, a left-handed person must either learn to do many things with the right hand or buy special equipment. For example, a left-handed person must either cut with the right hand or buy special scissors; either catch a ball with the right hand or buy a left-hander's mitt; either learn to play the complicated fingerboard of a guitar with the right hand or completely restring the guitar. But some things simply cannot be changed. For example, the handle on an adding machine is always on the right side. In most countries, the gearshift of a car is on the right side. Thus being left-handed means adapting to a right-handed world.

I. _____ Left handed   real hardship _____

   A. _____ negative _____
      1. _____ Latin   sinister _____
      2. _____ French gauche _____
      3. _____ english   negative _____
         a. _____ left out _____
         b. _____ others   right _____
         c. _____

B. _learn to do thing right here_

   1. _cut · with scissors_

   2. _Play the guitar_

   3. _Catch a ball_

C. _Can't be changed_

   1. _handle machine_

   2. _Gearshift of car_

Next to the Roman numeral I you should have put either the first or the last sentence. Next to A you should have put a version of the second sentence, such as "Word is negative." The next three sentences are examples of the negative uses of the word, so next to the first 1 should be "Latin word is *sinister*"; next to the first 2 should be "French word is *gauche*"; and next to the first 3 should be "Word in English is negative." The next three sentences are examples of how *left* is used in English as a negative word, so next to a should be "Left-handed compliment"; next to b should be "Left out"; next to c should be "Others right." Next to B you should have put "Learn to do things with right hand or buy special equipment." Next to the second 1 should be "Cut with scissors"; next to the second 2 should be "Catch a ball"; next to the second 3 should be "Play the guitar." Next to the C is the last major support: "Some can't be changed." Next to the third 1 you should have put "Handle of adding machine"; next to the third 2 you should have put "Gearshift of a car."

Judging Support

Once you recognize support, you must evaluate it. Is the author or other cited authority credible? Is the evidence adequate to persuade you of the author's point?

Evaluating Author's Credibility

Qualifications   Is the author or other authority knowledgeable about the subject? TV ads are notorious for using celebrities to endorse products even when the celebrity couldn't possibly have any expertise about the product. Whenever the author's qualifications are important, you should think about that person's experience, education, or other relevant factors.

Bias   Does the author or other authority have anything to gain or lose by taking a particular point of view? For example, when predicting whether housing prices in your city will go up or down, a real estate agent who is trying to sell you a house may reach very different conclusions from those of your stockbroker, who wants you to spend your money in the stock market instead of on a new house. Although they may have access to the same information, each might distort or select different facts, perhaps even subconsciously.

Fact Versus Opinion

When trying to evaluate what an author is saying, you must not only understand and evaluate the arguments, you must also be able to distinguish factual statements from opinions. One reason that people find it difficult to tell fact from opinion is that their own attitudes get in the way, clouding their judgment. For example, if you have always preferred classical music to popular music, you might decide that the statement "Classical music sounds better than popular music" is a fact. Of course, it isn't. A fact is something that everyone with an opportunity to observe would agree on. A fact can be proven. An example of a fact would be "All living things must die."

Mark the following statements *F* for fact and *O* for opinion.

_____ 1. The most densely populated state in the United States is New Jersey.

_____ 2. Cancer will eventually be curable.

_____ 3. Michelangelo was the world's greatest artist.

_____ 4. In her lifetime, one termite queen can produce over 300 million offspring.

_____ 5. The letter most used in the English Language is *e*.

The first, fourth, and fifth sentences are facts. Each can be proven. The second and third are opinions. We hope that cancer will be cured in the future, but no one can guarantee it, so it is just an opinion. There is no way to prove that one artist was greater than any other, so the third sentence must also be an opinion.

Clues to opinion come from such phrases as *I think, it seems,* and *everyone agrees that.* Clues to both fact and opinion can also come from your own experience. Think about whether a statement can be tested and proven. When you read, always evaluate whether an author is supporting his or her arguments with fact or opinion.

Evaluating Evidence

Let's say, for example, that you are trying to decide whether or not you should take Vitamin C to prevent or cure a cold. You have figured out that some experts think you should, and they present evidence for their point of view. Others who think you shouldn't also have evidence supporting their argument. What should you do? You might look at the evidence each group is presenting and evaluate it. Do they give facts, reasons, testimony, or examples? If the support is testimony, you must judge the credibility of the person giving testimony. Can you believe him or her? Is there someone equally credible on the other side? If the support is reasons, you must judge the logic of the reasoning involved. Article 12 in this unit will give you practice in recognizing logical errors. You can also compare the reasons given by the opposing point of view. If the support is examples, are they sufficient? Are they relevant to your situation? How might those who hold the opposite viewpoint respond to the examples? Facts can be omitted or distorted when given as evidence, and it is up to the reader to decide their validity for himself or herself. Even in scientific research, the facts often fail to justify the conclusions that are drawn. Article 17 in this unit has an exercise that will introduce you to the evaluation of research evidence.

In summary, you can't believe everything you read. Reading critically is essential to success in college and in life.

INCREASING READING FLEXIBILITY

Because they have to read so much, efficient reading is crucial for college students. But if your response is to say "I read _____ words per minute," you do not understand a basic principle of efficient reading. Good readers are flexible; they adjust their reading speeds. They read a textbook more slowly than the newspaper. They read Shakespeare more slowly than *Newsweek*.

The most important thing to keep in mind is the purpose of your reading. If you are trying to read and memorize textbook material for a test, you read much more slowly than if you are relaxing with a detective story or looking through the newspaper.

Types of Reading

There are four basic types of reading: study reading, rapid reading, skimming, and scanning. Each type is suited to a particular type of reading material and reading purpose, and each should be practiced at different speeds.

	Study Reading	Rapid Reading	Skimming	Scanning
Speed	Up to 250 wpm	250–800 wpm	Up to thousands of wpm	Up to thousands of wpm
Purpose	Thorough understanding and recall	Recreation, information, light reading	Survey, overview, review	Locating specific information
Types of Material	Textbooks, technical materials	Newspapers, magazines, novels	Any type	Any type

Use **study reading** on difficult textbook or technical material when your purpose is thorough understanding and/or memorization. Study reading rates usually do not exceed 250 words per minute. (Study reading is discussed in Unit III.)

Rapid reading should be used when your purpose is to get a general idea of what you read and when the material is not extremely complicated. Types of materials suitable for rapid reading incude newspapers, magazines, novels, and light nonfiction.

Skimming is quickly looking over a selection to get the general idea rather than reading every word. It is used (1) when surveying a chapter or article, (2) when all you need is a general overview, and (3) when reviewing something you once read to refresh your memory. To give you an example of skimming, we have emphasized some words in the following article. Read the dark print only; then, without looking back, answer the questions that follow the article.

> If you are seriously interested in a **car**, you should **haggle with the dealer** over the price. The sticker price on the window of a car is there because the law says it must be, but only a naive buyer accepts the sticker price as anything but a starting point for negotiations. Shop around, shop carefully, and **never pay the asking price**.
>
> You can easily **learn the dealer's cost for a new car** (invoice price) by buying an inexpensive guide titled **Edmund's New Car Prices**, available at bookstores and newsstands. Total the dealer's cost including options, and then **offer $125 to $200 above** this cost. You should aim to settle for **no more than $200 to $500 over** the dealer's cost for an **American** car, **or $500 for a foreign** car.
>
> A **good time to close** a deal is often **late Sunday night** (or the last night of the week the dealer is open) **or at the end of the month**. (Many dealerships offer bonuses to the person who has the best sales record at the end of the week or month.) It is good to **deal directly with the sales manager or assistant** manager, because this person is authorized to agree on a price.
>
> When you have settled on the car you want and have agreed with the salesperson on a price, you should **have the dealer put the agreement in writing before** you make a **deposit**. The order form for this agreement should **include a statement of the precise car** being bought, the **accessories** agreed on (if any), the **sales tax, registration fee**, and the **value of the trade-in** (if any). In addition, an **officer of the firm must sign** the order form or it has no legal value. The salesperson's signature means nothing; you may find that when the time comes to close the deal, you have been low-balled (promised a better deal than you are actually able to get) or high-balled (offered more on your trade-in than you will actually get). A person might be both high-balled and low-balled during the course of the negotiations. Both practices are very common among car dealers.

1. What is the article about? _____

2. What is the main idea? _____

3. How much should you pay for a new foreign car? _____

4. Who should you try to deal with? _____

The answers are (1) buying a car; (2) you can get a better deal if you know what you're doing; (3) no more than $500 over the dealer's cost; (4) manager or assistant manager.

Scanning is locating specific information, such as a name, a place, or a date. For example, when you look up something in the dictionary or in the telephone book, you are scanning. You run your eyes over the page and read only the information surrounding what you are looking for. You may also use scanning in textbooks — for example, when you are looking for a particular name or date in a chapter.

Factors in the Reader

In addition to your purpose and the type of material you are reading, factors in yourself also affect the rate at which you read.

One cause of slow reading is a small vocabulary. If you encounter many unfamiliar words, your thought processes will be interrupted. This will interfere with both speed and comprehension.

Another factor that influences reading rate is your comprehension skills. The ability to quickly identify the author's organization (subject, main ideas, and support) is essential to grasping the overall picture that he or she is trying to get across.

Your speed and comprehension will also increase if you have some familiarity with the concepts you will be reading about. Your background knowledge also affects your level of interest and, therefore, your ability to concentrate.

Finally, the way you read affects your speed and comprehension. Phrase reading — grouping words into meaningful phrases — allows you to read faster. Poor readers read word by word.

Poor | readers | read | like | this.

Good readers | read like this.

One way of overcoming word-by-word reading is to practice drawing lines between thought units, as in the second example above. After you have drawn lines, you can practice reading by looking at each unit rather than each word. Phrase reading also reduces some other common bad reading habits, such as habitually looking back at what you have just read.

11

Some Businesses Take Advantage of the Unwary

VOCABULARY PREVIEW

unwary (un wer′ē):   not cautious; unwatchful

accumulate (ə kyōōm′yə lāt′):   to pile up or collect

subversive (səb vʉr′siv):   tending or seeking to overthrow or destroy

discretionary (dis kresh′ən er′ē):   left to or regulated by one's own discretion or judgment

unsophisticated (ən sə fis′tə kā′tid):   lacking in experience; unworldly

deceitful (di sēt′fəl):   apt to lie or cheat; dishonest

fraudulent (frô′jə lənt):   based on or using a trickery or falsehood

prestigious (pres tij′əs):   having or imparting prestige or distinction

subtle (sut′l):   crafty; not obvious

terminate (tʉr′mə nāt′):   to put an end to; stop

audiophile (ô′dē ō fīl′):   a devotee of high-fidelity sound reproduction, as on record players

ploy (ploi):   an action intended to outwit someone; trick

insidious (in sid′ē əs):   secretly harmful; deceptive; sly

perpetrated (pʉr′pə trāt′id):   did (something evil or criminal)

traumatic (trô′ ma tik):   shocking; producing substantial and lasting damage

voided (void′id):   made ineffective or useless

trumped-up (trumpt up′):   devised by trickery; false

indicted (in dīt′id):   charged with a crime

punitive (pyōō′nə tiv)⁖   inflicting or concerned with punishment

fat, āpe, cär; ten, ēven; is, bīte; gō, hôrn, tōōl, look; oil, out; up, fʉr; chin, she; thin, *then*; zh, leisure; ŋ, ring; ə for *a* in *ago;* ′ as in *able* (ā′b'l)

SKILLS EXERCISE:
SKIMMING AND SCANNING

For explanation see pp. 157–158

A. **Skimming**. Take one minute to skim the following article. Run your eyes over the article to get a general idea of what it is about. Use the headings to help you organize your thoughts.

   1. After you have skimmed the article, write its main idea in your own words.

     _____

     _____

   2. Without looking back at the article, write three questions that you think will be answered by reading it.

     a. _____

     b. _____

     c. _____

B. **Scanning**. First, underline the key words in the following questions. Next, scan the article to find the answers, using the headings as guides. Quickly underline each answer and move to the next question. It should take you no more than three minutes to answer all of the questions. After you finish scanning for all ten answers, write them in the spaces below.

   1. What kind of people do companies take advantage of?

     _____

   2. What kind of advertising attracts people with one item, which, when you arrive at the store, you find is either sold out or of poor quality?

     _____

   3. What often happens with free gift offers?

     _____

   4. What is the name of the deceptive practice that involves mixing normally priced items with real markdowns?

     _____

   5. Is wholesale to the public cheaper than retail?

     _____

   6. To what kind of people is easy credit most appealing?

     _____

7. What kind of publication is involved when a company charges you to have your book published? _____

8. How much was a Los Angeles woman charged for unauthorized auto repair work? _____

9. What type of mail-order fraud asks you to send copies of a letter to friends? _____

10. What are the three rules the author suggests that you follow to avoid being taken advantage of? _____

Now read the article. Write your starting time here: _____

11

Some Businesses Take Advantage of the Unwary

J. Norman Swaton

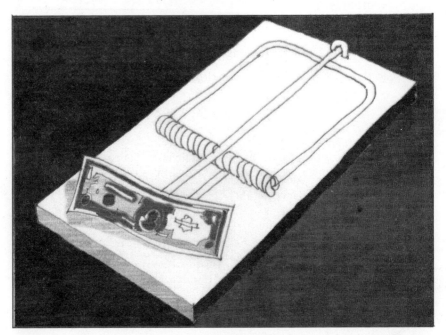

USINESS, AS POINTED out earlier, is an essential part of the American economy. Greed, apparently, is also an inescapable part of human nature, and this unfortunate combination can work against you in your efforts to accumulate investment capital just as much as inflation does.

There's nothing subversive about business going after discretionary funds. In fact, it's healthy and makes for progress in many ways. You, as consumer, are supposed to learn to play the game and exercise your free will to buy only those things that fit into your life plan. That part's simple enough. What muddies the picture are the countless companies that prey on the lonely, insecure, and immature (or at least unsophisticated) with advertising that effectively promises to fulfill needs and desires that can in no way be met through use of the product involved. The dishonesty of such practices is probably somewhat a matter of definition, and if the fantasy of satisfaction brings temporary pleasure at relatively little expense, there's probably no reason to mount a case against it. Women are going to spend money for *some* kind of pantyhose and whether it's the kind Joe Namath wears or just some unknown model is really a matter of little concern. Similarly, the clothing budget isn't affected too much if the dress shirts bought this month are the kind women on TV can't resist tearing from your body or plain old Sears page 395.

Actually, the last two statements are minor lies, as we'll see in a couple of chapters, but they serve here to make the point that some common business practices are less harmful than others. Puffery (flattering publicity or extravagant recommendation, according to the dictionary) is one thing, and has become an expected part of the marketing approach. But beyond this are still more deceitful and fraudulent practices that take billions of dollars out of the economy each year by taking advantage of unsophisticated people who believe the world is as honest as they are. We're going to look at some of the most common of these here because some of them might be unfamiliar to you. Knowing about them can make a considerable difference in how soon you reach your financial goals.

SOME COMMON DECEPTIONS TO WATCH FOR
The following are practices that usually can't be prosecuted under the law but that can take your dollars in sneaky, underhanded ways.

Bait and Switch Ads
These will probably be with us forever. "Singer Portable Sewing Machine — $29.95!" says the little ad in the classifieds or display section of the paper. The price is so great you run right down. If you call ahead, you'll be told they only have a few left so you'd better hurry because they can't hold them at that price. When you get there, of course, it's a rebuilt machine with no guarantee, which the salesperson either won't even bring out to show you or puts down so much you're ashamed you asked about it. What they do have, for a little more money, is the Dynamite Superfine free-arm machine that zigs, zags, and butters your toast.

Vacuum cleaners, refrigerators, television sets, freezers, meat, carpeting, even eyeglasses are sold this way. And the stores aren't always fly-by-night operations, either. Some of the most prestigious names in the department store field resort to the tactic. Some of the switches are so subtle you believe you did it yourself and actually feel pretty smart about it. The harm is that you are tricked into overspending — even if you receive value, which is usually not the case — and your budget is messed up for some time to come. Remember that whatever you spend in excess of what you hoped to spend comes right out of your investment capital and sets your plan back a corresponding length of time. If a merchant or salesperson you've invited to your home tries it on you, you're well advised to terminate the interview immediately and shop elsewhere.

False List Prices

This technique, which allows unjustified advertising claims of great discounts, is a common way of business in some lines. The hi-fi industry in the fifties became so addicted to this practice that national merchandising companies included the false list prices in their catalogs. The discounted "audiophile net" price was in fact the list price and it was virtually impossible to find any store that sold for either the false list or truly discounted prices. Competition and consumer education eventually eliminated this particular practice, and today examples of the phony list price are usually confined to individual brands and stores, although from time to time the "sticker price" on new automobiles becomes meaningless. Your best defense against this practice is careful shopping and comparison of prices at several dealers.

Phony Contest Awards

These may start out as a phone call advising you that your name has been selected as a contestant to receive a free this or that if you can answer two questions. The questions, of course, would make Groucho Marx blush. All you have to do to claim your free encyclopedia set is sign up for the reader service and the annual yearbooks. Cost? Strangely, about the same as the cost of the set with the other stuff thrown in. The same ploy works as a variation on the bait and switch: you receive a letter advising you you have won second prize or consolation prize in a contest you may or may not remember having entered (at a recent home show or county fair, for example). Your certificate is worth half or two-thirds the cost of a moderately priced sewing machine. When you try to buy it, you find there is no guarantee so you have to buy a service policy, or a cabinet, or instructions in sewing technique, all of which come free with the higher-priced, better-quality machine that zigs, zags, and butters toast.

Free Gifts

These often never appear. The gifts "have to be mailed out from our regional headquarters" or some such excuse when the salesperson arrives at your home. Whether the consumer buys or not, the free gift never quite makes it, but the family budget has been unnecessarily strained, or at least exposed to the probability of strain, through a deceptive advertising practice.

Phony Sales

This is a variation on the theme of false list prices because much, if not all, of the merchandise on sale is brought in for the event. Well-established department stores still do this, often mixing lower-priced merchandise with some legitimately marked-down goods. It's distressing to find that the sale price you paid for something is really more than its normal retail price, but it happens every day in stores all over the country. Refinements and variations include such practices as advertising a sale price on a 17-inch television set and showing a picture of a deluxe 25-inch. Another is the "going out for business" sale. The merchant will claim mere cuteness if brought to task for this deceitful substitution of words. More subtle still is the use of price comparisons such as "$20 value" in the obvious hope that the reader will take it to mean "$20 regular price," which, of course, it isn't.

Wholesale to the Public

This claim is by definition impossible. Wholesale is to retailers and retail is to the public. Still, millions of Americans daily buy from such stores in the belief they are saving money. Only when the price of an item is well established can such a claim be put to the test. Usually it fails, because the item can be bought from normal channels as cheaply and often with service that isn't available through the "wholesaler." A variation of this practice is the way some major manufacturers make a well-established product line of quality, and a very similar-appearing product line (often with a confusingly similar name) for sale in discount department stores. Luggage, typewriter, and sporting goods manufacturers are particularly guilty of this near-conspiracy, which leads consumers to believe they are getting a discount when in fact the product is sold for at least normal retail prices, considering the lowered quality.

Easy Credit

This one is usually accompanied by an advertisement to the effect that the seller of some item carries his own credit so you can qualify even if you're new in town, been bankrupt, and so on. It can be the most insidious victimization of all. It's always of most appeal to those who can least afford it, and the price is *high*. This is the subject of another whole chapter but it can't be mentioned too often as a lump in the oatmeal of life.

SOME PRACTICES TO BE WARY OF

Up to now we've been talking about sharp practices that manage to stay within the law. There are also countless full-blown frauds that are perpetrated on people every day. These are more traumatic in their impact on a financial program because they usually involve larger amounts of money — often the entire savings of a family — and more often than not the service or merchandise bought is worthless if it exists at all.

Unordered Merchandise

This is one of the cheapest of the scams and probably remains so because very few people are about to lay out more than a few dollars to cover a "COD" delivery for an absent neighbor. (When the neighbor comes home, of course, it turns out that nobody ordered anything in the first place and the box is probably empty in the second place.) A variation is the delivery of actual merchandise which wasn't ordered but then becomes the subject of repeated billings and threats of court action if payment isn't made as demanded. The law is on your side in most cases, but be sure to check with a lawyer if you're in doubt.

Vanity Publications

These can be relatively inexpensive if all you have to buy is a single copy of the book in which your biography is included as an outstanding biology student of the year, state PTA president, or retail hardware clerk of the week. An entirely different story is the $5,000 it may cost to get your book of poems "published" (quotes because *publication* implies intended sale and the vanity press industry intends to print only a few copies to stroke the frustrated ego of the author). Legitimate publishers never charge an author cash for publishing a work they intend to sell for a profit. Certain minor costs may by contract be charged to a royalty account, but the author never has to put up front money.

Auto Repair

Repair frauds are particularly effective in areas of mystery, such as automatic transmissions. Thousands of cases have been documented where a $3 or $4 part is installed in an automatic transmission in half an hour, and the customer charged $300 for his own repainted transmission as a "rebuilt." Guarantees are frequently voided by trumped-up situations which either never happened or are as totally unrelated as the wrong kind of gasoline being used. One of the world's largest retailers was recently indicted by a Los Angeles County grand jury for practices in some of its auto shops that included making unneeded repairs and charging for parts not installed. Fan belts are sometimes slashed by service station attendants and then pointed out as defective. One classic case in Los Angeles involved a woman who left her Mercedes in a dealer's repair shop for a new battery and got it back weeks later with a $1,900 bill for work unauthorized by her. At this writing, the courts have just settled a $90,000 award in her favor (including punitive damages intended as a warning to the repair industry), but an appeal has been filed by the dealer. The amount of time and money this cost the owner of the car (even though the attorney took the case on a percentage of award basis) is hard to measure, but she lost her apartment, car, and job in the process. Also, presumably, her taste for expensive European motor cars; she now drives a Datsun.

Anyone who has a competent mechanic who can be trusted should count this fact among the prime blessings of life.

Mail Order Frauds

These come in all sizes. At the cheap end are such scams as chain letters, which only take small amounts of money and large amounts of hope from the victim. "Send your dollar to the name at the top of the list. Add your name to the bottom of the list. Make ten copies of this letter and mail them to friends. In two weeks your name will be at the top of the list and thousands of people will be mailing their dollar to you." So the song goes, often laced with stories of tragedy befalling those who dared "break the chain." Mathematically, of course, the chain breaks itself in a few days, but neither that nor the illegality of the letters stops them.

At the other end are land sales that can cost thousands of dollars for property that ends up being on the side of a cliff, under a swamp, or two miles from the nearest water faucet.

A variation of mail order racketeering is the industry that advertises opportunities for wealth through running a mail order business from your home. "You can make millions as I have," is the typical approach. All you have to do is buy your merchandise from the self-professed wizard, and he'll share with you the secrets that made it all happen. Along the way you find out that you'll also need a catalog, and that's another two or three thousand, plus a mailing list, which he'll rent to you at a price, and a postage bill you wouldn't believe. Before long it becomes apparent that the way he made his million in mail order was from suckers like yourself.

Similar cons involving earthworms, chinchillas, rabbits, potted palms, stuffed dates, and unstuffed envelopes have been around forever. The one thing they all have in common is that you must buy something before you can start in business and watch the profits roll in. The problem is that the market always seems to be a little soft when your crop is ready to harvest, and the contract you thought you had for the buy back of the initial investment is a little tougher than you realized.

AVOIDING THE CON

The list of frauds and deceits is almost endless. Every year local police publicize them in newspapers to warn people of the possibility of being taken, and every year people who didn't get the word are taken anyway. It's impossible to learn all the varieties of scam, because new ones are made up every day. However, you can and should try to remember a few basic commonsense principles that will let you recognize that you are being hustled, even if you don't yet know just how. For example, these three rules can save you a lot of trouble and lost time in your progress toward financial goals.

1. *Never be forced into a hasty decision.* A salesperson who tries to convince you you have to decide right now or miss out is almost certainly a hustler. If it's good tonight, it'll be good in the morning. Sleep on it and see how it looks in the daylight. If he says he can't wait, you can be sure that you should.

2. *Don't believe you're getting a special deal.* Unless, of course, you know the seller personally (sometimes not even then!). If the deal is because you've somehow been singled out to star in an advertising campaign, get the person's license number if you can and call the police. Chances are excellent he or she is trying to pick your pockets.

3. *Don't buy something expensive to save money.* There's an old story about a weary housewife who decided to pass on the freezer full of beef because ". . . we're already paying for our foreign car with what we save on gasoline, our television with what we save on movies, our washer-dryer with what we save on laundry bills, and our sewing machine with what we save on clothes. We really can't afford to save any more right now." Unless actual experience shows that you'll really save money every month — and that means your cost *including the payment* will be less — you may be saving money in the long run but perishing in the short run. Any salesperson who doesn't see it that way is not your friend, no matter what it says on his business card.

2800 words

Write your ending time here: _____

Subtract your starting time: _____

Total time: _____

Check the Rate Chart in the back of the book to find out how many words per minute you have read, and then record your score on the Progress Chart.

ANSWERS TO SKIMMING QUESTIONS
1. Your answer should be similar to the correct answer for question 2 in the Comprehension Check.

2. Write the answers to your skimming questions here.

    a. _____

    b. _____

    c. _____

11

Some Businesses Take Advantage of the Unwary

COMPREHENSION CHECK
Circle the letter before the best answer to each question below. Don't look back at the article.

Subject and Main Idea

1. The subject is
    a. consumer education.
    b. deceptive practices by business.
    c. how to avoid being cheated.
    d. what to do if you are ripped off.

2. The main idea is that
    a. the government should have stricter consumer protection laws.
    b. consumers who are deceived by shady business practices are immature or insecure.
    c. there are many dishonest business practices.
    d. it is important for consumers to recognize shady business practices.

Details

3. Puffery is
    a. flattering publicity.
    b. legal cheating.
    c. an illegal business practice.
    d. avoided by advertisers.

4. Bait and switch ads
    a. try to get you to buy shoddy merchandise.
    b. try to get you to buy merchandise that is more expensive than the merchandise that was advertised.
    c. are used only by fly-by-night operations.
    d. lie about the price of merchandise.

5. "Wholesale to the public" deceptions are
    a. not really dishonest.
    b. always easy to check out.
    c. illegal.
    d. legal.

6. Which of the following practices is illegal?
    a. false list prices
    b. phony contest awards
    c. free gifts
    d. unordered merchandise

Inferences

7. The author implies that the use of shady business practices
    a. should be stopped.
    b. would not occur under socialism.
    c. is unavoidable.
    d. is increasing.

8. If you have been "baited-and-switched" but the merchandise still looks like a good buy, you should
    a. grab it.
    b. refuse it and call the police.
    c. give the store a bad check for it.
    d. go home and think about it.

9. In general, consumers should
    a. be trusting.
    b. be suspicious.
    c. be deceptive.
    d. retain a lawyer.

10. If you are offered an appliance for $200 that the store calls "a $500 value," you should
    a. check the price in other stores.
    b. buy it.
    c. refuse to do business with this store.
    d. report the store to a consumer protection agency.

QUESTIONS FOR ANALYSIS AND APPLICATION

1. Summarize the principles discussed in the selection for avoiding cons.

2. Describe an example, from a newspaper or magazine, of one of the deceptive business practices discussed in the article.

VOCABULARY IN CONTEXT
Multiple Choice
Circle the letter before the best definition of each underlined word or phrase.

1. Being in a car accident is a very traumatic experience.
    a. unpleasant   b. disturbing   c. shocking
    d. uncomfortable

2. When people aren't careful to pay bills as they receive them, bills tend to <u>accumulate</u>.
   a. collect   b. diminish   c. scatter   d. lessen

3. The manager of the 7-11 food store used the <u>ploy</u> of telling the thief he had pushed a button which contacted the police.
   a. feat   b. idea   c. practice   d. trick

4. During economic recessions, businesses are forced to <u>terminate</u> the employment of many individuals.
   a. initiate   b. end   c. slow   d. free

5. Most young children are <u>unsophisticated</u> and often charming.
   a. unworldly   b. smooth   c. adorable   d. loving

6. Being forced to sit in the corner with a dunce cap on is now considered too <u>punitive</u> a practice in public elementary schools.
   a. rewarding   b. punishing   c. educational
   d. threatening

7. A <u>deceitful</u> friend can hurt you more than an obvious enemy.
   a. dishonest   b. old   c. distant   d. loyal

8. It is wrong for a police officer to arrest someone on <u>trumped-up</u> charges.
   a. serious   b. weak   c. unimportant   d. false

9. <u>Unwary</u> visitors to big cities like New York might get mugged walking down dark alleys.
   a. careful   b. unwatchful   c. new   d. watchful

Fill-in
Write the best word from this list in the blank in each sentence below:

subversive   discretionary   perpetrated   subtle

audiophiles   fraudulent   voided   insidious

prestigious   indicted

10. Double agents in important government security positions are the most _____ threat of all to national security.

11. In nations with unstable governments, there are often _____ movements.

12. Going on a cruise instead of visiting relatives uses more _____ funds.

13. John Dillinger _____ so many evil acts during the 1920s that he was declared public enemy number one by the FBI.

14. _____ were very pleased when compact discs replaced records because of the superior quality of sound.

15. In the old west there were fake doctors who sold useless "medicine" by making _____ claims that the product could cure any emotional or physical ailment.

16. When you are trying to get someone to do you a favor, a _____ approach often works best.

17. One of the most _____ universities in the United States is Harvard University.

18. Gangster Al Capone was _____ and sent to jail for tax evasion in the 1920s.

19. A _____ check cannot be cashed.

SKILLS EXERCISE:
CRITICAL READING
Inferences

For explanation see pp. 149–152

If you can draw any of the following conclusions from the article, write *yes* in the blank before the statement. If you cannot, write *no* in the blank.

yes   1. A lot of advertising is deceptive.

yes   2. People respond to advertising hoping to get the best deal possible.

yes   3. Careful buyers are taken advantage of less often.

yes   4. Whether a business practice is honest or dishonest is not always clear-cut.

_No_   5. All offers you receive by mail are misleading.

_No_   6. All of the practices mentioned in the article are illegal.

yes   7. Bait and switch ads are very difficult to stop.

_No_   8. False list prices are not very common today.

_No_   9. None of these sales practices are done by reputable stores.

_No_   10. The "unordered merchandise scam" doesn't usually involve large appliances such as refrigerators, television sets, or dishwashers.

12

Critical Thinking: Recognizing Fallacies

VOCABULARY PREVIEW

fallacies (fal′ə sēz):   errors in reasoning; flaws or defects in argument

cite (sīt):   quote; mention by way of example, proof, and so on

refute (ri fyo͞ot′):   to prove to be false or wrong

geneticist (jə net′ə sist):   a specialist in the branch of biology that deals with heredity

relevant (rel′ə vənt):   relating to the matter under consideration; to the point

authoritative (ə thôr′ə tāt′iv):   based on competent authority

valid (val′id):   based on evidence or sound reasoning

alleged (ə lejd′):   not actual; so-called; claimed

bewitching (bi wich′iŋ):   enchanting, delightfully irresistible; fascinating

dawdling (dôd″l iŋ):   wasting time in unimportant activities; being slow

attributing (ə trib′yo͞ot iŋ):   thinking of as belonging to

lauded (lôd′id):   praised

fat, āpe, cär; ten, ēven; is, bīte; gō, hôrn, to͞ol, look; oil, out; up, fʉr; chin, she; thin, *then*; zh, leisure; ŋ, ring; ə for *a* in *ago;* ` as in *able* (ā′b`l)

SKILLS EXERCISE:
SKIMMING AND SCANNING

For explanation
see pp. 157–158

A. *Skimming.* Take one minute to skim the following article. Run your eyes over the article to get a general idea of what it is about. Use the headings to help you organize your thoughts.

1. After you have skimmed the article, write its main idea in your own words. _____

_____

2. Without looking back at the article, write three questions that you think will be answered by reading it.

a. _____

b. _____

c. _____

B. *Scanning.* First, underline the key words in the following questions. Next, scan the article to find the answers, using the headings as guides. Quickly underline each answer and move to the next question. It should take you no more than three minutes to answer all of the questions. After you finish scanning for all ten of the answers, write them in the spaces below.

1. How many fallacies are discussed? _____

2. What is one of the two tests of Appeal to Authority?

_____

3. How many types of fallacies with statistics are discussed?

_____

4. How did the author get the statistics on the number of mosquitoes hatched in Ontario? _____

5. What was the Cincinnati Reds example used to illustrate?

_____

6. What was the Zolon growth rate? _____

7. What do the words *ad hominem* mean? _____

8. What basketball team did Bill Bradley play for? _____

9. What does an ad hominem attack tend to be used for?

_____

10. On what type of fallacies are many superstitions based?

_____

Now read the article. Write your starting time here: _____

12

Critical Thinking: Recognizing Fallacies

Rudolph F. Verderber

A LTHOUGH BOOKS WRITTEN ABOUT ARGUMENT list other valid types of reasoning and often discuss ten or twenty common fallacies, we do not have the space to cover them all here. . . . I wish to focus on five common fallacies that you are likely to find.

HASTY GENERALIZATION

One of the most common thinking fallacies is called *hasty generalization*, which results from a shortage of data. Conclusions from hasty generalization fail to meet the test of sufficient instances cited. In real-life situations, we are likely to find people making generalizations based on only one, or at most a few, examples. For instance, in support of the argument that teenagers favor marijuana decriminalization, a person might cite the opinions of two teenagers who live next door. Yet, the cross-section for that sample is neither large enough nor representative enough. In a speech, the argument may sound more impressive than it is, especially if the speaker dramatizes the one example. But you can refute the argument as a hasty generalization.

Thus, if a speaker presents a generalization with no data, or with extremely little data, you will want to question the reasoning on that basis alone. Although students in a public speaking class should not make the mistake of hasty generalization in a speech, you may find opportunities to refute arguments on that basis.

APPEALS TO AUTHORITY

An *appeal to authority* is a fallacy based on the quality of the data. When people support their arguments with the testimony of an authority, you can refute it as being fallacious if the use of the testimony fails to meet either of two tests: (1) If the source is not really an authority on the issue or (2) if the content of the testimonial is inconsistent with other expert opinion.

Let us consider cases in which the source is not truly an authority. Advertisers are well aware that because the public idolizes athletes, movie stars, and television performers, people are likely to accept their word on subjects they may know little about. So when an athlete tries to get the viewer to purchase perfume, the athlete's argument is a fallacy.

175

Although the fallacy of authority may be easy to recognize in a television ad, other examples of the fallacy may not be so easy to recognize. Economists, politicians, and scientists often comment on subjects outside their areas of expertise; sometimes neither they nor we realize how unqualified they are to speak on such subjects. A scientist's statement is good evidence only in the science in which he or she is an expert. Thus, a geneticist's views on the subject of the world food supply may or may not be fallacious, depending on the point he or she is trying to make.

The other test is whether the content of the testimonial is contrary to other expert opinion. Even when an authority states an opinion relevant to his or her area of expertise, that opinion may be fallacious if the opinion is one that is not supported by a majority of other authorities in that field. If a space biologist says that there must be life similar to ours on other planets, his or her opinion is no more logical proof than any other opinion; it is not even an authoritative opinion if a majority of other equally qualified space biologists believe otherwise. If you look long enough you can always find someone who has said something in support of even the most foolish statement. Avoid the mistake of accepting any statement as valid support just because some alleged authority is cited as the source.

APPEALS BASED ON STATISTICS

Fallacies in the use of statistics may be based on the quantity of data, quality of data, or reasoning from data. Statistics are nothing more than large numbers of instances; but statistics seem to have a bewitching force — most of us are conditioned to believe that instances cast in statistical form carry the weight of authority. Yet, the potential fallacies from statistics are so numerous that there is no way we can do total justice to the subject in this short analysis. The old saying, "Figures don't lie, but liars figure," is so applicable to the general use of statistics that you must be particularly careful with their use. To be safe, you should look at any statistical proof as potentially fallacious. Even statistics that are used honestly and with the best of motives still may be fallacious, because the clear, logical use of statistics is so difficult.

As you examine arguments supported with statistics, look for the following:

1. *Statistics that are impossible to verify.* If you are like me, you have read countless startling statements such as, "Fifteen million mosquitoes are hatched each day in the Canadian province of Ontario" or "One out of every seventeen women in ancient Greece had six fingers." Now, do not quote these — I made them up; but they are no more unlikely than many other examples I have seen. The fact is that we have no way of verifying such statistics. How does anyone count the number of mosquitoes hatched? How can we test whether

anyone counted the fingers of ancient Greek women? Statistics of this kind are startling and make interesting conversation, but they are fallacious as support for arguments.

2. *Statistics used alone.* Statistics by themselves do not mean much. For example, "Last season the Cincinnati Reds drew approximately 1.7 million fans to their seventy home games." Although at face value this sounds like (and it is) a lot of people, it does not tell much about the club's attendance. Is this figure good or bad? Was attendance up or down? Statistics often are not meaningful unless they are compared with other data.

3. *Statistics used with unknown comparative bases.* Comparisons of statistics do not mean much if the comparative base is not given. Consider the statement, "While the Zolon growth rate was dawdling along at some 3 percent last year, Allon was growing at a healthy 8 percent." This statement implies that Allon is doing much better than Zolon; however, if Zolon's base was larger, its 3 percent increase could be much better than Allon's 8 percent. We cannot know unless we understand the base from which the statistic was drawn.

AD HOMINEM ARGUMENT

An *ad hominem argument* is a fallacy occurring with an attack on the person making the argument rather than on the argument itself. Literally, *ad hominem* means "to the man." For instance, if Bill Bradley, the highly intelligent and very articulate former New York Knicks basketball player, presented the argument that athletics are important to the development of the total person, the reply, "Great, all we need is some jock justifying his own existence" would be an example of an ad hominem argument.

Such a personal attack often is made as a smokescreen to cover up a lack of good reasons and evidence. Ad hominem name-calling is used to try to encourage the audience to ignore a lack of evidence. Make no mistake, ridicule, name-calling, and other personal attacks are at times highly successful, but they almost always are fallacious.

QUESTIONABLE CAUSE

Another common thinking fallacy is *questionable cause.* . . . It is human nature to look for causes for events. If we are having a drought, we want to know the cause; if the schools are in financial trouble, we want to know the cause; if the crime rate has risen during the year, we want to know the cause. In our haste to discover causes for behavior, we sometimes identify something that happened or existed before the event or at the time of the event, and label that something as the cause of the event. This tendency leads to the fallacy of questionable cause.

Think of the people who blame loss of money, sickness, and problems at work on black cats that ran in front of them, or mirrors that broke, or ladders they walked under. You recognize these as superstitions. Nevertheless, they are excellent examples of attributing causes to unrelated events.

Superstitions are not the only examples of questionable cause. Consider a situation that occurs yearly on many college campuses. One year a coach's team has a winning year, and the coach is lauded for his or her expertise. The next year the team does poorly and the coach is fired. Has the coach's skill deteriorated that much in one year? It is quite unlikely. But it is much easier to point the finger at the coach as the cause of the team's failure than to admit that the entire team or the program itself is inferior. The fact is that examples of this kind of argument are frequent.

If you believe that the data alone are not important or significant enough to bring about the conclusion, then you can question the reasoning on that basis. You should keep in mind that an event is seldom a result of a single cause. Attribution of an event to one cause is almost always fallacious. When you find a speaker or writer attempting this form of argument, you should refute it on the basis of weakness in reasoning.

1700 words

Write your ending time here: _____

Subtract your starting time: _____

Total time: _____

Check the Rate Chart in the back of the book to find out how many words per minute you have read, and then record your score on the Progress Chart.

ANSWERS TO SKIMMING QUESTIONS

1. Your answer should be similar to the correct answer for question 2 in the Comprehension Check.

2. Write the answers to your skimming questions here.

    a. _____

    b. _____

    c. _____

12

Critical Thinking: Recognizing Fallacies

COMPREHENSION CHECK
Circle the letter before the best answer to each question below. Don't look back at the article.

Subject and Main Idea
1. The subject of the article is
   a. how to refute an argument.
   b. a definition of fallacies.
   c. five common errors in reasoning.
   d. why people commit fallacies.

2. The main idea is that
   a. fallacies are errors in logic.
   b. five common fallacies frequently occur in arguments.
   c. everyone makes mistakes.
   d. most arguments are faulty.

Details
3. The fallacious use of statistics consists of
   a. using statistics that are impossible to verify.
   b. using statistics without other related data.
   c. not giving the base on which the statistic is drawn.
   d. all of the above.

4. A type of fallacy *not* discussed in the article is
   a. hasty generalization.
   b. ad populum argument.
   c. questionable cause.
   d. ad hominem argument.

5. The coach being fired because the team did not win was used as an example of
   a. questionable cause.
   b. ad hominem argument.
   c. hasty generalization.
   d. appeals to authority.

179

6. The type of fallacy that presents an insufficient and nonrepresentative sample is
   a. appeal to authority.
   b. questionable cause.
   c. hasty generalization.
   d. none of the above.

Inferences
7. Saying "The increase in television violence results in more violence on the streets" is an example of
   a. ad hominem argument.
   b. hasty generalization.
   c. questionable cause.
   d. faulty statistics.

8. Football players are probably authorities on
   a. sports injuries.
   b. most professional sports.
   c. football equipment.
   d. which deodorant is most effective.

9. The reason that fallacies are so common is that
   a. our society has brainwashed us.
   b. we often don't think critically.
   c. people are afraid of authority.
   d. people will believe anything they're told.

10. Saying that an opponent is soft on communism is an example of
    a. appeal to authority.
    b. faulty statistics.
    c. hasty generalization.
    d. ad hominem argument.

QUESTIONS FOR ANALYSIS AND APPLICATION
1. Why do you need to know how to refute fallacies?

2. Find six advertisements on TV or in magazines that commit some of the fallacies discussed in this article. Identify the type of fallacy and explain what is faulty about the logic.

VOCABULARY IN CONTEXT

Multiple Choice
Circle the letter before the best definition of each underlined word or phrase.

1. One of many historical <u>fallacies</u> still believed today is that Horace Greeley was the first to say "Go west, young man," while it was actually John Soule that coined the phrase.
   a. false ideas   b. truths   c. religious teachings
   d. moral laws

2. Nutritionists often <u>refute</u> the statement that hot meals are better for you than cold ones.
   a. report   b. prove   c. disprove   d. suggest

3. In term papers, one must <u>cite</u> sources in footnotes in order to avoid being accused of illegally copying material.
   a. refer to   b. confuse   c. avoid   d. create

4. There are <u>valid</u> arguments on both sides of most issues.
   a. important   b. logically correct   c. illogical   d. varied

5. Dr. Christiaan Barnard was <u>lauded</u> for performing the first human heart transplant.
   a. blamed   b. criticized   c. credited   d. praised

Fill-in
Write the best word from this list in the blank in each sentence below:

geneticist   dawdling   attributing   alleged

authoritative   relevant   bewitching

6. Seeing a _____ before having children is important for couples with inherited problems in their family history.

7. _____ at work instead of being efficient can get you fired.

8. Tomatoes were once _____ to be poison-ous fruits.

9. General Colin Powell is an _____ source on politics in the Middle East.

10. The _____ girl captured the young man's heart.

11. In sales, verbal ability and enthusiasm are _____ to success.

12. _____ his success to his mother, the author dedicated the book to her.

SKILLS EXERCISE:
CRITICAL READING
Inferences

For explanation see pp. 149–156

If you can draw any of the following conclusions from the article, write *yes* in the blank before the statement. If you cannot, write *no* in the blank.

_____ 1. Companies with good products take great pains to avoid using fallacious advertising.

_____ 2. You will never find fallacious ideas in a newspaper.

_____ 3. The short nature of commercials encourages the use of hasty generalization.

_____ 4. The use of numbers and statistics has a powerful impact on people in our society.

_____ 5. Everyone commits fallacies at one time or another.

_____ 6. Because people are becoming more aware of fallacious advertising, we can expect less of it in the future.

_____ 7. The five fallacies discussed are the only important ones.

_____ 8. Some fallacious arguments are convincing.

_____ 9. Sponsors should never use movie stars or athletes to advertise their products because these people are rarely authorities on anything.

_____ 10. The author probably advised his students to avoid using statistics in their speeches or writing.

Judging Support: Evaluating Evidence

A. Logical Reasoning

Identify the following types of fallacies by writing the appropriate symbol in the blank before each sentence.

AA   appeal to authority (popularity or traditional wisdom)
AH   ad hominem argument
AS   appeal through faulty statistics
HG   hasty generalization
QC   questionable cause

_AH_ 1. People who don't agree with me are idiots.

_QC_ 2. I got sick last night; it must have been something I ate.

_HG_   3. More school children are losing their ability to distinguish right from wrong. Just look at the vandalism that occurred at Middletown Elementary School.

_AS_   4. There are more bugs in the United States than anywhere else in the world.

_AA_   5. Joe Smoo, the famous basketball player, says that Swiss Mush is the breakfast cereal that makes champions.

_AS_   6. One out of every three people in prehistoric times was killed by a dinosaur.

_HG_   7. Detergent X must be better than detergent Y because it cleaned this stain better.

_QC_   8. The pollution is terrible. See how everyone is coughing?

_AA_   9. Jean Kelley, who plays Dr. Janet Jones on the *Guiding Gift*, says that Aspergrim relieves headaches five times faster than any other aspirin or nonaspirin product.

_AH_   10. The only people who favor eating "health foods" are crackpots and faddists.

B. Appeal to Authority

Listed below are three celebrities and six issues. After each issue, write the name of the person you would trust as an authority on that subject. If none of them is an authority on the subject, write *none*.

Celebrities: Magic Johnson   Bruce Springsteen   Meryl Streep

Issues:

cancer research _____

acting techniques _____

guitars _____

deodorant _____

investments _____

basketball shoes _____

13

The New (and Still Hidden) Persuaders

VOCABULARY PREVIEW

stimulation (stim'yə lā'shən):   arousal or excitement

dilation (dī lā'shən):   expansion; act of becoming wider or larger

disgruntled (dis grunt'′ld):   irritated or discontented

gauging (gāj'iŋ):   measuring

electrodes (i lek'trōdz):   terminals by which electricity enters and leaves a battery

emits (i mits'):   sends out; gives forth; discharges

psycholinguistic (sī'kō liŋ gwis'tik):   pertaining to the psychology of language

segmentation (seg'mən tā'shən):   separation into parts

imagery (im'ij rē):   mental pictures

epitomizing (i pit'ə mīz'iŋ):   typifying

brogue (brōg):   dialectical pronunciation, especially that of English by the Irish

concocted (kən käkt'əd):   invented, made by combining ingredients

striations (strī ā'shənz):   thin lines, bands, or grooves

subliminal (sub lim'ə n'l):   below the threshold of conscious awareness

seduction (si duk'shən):   temptation; persuasion

ostensibly (äs ten'sə blē):   apparently; seemingly

consistency (kən sist'ən sē):   texture, such as firmness or thickness

audible (ô'də b'l):   loud enough to be heard

fat, āpe, cär; ten, ēven; is, bīte; gō, hôrn, tōōl, look; oil, out; up, fʉr; chin, she; thin, then; zh, leisure; ŋ, ring; ə for *a* in *ago;* ' as in *able* (ā'b'l)

SKILLS EXERCISE: SKIMMING AND SCANNING

For explanation see pp. 157–158

A. *Skimming.* Take one minute to skim the following article. Run your eyes over the article to get a general idea of what it is about.

   1. After you have skimmed the article, write its main idea in your own words. _____

      _____

   2. Without looking back at the article, write three questions that you think will be answered by reading it.

      a. _____

      b. _____

      c. _____

B. *Scanning.* First, underline the key words in the following questions. Next, scan the article to find the answers. Quickly underline each answer and move to the next question. It should take you no more than three minutes to answer all of the questions. After you finish scanning for all ten of the answers, write them in the spaces below.

   1. Today, the advertising world has turned to what for clues to our feelings? _____

   2. What does a pupillometer measure? _____

   3. What caused the eye dilation in the ad for frozen french fries?

      _____

   4. What part of the voice does one machine analyze? _____

   5. What do electrodes measure? _____

   6. How does cleanliness rank on the scale of reasons to buy soap?

      _____

   7. Scientists have been able to speed up the voice by how much, without the person sounding like Donald Duck? _____

   8. Did women prefer the jars of cold cream with the circles or the triangles on them? _____

   9. Are women or men more aroused by nudity in an ad? _____

   10. What emotional need did American Telephone and Telegraph try to meet with its "Reach out and touch someone" campaign?

      _____

Now read the article. Write your starting time here: _____

13

The New (and Still Hidden) Persuaders

Vance Packard

P EOPLE KEEP ASKING ME what the hidden persuaders are up to nowadays. So, for a few months, I revisited the persuasion specialists. The demographers and motivational researchers, I found, are still very much with us, but admen today are also listening to other kinds of behavior specialists. It's a less wacky world than 20 years ago perhaps, but more weird.

Admen seek trustworthy predictions on how we the consumers are going to react to their efforts. Years ago they learned that we may lie politely when discussing ads or products, so, increasingly, the advertising world has turned to our bodies for clues to our real feelings.

Take our eyes. There is one computerized machine that tracks their movement as they examine a printed ad. This spots the elements in the ad that have the most "stopping power." For overall reactions to an ad or commercial, some admen have been trying the pupillometer, a machine that measures the pupil under stimulation.

The pupil expands when there is arousal of interest, although this can lead to mistaken conclusions. A marketer of frozen french fries was pleased by reports of significant dilation during its TV ad. But further analysis indicated that it was the sizzling steak in the ad, not the french fries, that was causing the dilation. What's more, the pupillometer cannot tell whether a viewer likes or dislikes an ad. (We are also aroused by ads that annoy us.) This caused some of its users to become disgruntled, but others stick with it as at least helpful. Arousal is *something*. Without it the admen are inevitably wasting money.

There are also machines that offer voice-pitch analysis. First, our normal voices are taped and then our voices while commenting on an ad or product. A computer reports whether we are offering lip service, a polite lie or a firm opinion.

In the testing of two commercials with children in them, other kids' comments seemed about equally approving. The mechanical detective, however, reported that one of the commercials simply interested the kids, whereas the other packed an emotional wallop that they found hard to articulate.

Viewing rooms are used to try out commercials and programs on off-the-street people. Viewers push buttons to indicate how interested or bored they are.

One technique for gauging ad impact is to measure brain waves with electrodes. If a person is really interested in something, his brain emits fast beta waves. If he is in a passive, relaxed state, his brain emits the much slower alpha waves. An airline has used brain-wave testing to choose its commercial spokesman. Networks have used the test to check out actors and specific scenes in pilot films that need a sponsor.

Admen also seek to sharpen their word power to move us to action. Some have turned to psycholinguistics — the deep-down meaning of words — and to a specialty called psychographic segmentation.

A few years ago Colgate-Palmolive was eager to launch a new soap. Now, for most people, the promise of cleanliness ranks low as a compelling reason for buying soap. It's assumed. So soap makers promise not only cleanliness but one of two gut appeals — physical attractiveness (a tuning up of complexion) or a deodorant (a pleasant smell).

Colgate-Palmolive turned to psychographic segmentation to find a position within the "deodorant" end of the soap field. The segmenters found a psychological type they called Independents — the ambitious, forceful, self-assured types with a positive outlook on life, mainly men, who like to take cold showers.

Their big need, over and above cleanliness, was a sense of refreshment. What kind of imagery could offer refreshment? Colgate researchers thought of spring and of greenery and that led them to think of Ireland, which has a nationally advertised image epitomizing cool, misty, outdoor greenery.

So the Colgate people hired a rugged, self-assured male with a bit of a brogue as a spokesman and concocted a soap with green and white striations. The bar was packaged in a manly green-against-black wrapper (the black had come out of psychological research), and they hailed it as Irish Spring — now a big success in the soap field.

Advertising people have long fretted about not being able to say much in a 15- or 30-second commercial. So they experimented with faster talking. Typically, when you run a recorded message at speeds significantly faster than normal you get Donald Duck quackery. But psychologists working with electronic specialists came up with a computerized time-compression device that creates a normal-sounding voice even when the recording is speeded up by 40 percent. Research has also indicated that listeners actually preferred messages at faster-than-normal speed and remembered them better.

Meanwhile, at one of the world's largest advertising agencies, J. Walter Thompson, technicians forecast that by 1990 many TV messages will be coming at us in three-second bursts, combining words, symbols and other imagery. The messages will be almost subliminal.

The subliminal approach is to get messages to us beneath our level of awareness. It can be a voice too low for us to hear consciously. It can be a message flashed on a screen too rapidly for us to notice, or a filmed message shown continuously but dimly. It can even be a word such as SEX embedded in the pictures of printed ads.

Subliminal seduction has been banned by most broadcasters, but nothing prevents its use in stores, movies and salesrooms. Several dozen department stores use it to reduce shoplifting. Such messages as "I am honest, I will not steal" are mixed with background music and continually repeated. One East Coast retail chain reported a one-third drop in theft in a nine-month period.

The sale of imagery and symbols continues to fascinate admen. In one experiment, 200 women were questioned, ostensibly about color schemes in furniture design. For their co-operation the women were given a supply of cold cream. They were to take home and try out two samples. When they came back for their next advice-giving session, they would be given an ample supply of the cold cream of their choice.

Both sample jars were labeled "high-quality cold cream." The cap of one jar had a design with two triangles on it. The cap of the other jar had two circles. The cold cream inside the jars was identical, yet 80 percent of the women asked for the one with the circle design on the cap. They liked the consistency of that cream better. They found it easier to apply and definitely of finer quality. All because, it seems, women prefer circles to triangles.

The use of sexuality in the media has become standard. Interestingly, a research report stated that women now are more aroused by nudity in ads than men. This may account for one twist recently employed by admen. In 1980, a highly successful campaign for men's Jockey-brand underwear was aimed at women, based on the finding that women often buy clothing for their mates.

For this campaign the star was the handsome pitcher of the Baltimore Orioles, Jim Palmer. In the ads he was nude except for the snug-fitting Jockey briefs. Sales soared — as did Palmer's female fan mail.

Today, as when I first reported on persuasion techniques in advertising, our hidden needs are still very much on admen's minds. One need that has grown greatly in two decades — perhaps because of all the moving and the breaking of families — is warm human contact.

The American Telephone and Telegraph Company used this need to generate more long-distance calls. Historically, such calls were associated with accidents, death in the family and other stressful situations. AT&T wanted long-distance calling to become casual spur-of-the-moment fun. Hence the jingle, "Reach out, reach out and touch someone," played against various scenes filled with good friendship.

Then there was a manufacturer of hay balers who sought more farmers to buy his machine. Psychologist Ernest Dichter, an old master at persuasion, came up with a technique based on the theory that instant reward is better in creating a sense of achievement than long-delayed reward — in this case a check for the hay two months later.

Dichter recommended attaching a rear-view mirror and a bell to the baler. Every time a bundle of hay was assembled as the machine moved across a hayfield, the farmer could see it in the mirror. And when the bale dropped onto the field the bell rang. Thus the reward was not only instant but visual and audible. Farmers loved it. And so did the manufacturer, who started ringing up the hay-baler sales.

1450 words

Write your ending time here: _____

Subtract your starting time: _____

Total time: _____

Check the Rate Chart in the back of the book to find out how many words per minute you have read, and then record your score on the Progress Chart.

ANSWERS TO SKIMMING QUESTIONS

1. Your answer should be similar to the correct answer for question 2 in the Comprehension Check.

2. Write the answers to your skimming questions here.

    a. _____

    b. _____

    c. _____

13

The New (and Still Hidden) Persuaders

COMPREHENSION CHECK

Circle the letter before the best answer to each question below. Don't look back at the article.

Subject and Main Idea

1. The subject of the article is
   a. new advertising research and methods.
   b. the process of mind control.
   c. advertising.
   d. dishonest advertising techniques.

2. The main idea is that
   a. advertisers use research to influence our buying habits.
   b. the Irish Spring soap campaign was carefully organized.
   c. new products are created by advertisers.
   d. people are easily manipulated by advertisers.

Details

3. Packard says that
   a. persuasive techniques are immoral.
   b. advertising companies have been seeking trustworthy predictors for years.
   c. advertising technology has not changed in the past twenty years.
   d. people can tell you how they are influenced by ads.

4. Women
   a. are more easily influenced by ads than men are.
   b. buy soap because it promises cleanliness.
   c. make more long-distance calls than men do.
   d. are more aroused by nudity in ads than men are.

5. Women buy cold cream mainly on the basis of
   a. consistency.
   b. price.
   c. packaging.
   d. sex appeal.

6. Subliminal advertising
   a. is illegal in department stores.
   b. is useful in department stores.
   c. doesn't work.
   d. is illegal in movies.

Inferences

7. Packard probably wrote the article because he
   a. is a top adman.
   b. wants laws against this kind of advertising.
   c. wants people to shop more wisely.
   d. wants to legalize subliminal advertising on TV.

8. The short length of TV commercials has
   a. made advertisers use subliminal advertising.
   b. led to some new electronic techniques.
   c. made advertisers happy.
   d. discouraged consumer buying.

9. The Irish Spring example shows that independent men
   a. buy most of the soap for the household.
   b. can also be influenced by advertising.
   c. are more easily manipulated than women.
   d. want soaps from foreign countries.

10. Unconscious needs
    a. can be used to increase product sales.
    b. are more common in Americans than in people from
       other countries.
    c. are abnormal.
    d. don't really affect us very much.

QUESTIONS FOR ANALYSIS AND APPLICATION

1. People in many foreign countries criticize the United States for selling too many products on the basis of a gimmick rather than quality. Do you think they are justified in these attacks? Why or why
   not?

2. Why do you purchase the following items?

Product	Brand	Reason You Buy It	What Other Brands Have You Tried?
soup			
detergent			
soap			
toothpaste			

Do you think your purchasing decisions are swayed by advertising?
Explain your answer.

VOCABULARY IN CONTEXT
Multiple Choice
Circle the letter before the best definition of each underlined word.

1. Summer camp provided the young boys with all the stimulation they needed.
   a. excitement   b. nourishment   c. quiet   d. amusement

2. Scientists now believe that dilation of the pupils is an indication that a person is lying.
   a. contraction   b. expansion   c. blinking   d. watering

3. Following April fifteenth, income tax day, many taxpayers feel disgruntled about paying so much of their incomes to the government.
   a. dissatisfied   b. joyous   c. confused   d. helpless

4. An applause meter was one means used to gauge the audience's responses to different endings of *Star Wars* before the final ending was chosen for public viewing.
   a. increase   b. reduce   c. see   d. measure

5. If the electrodes on a car battery are not kept clean, the car may not start.
   a. wires   b. terminals   c. sides   d. joints

6. Bats emit screeching sounds as a form of radar.
   a. hear   b. take in   c. call off   d. send out

7. The segmentation of the brain into two hemispheres makes it look something like a walnut.
   a. division   b. viewing   c. unification   d. creation

8. Imagery can assist anyone in remembering the plot of a story.
   a. writing   b. mental picturing   c. drawing
   d. repetition

9. Clark Gable epitomized people's image of the Hollywood star in that he was rich, handsome, intelligent, and married to a beautiful woman whom he loved.
   a. contradicted   b. hated   c. idolized   d. typified

Fill-in
Write the best word from this list in the blank in each sentence below:

psycholinguistics   brogue   concocted   striations

subliminal   seduction   ostensibly   consistency   audible

10. Sounds with extremely high frequencies are

   _____ only to animals.

11. In the comic books, Diana Prince is _____
a plain woman but changes into the beautiful Wonder Woman to
fight the enemies of the United States.

12. She broke her diet because she could not stand the _____
of the chocolate dessert.

13. Actors who play Catholic priests frequently speak with an Irish

_____ to sound more authentic.

14. Rocks with _____ of different shades
were usually formed in layers.

15. Chop suey was _____ by a San Francisco
restaurant owner as a way to serve leftovers.

16. The _____ flashing of the word *popcorn*
during a movie was supposed to make people buy more during
intermission.

17. Jello should chill to a firm _____ before
being eaten.

18. The way children learn to label St. Bernards and Chihuahuas as
dogs and Siamese and Persians as cats is a concern of

_____ .

SKILLS EXERCISE:
CRITICAL READING
Inferences

*For explanation
see pp. 149–156*

If you can draw any of the following conclusions from the article,
write *yes* in the blank. If you cannot, write *no* in the blank.

_____ 1. The hidden persuaders are successful in influencing
our decisions.

_____ 2. All of the hidden persuaders' techniques are illegal.

_____ 3. People's decisions about which products they buy are
always conscious.

_____ 4. The pupillometer will soon become part of lie
detector tests.

_____ 5. The meanings of people's reactions to the pupillometer
are always clear.

_____ 6. The machinery that the author discusses is
relatively new.

_____ 7. Physical changes in the body reflect our feelings.

_____ 8. Packard began analyzing advertising techniques many
years ago.

_____ 9. The new machinery is more effective with adults who have formed strong opinions than with children.

_____ 10. People have other reasons for buying a product besides its quality.

Author's Purpose:
Word Choice

An author chooses words carefully to make his or her point and some-times also to add to the reader's interest. For example, Tony Randall in Article 1 says, "if they [words] are drugs, I'm a hopeless addict — and I hope to get you hooked, too!" He means that he is very interested in words, but the use of the drug-addiction image strengthens his point and creates a vivid image in the reader's mind.

A. The sentences below contain quotations from this book. Translate each underlined phrase into everyday language. In other words, write what you think the author means.

1. "Careful — you don't want them to think you're a stuffed shirt." (Article 1)

   Meaning: _____

2. "This [easy credit] is the subject of another whole chapter but it can't be mentioned too often as a lump in the oatmeal of life." (Article 11)

   Meaning: _____

3. "Anyone who has a competent mechanic who can be trusted should count this fact among the prime blessings of life." (Article 11)

   Meaning: _____

4. "[Independents] . . . mainly men who like to take cold showers." (Article 13)

   Meaning: _____

5. "Psychologist Ernest Dichter, an old master at persuasion, came up with a technique . . ." (Article 13)

   Meaning: _____

6. "The mechanical detective, however, reported that one of the commercials simply interested the kids, whereas the other packed an emotional wallop that they found hard to articulate." (Article 13)

   Meaning: _____

B. Below are four famous phrases from presidential speeches. We remember them because they are vivid. Put each into your own words.

1. "Speak softly, but carry a big stick." (Theodore Roosevelt)

_____

2. "Let us have faith that right makes might." (Abraham Lincoln)

_____

3. "The buck stops here." (Harry Truman)

_____

4. "If you call a tail a leg, how many legs has a dog? Five? No, calling a tail a leg doesn't make it a leg." (Abraham Lincoln)

_____

5. "Conformity is the jailer of freedom and the enemy of growth." (John Kennedy)

_____

C. Now try your hand at making sentences more vivid. Below are five "clear but dull" sentences. Each is based on an idea that was vividly presented by the author of the article. Look at the sentences in section A or back to the article from which the idea was drawn to give you ideas about how to make the sentences more interesting. Write words or phrases that are more vivid than the underlined word or phrase below.

1. "These [ads] will probably be with us forever." (Article 11)

_____

2. The ad using Jim Palmer was successful. (Article 13)

_____

3. "Good sleepers" fall asleep within ten minutes after going to bed. (Article 9)

_____

4. He awoke in a bad mood. (Article 5)

_____

5. "That's crazy!" I replied. (Article 4)

_____

14

Making the Most of Your Time in Front of an Audience

VOCABULARY PREVIEW

ovation (ō vā'shən):   enthusiastic applause

grist (grist):   anything that one can use profitably

pertinent (pur't'n ənt):   having some connection with the matter at hand; to the point

eloquence (el'ə kwəns):   speech or writing that is expressive, forceful, graceful, and persuasive

sham (sham):   fraud or imitation

edited (ed'it id):   prepared for public presentation

onslaught (än'slôt):   violent attack

lorries (lôr'ēz):   British word for trucks

plodded (pläd'id):   walked or moved heavily and with effort

comparatively (kəm par'ə tiv lē):   in comparison to something else; relatively

humdrum (hum'drum):   dull, boring

ad lib (ad lib'):   to make up and perform without any preparation

fat, āpe, cär; ten, ēven; is, bīte; gō, hôrn, tōōl, look; oil, out; up, fur; chin, she; thin, *then*; zh, leisure; ŋ, ring; ə for *a* in *ago;* ' as in *able* (ā'b'l)

SKILLS EXERCISE: SKIMMING AND SCANNING

For explanation see pp. 157–158

A. *Skimming.* Take one minute to skim the following article. Run your eyes over the article to get a general idea of what it is about. Use the headings to help you organize your thoughts.

1. After you have skimmed the article, write its main idea in your own words. _____

   _____

2. Without looking back at the article, write three questions that you think will be answered by reading it.

   a. _____

   b. _____

   c. _____

B. *Scanning.* First, underline the key words in the following questions. Next, scan the article to find the answers. Quickly underline each answer and move to the next question. It should take you no more than three minutes to answer all of the questions. After you finish scanning for all ten of the answers, write them in the spaces below.

1. Name the president whose speeches the author read. _____

2. What must you look for for your speech? _____

3. What is the name of the journalism school at Northwestern University? _____

4. How must you think? _____

5. Who improved the process of steelmaking and founded The Cooper Union in New York City? _____

6. How many steps are there in preparing a good speech? _____

7. What is the first step in preparing a good speech? _____

8. Where should you present your speech when practicing?

   _____

9. How many suggestions are there from people who succeed?

   _____

10. What is the fourth suggestion? _____

14

Making the Most of Your Time in Front of an Audience

Art Brown

FOR MANY YEARS, I earned my living in Washington mostly as a speechwriter.

I must have been born timid, for it never appealed to me to stand up before a crowd and make a speech. But it always seemed easy and natural for me to provide ammunition for anyone I happened to know who wanted to give a speech to get elected to office or something.

After I got to writing speeches professionally, I read and studied great speeches — speeches that have lived — speeches, for example, by Abraham Lincoln, Patrick Henry, Daniel Webster, and Winston Churchill.

In time, I learned something about the feel of an effective speech and about how to construct an effective speech.

And by working with experienced speakers, by talking with them, by learning from them what makes a speech go across, and by watching them in action, I learned something about how to deliver a speech.

Those are my qualifications for offering you a few tips on "How to Make the Most of Your Time before an Audience."

ONLY ONE WAY TO JUDGE A SPEECH

You would like to produce a speech that will get a standing ovation from the audience, that will make headlines in the press, that will be printed in *Vital Speeches,* and that can be put out in booklet form. If it wins a Freedoms Foundation award, so much the better.

But, when you come right down to it, there is only one way for you to judge whether a speech you make is a good speech: It's a good speech when it accomplishes its purpose.

So, in preparing a speech, the very first thing for you to do is to determine exactly what you want the speech to accomplish.

Just what is its purpose? Why are you giving the speech?

What message do you want to present to your listeners? What do you want them to do about it?

What resistances are you going to be up against? How can you overcome those resistances?

What questions are you likely to be asked? How can you answer those questions briefly and convincingly?

The next thing for you to do is to learn as much as you possibly can about your audience, their organization, their interests, their problems, their needs.

When you address them, you want to feel right at home with them; you want to see things from their point of view.

LOOK FOR GRIST FOR YOUR SPEECH

Now, the thing you have to do is to be on the continual lookout for grist for your speech. You not only need pertinent facts and figures, but you also need items that you can use to brighten up your talk, to support the points you make, and to give your speech added interest and a change of pace from time to time: illustrations, anecdotes, jokes, humorous lines, and suitable quotations.

When I was a student at the Medill School of Journalism at Northwestern University, an editorial writer on *The Chicago Tribune,* who was lecturing in class one day, told the students how he was always looking for items for possible use in his editorials. He told us his method for keeping those items together in one place where he could put his hand on a particular one when he needed it.

Instead of filing the items by subject, he kept them in a folder, with the most recent item on top. Whenever he added a new one, he took a moment to leaf through those that were already there — and that refreshed his memory, so that he was able to find a particular item in a hurry when he wanted it.

That's a simple little technique which I have found to be practical, and I pass it on to you.

THINK HARD, DEEP, AND LONG

The really important thing, however, in preparing a speech is to think the subject through hard enough, deep enough, and long enough to make the whole thing jell in your mind and hold together.

Herbert Corey, who had been an overseas correspondent and who, when I knew him, was back in Washington writing magazine articles and working on a book, told me that his secret of writing something was to gather the material on the subject, and then to put it in his mind and "cook it."

"Unless you've got a deadline to meet," he said, "don't start writing anything until it's ready to write itself."

Peter Cooper, the inventor, had somewhat the same idea. Among other things, he improved the process of steelmaking, built one of the earliest locomotives in this country, played an important part in the laying of the Atlantic cable, and founded The Cooper Union in New York City.

"EVENTUALLY THE ANSWER COMES"

Peter Cooper's working slogan was, "Eventually the answer comes."

I have that line typed out and pasted on the front of my typewriter.

It's comforting to know that when you are writing a speech or anything else, and when you use your head and think about the job at hand hard enough and long enough, "Eventually the answer comes."

Montaigne knew the truth of that. In his *Essays*, he says:

"I hear some making excuses for being unable to express themselves, and pretending to have their heads full of many fine things but, for want of eloquence, being unable to produce them; that is a sham. . . . For my part, I hold, and Socrates makes it a rule, that whoever has in his mind a vivid and clear idea will express it. 'The matter seen, the words freely follow.'"

HOW TO PREPARE A GOOD SPEECH

These, then, are tips on how to prepare a good speech:

1. Know exactly what you want your speech to accomplish.

2. Learn as much as you can about your audience, so that you will be able to see things from the viewpoint of your listeners.

3. Know the questions your listeners are likely to ask, and know how to answer those questions convincingly.

4. Be continually on the lookout for grist for your speech.

5. Think the subject through hard, deep, and long, so that it organizes itself and holds together — a most important step.

TAKE PLENTY OF TIME TO REHEARSE

Now, after you have written your speech, and after you have edited it and polished it, take plenty of time to rehearse it.

Tape record your speech and play it back to yourself. Listen to how you emphasize certain words — verbs and nouns in particular — or how you fail to emphasize certain words that you should.

If there are any stumbling blocks for you in your speech, get rid of them.

Rehearse your speech until you almost know it by heart.

LOOK AT YOURSELF IN A MIRROR

Winston Churchill worked for 40 years to master the art of writing a speech — and to learn how to write a sentence that would have each phrase in its proper place so that the sentence would move directly ahead and not backtrack, and so that the sentence would say what it was meant to say and have the proper cadence and flavor.

Here is an example of a Churchill sentence — from his Dunkirk speech:

"Behind this armored and mechanized onslaught came a number of German divisions in lorries, and behind them again, there plodded — comparatively slowly — the dull brute mass of the ordinary German Army and German people, always so ready to be led to the trampling down in other lands of liberties and comforts which they have never known in their own."

But Churchill did not depend entirely on his ability as a thinker and a writer. He depended also on his ability to speak before an audience. And throughout his whole career, he would never deliver a speech without first rehearsing it before a mirror. He wanted to see himself in action.

WHAT THOSE WHO SUCCEED SUGGEST

Here are some suggestions from successful speakers. You doubtless know all of these things already, but it doesn't do any harm to be reminded of them.

1. When you deliver a speech, be relaxed; the world is not coming to an end. Be yourself.

2. Strive for audience contact. That's what you're there for. Look right at individuals in the audience as you talk to them. Watch for their reaction.

3. Don't read your speech in a humdrum fashion. That's the worst thing in the world to do; it kills the speech. You are thoroughly familiar with the script. Use it only as a guide. Ad lib when you feel like it.

4. In your opening remarks, it's a good idea not to start off by talking about yourself. Put your listeners in the picture right away by talking about them.

Instead of saying, "It's a great pleasure for me to be here on this occasion . . .", say something like this: "You people who are in this room here today perhaps know more about the subject that we will be discussing than any other group in America." Or, say whatever is appropriate and true, so long as you are talking about them and not about yourself.

5. As you go along, however, address your listeners as "we," rather than as "you." The reason for doing so is to avoid sounding preachy, to avoid giving them the impression that you are trying to tell them what they should or should not do.

    You are not trying to force your ideas on them. You are simply letting them know that, after weighing all the facts in the case, you have come to certain conclusions about the situation — conclusions which you believe to be sound. Your job is to win your listeners over to your way of thinking — or to give them information that will be helpful to them in their thinking.

    It is more effective for you to say, "It seems to me," or, "As I see it," than it is to give your listeners the impression that you think you know all the answers.

6. A good way to launch the question-and-answer session is to say something like this:

    "What one single question do you have in mind that you would like to have answered here today — what one question, if you could get the answer, would make you glad you came to this meeting?"

7. If you don't know the answer to a question, just say: "I don't know — but if you will see me after this meeting, I will get your address and then, after I get back home, I will try to get the answer for you and send it to you."

LET THEM KNOW YOU ARE GLAD

More than one successful speaker has told me that the best way to give a speech is to be fully prepared, and then when you are before the audience, to let them know by your whole manner and your whole being that it gives you a lift to be there.

    When they know that you are really glad to be there, they are really glad to be there.

    They listen with interest to what you have to say.

    They get something out of it.

    They remember what you tell them.

    They are influenced by it.

    And once more, you have made the most of your time before an audience.

1900 words

Write your ending time here: _____

Subtract your starting time: _____

Total time: _____

Check the Rate Chart in the back of the book to find out how many words per minute you have read, and then record your score on the Progress Chart.

ANSWERS TO SKIMMING QUESTIONS

1. Your answer should be similar to the correct answer for question 2 in the Comprehension Check.

2. Write the answers to your skimming questions here.

    a. _____

    b. _____

    c. _____

14

Making the Most of Your Time in Front of an Audience

COMPREHENSION CHECK
Circle the letter before the best answer to each question below. Don't look back at the article.

Subject and Main Idea
1. The subject of the article is
   a. writing speeches for famous people.
   b. preparing a speech.
   c. famous people's speeches.
   d. becoming a good speaker.

2. The main point is that
   a. preparing a speech is hard work.
   b. there are specific techniques for preparing and presenting a good speech.
   c. you only improve your speaking ability by speaking.
   d. you must rehearse a speech many times to be good.

Details
3. Brown was a
   a. good speaker.
   b. professional speechwriter.
   c. politician.
   d. college professor.

4. A speech is successful only if it
   a. makes newspaper headlines.
   b. begins with the speaker telling his or her qualifications.
   c. accomplishes its purpose.
   d. gets politicians elected.

5. Brown suggests that you
   a. emphasize adjectives, not nouns and verbs, when speaking.
   b. begin writing the speech immediately to save time.
   c. analyze the audience before you begin to write.
   d. avoid writing speeches that contain a lot of factual material, because they are boring.

205

6. A good speech should be
    a. memorized.
    b. read from a manuscript.
    c. almost known by heart.
    d. unrehearsed so it sounds more natural.

Inferences

7. A good speaker
    a. has good speechwriters.
    b. knows his or her audience.
    c. studies other speeches by famous politicians of the past.
    d. only writes a speech once, because it is right the first time.

8. To be a good speechwriter, you
    a. must be a good speaker.
    b. must overcome being timid.
    c. must not worry about how or to whom the speech is presented.
    d. need to understand what different audiences expect.

9. A good speech
    a. cannot be written to meet deadlines.
    b. is more than a mass of factual material.
    c. amuses an audience.
    d. doesn't have to be rewritten.

10. Making the most of your time in front of an audience
    a. comes naturally to most speakers.
    b. means presenting speeches that are good enough to be printed
       in *Vital Speeches.*
    c. requires taking college speech courses.
    d. means writing and presenting a speech that meets your goals
       and your audience's needs.

QUESTIONS FOR ANALYSIS AND APPLICATION

1. A team of readers interviewed 3,000 Americans and found that the
   fear of public speaking was greater than any other fear. Why do you
   think this is so?

2. Beyond the article's suggestions for preparing and delivering a
   speech, what can be done to help people who are afraid of speaking?
   Where could a person who is not good at public speaking go to improve those skills?

VOCABULARY IN CONTEXT
Multiple Choice
Circle the letter before the best definition of each underlined word.

1. Elvis Presley received <u>an ovation</u> at the end of the concert.
   a. criticism   b. booing   c. extended applause
   d. a paycheck

2. The defense attorney's summation was <u>pertinent</u> to the judge's decision to free the defendant.
   a. contrary   b. related   c. opposed   d. unrelated

3. Martin Luther King's <u>eloquence</u> in his speech "I Have A Dream" placed him among the best speakers of the twentieth century.
   a. genius   b. quickness   c. awkwardness
   d. expressiveness

4. Books must be <u>edited</u> to eliminate errors in spelling and grammar and also to eliminate confusion.
   a. copied   b. carefully reviewed   c. written
   d. censored

5. Camels can <u>plod</u> for days across the desert without food or water because they can live off the fat in their humps.
   a. prance   b. go   c. move quickly   d. walk heavily

6. Albino frogs are <u>comparatively</u> rare, occurring much less frequently than human quintuplets.
   a. not very   b. usually   c. relatively   d. occasionally

Fill-in

Write the best word from this list in the blank in each sentence below:

grist   **ad lib**   **lorries**   **onslaught**   **humdrum**   **sham**

7. _____ are used to transport goods from one place to another.

8. Actors have to _____ when they forget their lines on stage.

9. General Custer's soldiers all died because they could not withstand the _____ of the Sioux.

10. Johnny Carson often uses current news items as

_____ for his jokes.

11. Rich people often wear _____ jewels in public while keeping their real jewelry in a safe.

12. The _____ rhythm of the Brahms lullaby has lulled infants to sleep for the last 150 years.

SKILLS EXERCISE:
CRITICAL READING
Inferences

For explanation
see pp. 149–156

Decide whether or not you can infer the following statements. If you can infer the statement, answer *yes*. If you cannot infer the statement from the article, answer *no*.

_____ 1. Mr. Brown has written many speeches.

_____ 2. Mr. Brown is a politician in Washington, D.C.

_____ 3. Effective speeches have certain qualities in common.

_____ 4. You should judge a speech by how much the audience likes it.

_____ 5. Good speeches use materials beyond facts and figures.

_____ 6. The author was a writer for a large newspaper in Chicago.

_____ 7. Writing a speech takes time because you may have to leave it and come back to it later.

_____ 8. Knowing all you can about your audience helps you in speaking.

_____ 9. You must try to guess what the audience might be thinking.

_____ 10. Listeners can be influenced by even small things such as the pronouns you choose.

Judging Support: Evaluating Author's Credibility

Qualifications   Several of the authors of articles in this book take positions as authorities on the subject they write about. For each author listed below, look at the article and see if you can determine what his qualifications are. Some of the authors are introduced in a short statement on the survey page preceding the article; in other cases, the author's qualifications are mentioned in the article. Rate the author's credibility on a scale of 1 to 5; 1 designates the lowest credibility and 5 designates the highest.

Author	Article	Qualifications	(1-5) Credibility
Tony Randall	1. How to Improve Your Vocabulary	_____	_____
Edward T. Thompson	3. How to Write Clearly	_____	_____
Jan Stussy	4. The Many Miracles of Mark Hicks	_____	_____
Vance Packard	13. The New (and Still Hidden) Persuaders	_____	_____
Art Brown	14. Making the Most of Your Time in Front of an Audience	_____	_____

15

Over-the-Counter Addictions

VOCABULARY PREVIEW

withdrawal (wi*th* drôl'):   the body's negative mental and physical reactions to the stopped usage of an addictive drug

substance (sub'stəns):   a drug, especially one whose use is regulated by law

pharmacologist (färm'ə käl'ə gist):   a scientist dealing with the effect of drugs on living organisms

cold turkey (kōld tʉr'kē):   (slang) the abrupt and total stopped usage of a drug by an addict

stimulant (stim'yə lənt):   something that rouses or excites to activity or increased activity

psychic (sī'kik):   concerning the mind; psychological; mental

die-hard (dī'härd'):   a person stubbornly resistant to new ideas, reform, and so on

aftermath (af'tər math'):   a result, especially an unpleasant one; aftereffect

abruptly (ə brupt'lē):   suddenly; unexpectedly

agitation (aj'ə tā'shən):   disturbance or excitement caused by emotional or physical factors

tolerance (täl'ər əns):   the natural or developed ability to resist the effects of the continued or increasing use of a drug

binging (binj'ŋ):   doing something excessively

bulimia (bə lē'mē ə):   an eating disorder characterized by binging and forcing oneself to eliminate large amounts of food

degenerate (di jen'ə rāt'):   to lose former, normal, or higher qualities; to decline

generic (jə ner'ik):   medication or other product that doesn't have a trademark

tout (tout):   to claim to be of great worth; praise

chronic (krän'ik):   lasting a long time or coming back often: said of a disease; continuing indefinitely; habitually

habitual (hə bich'oo wəl):   much seen, done, or used: usual; done or acquired by habit

plague (plāg):   to harrass; trouble; torment

fat, āpe, cär; ten, ēven; is, bīte; gō, hôrn, tōōl, look; oil, out; up, fʉr; chin, she; thin, *then*; zh, leisure; ŋ, ring; ə for *a* in *ago*; ' as in *able* (ā'b'l)

SKILLS EXERCISE:
SKIMMING AND SCANNING

For explanation
see pp. 157–158

A. *Skimming.* Take one minute to skim the following article. Run your eyes over the article to get a general idea of what it is about. Use the headings to help you organize your thoughts.

1. After you have skimmed the article, write its main idea in your own words. _____

   _____

2. Without looking back at the article, write three questions that you think will be answered by reading it.

   a. _____

   b. _____

   c. _____

B. *Scanning.* First, underline the key words in the following questions. Next, scan the article to find the answers, using the headings as guides. Quickly underline each answer and move to the next question. It should take you no more than three minutes to answer all of the questions. After you finish scanning for all ten of the answers, write them in the spaces below.

1. Name three of the types of drugs discussed in the article.

   _____

2. What do you experience if you stop using a substance that you are addicted to? _____

3. What is considered an extensive period for using sleeping pills?

   _____

4. What is a natural sleep inducer? _____

5. What are diet pills supposed to do? _____

6. What is the active ingredient in many top-selling diet pills?

   _____

7. What is the active ingredient in most stay-awake products?

   _____

8. To kick the habit, what type of laxative does Dr. Schuster suggest using? _____

9. How do eyedrops reduce redness? _____

10. Instructions on nasal sprays give a time limit of how long for usage? _____

Now read the article. Write your starting time here: _____

15

Over-the-Counter Addictions

Jean Laird

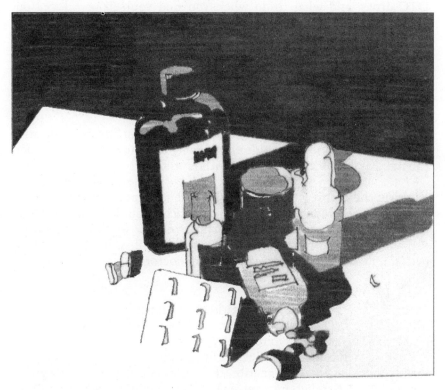

ARE YOU A JUNKIE? Millions are and don't realize it. These innocent addicts are hooked on many of the same remedies you'll find sitting in your medicine chest. Here's how to protect your family.

IT CAN HAPPEN TO ANYONE

Most folks wouldn't dream of ignoring the directions that come with a prescription medicine. Yet we adopt a dangerously casual attitude regarding over-the-counter (OTC) drugs. "How dangerous can they be," we reason, "when even a child can buy them?"

In fact, OTC remedies like laxatives and sleeping aids are still drugs, and they exert a powerful effect on our bodies. Used properly, these products are safe and usually very effective. However, when they are misused, these same drugs can turn on us. Even though they might not make you "high," some OTC drugs can be powerfully addicting.

"If you experience physical or psychological withdrawal symptoms after you stop using a substance," notes Joe Graedon, pharmacologist and author, "then you are addicted." The problems connected with these addictions can prove far more hazardous than the ailment you are trying to treat.

Here's how to help you and your family stay on friendly terms with OTC drugs, and what to do when you find yourself or a loved one addicted.

SLEEPING PILLS

OTC sleep aids are approved by the FDA "for occasional use only." By taking them for an extended period — more than two weeks — you risk becoming dependent on them, warns Gerald Rachanow, deputy director of the FDA's Division of Over-the-Counter Drugs.

These products are actually antihistamines, an allergy medication that causes sleepiness as a side effect. Long-term use of these products can make it difficult to fall asleep without them.

Kicking the Habit   Quit cold turkey, even if that means a few nights of restless sleep. Moderate daily exercise is a natural sleep inducer; avoid caffeine (it's in chocolate and some soft drinks, as well as in coffee and tea) and stimulant medicines (check the label). If your sleep problems persist for more than two weeks, see your doctor.

DIET PILLS

Especially popular with teenage girls, OTC diet pills are a $110-million-a-year business. These products do not directly cause weight loss. Instead, they are supposed to reduce appetite, making it easier to stick to a sensible, reduced-calorie diet. Although there is some evidence that these products decrease appetite, they remain controversial. Right in the middle of the diet-aid controversy is phenylpropanolamine (PPA), the active ingredient in many top-selling products. Research indicates that for about one-third of people, PPA causes a temporary increase in blood pressure. Healthy individuals can weather the increase without danger; people with high blood pressure face a much greater risk.

Dr. Michael H.M. Dykes also warns that diet-pill users risk "psychic dependence and other undesirable side effects." Use these products only as long as weight loss continues without side effects (fluttering heart, dizziness, and nausea) and without the need for higher doses, usually four to six weeks.

Kicking the Habit   If you have been taking OTC diet pills for longer than six weeks — or if you experience any side effects — stop using these products immediately. Otherwise, you can safely taper off.

STIMULANTS

Most die-hard coffee lovers are familiar with the unpleasant aftermath of quitting their brew abruptly. Headaches and agitation are common withdrawal symptoms. The offending agent, caffeine, is also the active ingredient in most OTC stay-awake products. Stop taking these pills abruptly and you'll likely experience the same symptoms.

What's more, according to psychologist Dr. Steven Levy, author of *Managing the Drugs in Your Life,* the body develops a tolerance for caffeine, requiring more and more to get the same stimulating effect. The bigger your caffeine habit, the worse the withdrawal symptoms you will experience.

Kicking the Habit   Most experts recommend tapering off the pills and avoiding other sources of caffeine.

LAXATIVES

Even with clear warnings on the packages that "frequent or continued use may result in dependency," laxatives are among the most widely abused OTC drugs. The most tragic abusers are young people — mostly women — who use laxatives in a misguided attempt to maintain their weight while binging on high-calorie foods. This practice, called bulimia, can cause severe illness or even death.

Most laxative abusers, however, began taking the products for good reason, but just didn't know when to stop. These folks soon discovered the unpleasant facts of laxative abuse.

Dr. Marvin M. Schuster, gastroenterologist at Johns Hopkins School of Medicine, says the most habit-forming laxatives contain phenolphthalein. This chemical works by irritating the nerves that cause intestinal muscles to contract. "Eventually," Dr. Schuster warns, "these nerve cells can permanently degenerate. The intestine actually becomes partially paralyzed, making constipation worse than it was before you took the laxatives."

Kicking the Habit   Dr. Schuster advises using a bulk-type laxative, which works more naturally than the stimulant types containing phenolphthalein. Common brand names of bulk-type laxatives include Fiberall and Metamucil; or look for less expensive generic and store brands containing psyllium fiber.

EYE DROPS

Some eye drops — notably those that tout their ability to reduce redness — contain drugs that constrict the blood vessels in the eyes, which makes the eyes appear whiter. Using eye drops occasionally is safe. However, using these products for more than three days only makes the redness worse. You may find you are having to use them every few hours. Cutting back leaves your eyes redder than they started out.

Kicking the Habit   The best way is to taper off. If you are really worried about chronic eye redness, see a doctor.

NASAL SPRAYS

Habitual users of nasal spray often find it is very difficult to stop. That's why instructions on nasal sprays warn against use for more than three days. If you get addicted, you'll find you can't breathe through your nose without them; congestion, sneezing, and a runny nose may plague you constantly.

How to Kick the Habit   To wean yourself from nasal spray addiction, Dr. C. Edwin Webb, pharmacist and Director of Professional Affairs of the American Pharmaceutical Association, advises switching from long-lasting, 12-hour brands of spray to short-acting forms, then going on to children's formula, decreasing the number of uses of each product as you go along.

1000 words

Write your ending time here: _____

Subtract your starting time: _____

Total time: _____

Check the Rate Chart in the back of the book to find out how many words per minute you have read and then record your score on the Progress Chart.

ANSWERS TO SKIMMING QUESTIONS

1. Your answer should be similar to the correct answer for question 2 in the Comprehension Check.

2. Write the answers to your skimming questions here.

    a. _____

    b. _____

    c. _____

15

Over-the-Counter Addictions

COMPREHENSION CHECK
Circle the letter before the best answer to each of the following questions. Don't look back at the article.

Subject and Main Idea
1. The subject of the article is
   a. drug addictions.
   b. the advantages of over-the-counter drugs.
   c. addiction to over-the-counter drugs.
   d. children's addictions to over-the-counter drugs.

2. The main idea is that
   a. drugs are dangerous.
   b. over-the-counter drugs should be banned.
   c. over-the-counter drugs can be habit forming.
   d. all drugs should be prescribed by a doctor.

Details
3. "OTC" stands for
   a. once-toxic chemicals.
   b. the government agency that regulates drugs.
   c. overly taken chemicals.
   d. over-the-counter.

4. The ingredient in sleeping pills that causes sleepiness is actually
   a. an appetite depresser.
   b. an antidepressant.
   c. an allergy medication.
   d. poisonous.

5. Diet pills
   a. are usually effective.
   b. are especially popular with teenage girls.
   c. directly cause weight loss.
   d. contain a form of cocaine.

6. Long-term use of laxatives can result in
   a. heart attacks.
   b. loss of appetite.
   c. an increase in blood pressure.
   d. partial paralysis of the intestine.

Inferences

7. You can infer from the article that
   a. the author wants these drugs taken off the market.
   b. the author feels that most people don't realize how dangerous these drugs can be.
   c. doctors should prescribe all sleeping medications.
   d. people should not buy over-the-counter drugs because they are too dangerous.

8. The author implies that
   a. it is easy to stop using over-the-counter medication.
   b. you should see a doctor before using over-the-counter drugs.
   c. people are more careless with over-the-counter drugs than with prescribed medication.
   d. all of the above are true.

9. The over-the-counter addicts
   a. are usually teenagers.
   b. often don't recognize they have a problem.
   c. usually die from the addiction because they can't stop.
   d. will usually become prescription or illegal drug addicts.

10. You can infer from the article that
   a. people can rarely recognize the side effects of these drugs.
   b. some people have personalities that lead to these addictive behaviors.
   c. we can safely use over-the-counter drugs if we follow the instructions.
   d. the drug companies are legally responsible for the problem.

QUESTIONS FOR ANALYSIS AND APPLICATION

1. Name at least two ways over-the-counter medications can be made safer.

2. Compare and contrast the issues involved with the abuse of legal (over-the-counter and prescription) and illegal drugs. Consider at least two of the following: costs, legal penalties, medical treatment, effects on family, effects on the workplace.

VOCABULARY IN CONTEXT
Multiple Choice
Circle the letter before the definition of each underlined word or phrase.

1. Experts often say that <u>chronic</u> television viewing is harmful to the mental development of children.
   a. intense   b. habitual   c. occasional   d. casual

2. Migraine headaches <u>plague</u> millions of people in the United States.
   a. surprise   b. endanger   c. please   d. torment

3. The car stopped <u>abruptly</u> when the driver saw the young child running into the street.
   a. cautiously   b. suddenly   c. quietly   d. slowly

4. In the <u>aftermath of</u> an earthquake, it is important to have previously stored supplies, because things such as food, water, and medical supplies may not be available.
   a. thrill before   b. aftereffect of   c. process of
   d. afterworld near

5. Wearing garlic around your neck was once <u>touted</u> as a way to ward off evil spirits.
   a. proven   b. assured   c. praised   d. given

6. Constant <u>binging on</u> your favorite foods might indicate a problem.
   a. little use of   b. purchasing of   c. excessive use of
   d. avoidance of

7. Many alcoholics find that rather than cutting down on their amount of drinking, the only way they can really stop is to quit <u>cold turkey</u>.
   a. immediately and completely   b. slowly and carefully
   c. under a doctor's care   d. as part of a support group

8. Some people develop a <u>psychic</u> dependence on television soap operas and must watch them every day.
   a. strong   b. mental   c. physical   d. constant

9. The <u>agitation</u> of knowing that a difficult task lies ahead can keep you awake all night.
   a. pleasure   b. disturbance   c. disappointment   d. fear

Fill-in
Write the best word from this list in the blank in each sentence below:

withdrawal   pharmacologists   bulimia   generic   habitual

degenerates   tolerance   substance   die-hard   stimulants

10. Most people's hearing _____ as they become older.

11. Teenagers are often criticized for their _____ talking on the telephone.

12. After years of use, most people build up a _____ to coffee, cigarettes, or even prescribed medications, requiring a greater amount to achieve the same effect.

13. Because the nicotine in cigarettes causes people to become addicted, heavy smokers who try to stop smoking experience

_____ symptoms.

14. _____ abusers can come from all age groups and economic backgrounds.

15. Many college students use _____ such as No-Doz so that they can study late into the night.

16. A _____ Republican will never vote for a Democratic candidate.

17. _____ are only now finding out about the damaging effects of second-hand smoke on nonsmokers' lungs.

18. _____ is a serious eating disorder more commonly suffered by teenage girls than other people.

19. _____ aspirin can be bought at a drug store for less money than the name-brand equivalent.

SKILLS EXERCISE: CRITICAL READING
Argumentation and Support

> For explanation see pp. 152–154

A. Fill in the supporting statements for the following argument:

1. Laxatives are among the most widely abused OTC drugs.

   a. _____

   b. Constipated people

2. There are steps to kicking the habit of using sleeping pills.

   a. _____

   b. _____

   c. _____

   d. _____

   e. _____

B. In the following exercise, fill in the main argument:

1. _____

   a. If you get addicted you'll find you can't breathe through your nose without them.

   b. Congestion, sneezing, and a runny nose may plague you constantly.

2. _____

   a. Taper off the eye drops.

   b. If worried, see a doctor.

16

Newspapers

SKILLS EXERCISE:
SKIMMING AND SCANNING

For explanation
see pp. 157–158

A. *Skimming.* Take one minute to skim the following article. Run your eyes over the article to get a general idea of what it is about.

  1. After you have skimmed the article, write its main idea in your own words. _____

  _____

  2. Without looking back at the article, write three questions that you think will be answered by reading it.

  a. _____

  b. _____

  c. _____

B. *Scanning.* First, underline the key words in the following questions. Next, scan the article to find the answers. Quickly underline each answer and move to the next question. It should take you no more than three minutes to answer all of the questions. After you finish scanning for all ten of the answers, write them in the spaces below.

  1. Besides newspapers, what other medium provides news? _____

  2. How many seconds would it take you to read the information contained in a ten-minute TV broadcast? _____

  3. Approximately how many words are in the Sunday *New York Times?* _____

  4. How are headline stories organized? _____

  5. What world organization is mentioned in the article? _____

  6. Name a famous national columnist who writes humorous articles. _____

  7. What two cities are sources for gossip columns? _____

  8. Who is the serious columnist for *The New York Times?* _____

  9. What are the last names of four other serious columnists who are mentioned? _____

  10. What city is a source for political columns? _____

The following selection is taken from a chapter called "Newspapers and Magazines" in a textbook on the techniques of reading. It discusses the reading techniques most appropriate for newspapers.

Now read the article. Write your starting time here: _____

16

Newspapers

Horace Judson

WHAT NEWSPAPER DO YOU READ? Have you ever examined it closely, compared it with others? Have you ever stopped to consider just how you read it?

A good modern newspaper is an extraordinary piece of reading. It is remarkable first for what it contains: the range of news from local crime to international politics, from sports to business to fashion to science, and the range of comment and special features as well, from editorial page to feature articles and interviews to criticism of books, art, theater, and music. A newspaper is even more remarkable for the way one reads it: never completely, never straight through, but always by jumping from here to there, in and out, glancing at one piece, reading another article all the way through, reading just a few paragraphs of the next. A good modern newspaper offers a variety to attract many different readers, but far more than any one reader is interested in. What brings this variety together in one place is its topicality, its immediate relation to what is happening in your world and your locality now. But immediacy and the speed of production that goes with it means also that much of what appears in a newspaper has no more than transient value. For all these reasons, no two people really read the same paper: what each person does is to put together, out of the pages of that day's paper, his own selection and sequence, his own newspaper. For all these reasons, reading newspapers efficiently, which means getting what you want from them without missing things you need but without wasting time, demands skill and self-awareness as you modify and apply the techniques of reading. . . .

Or do you get your news from television? TV news and commentary has obvious values of immediacy and vividness. Its drawbacks are not so obvious, but are considerable. Broadcast news programs necessarily are highly simplified and condensed. They are also inflexible, giving you no choice to get less or more information than brief capsules about each item. No matter how vivid the pictures, the information that explains them is limited to the lock-step speed of speech: leaving out the commercials, a ten-minute broadcast can contain no more information than

223

you should be able to read in about 90 seconds. Television news is essential and inescapable today; but its limitations are built into the way broadcasting works, and therefore make newspapers more important than ever.

As always, so with newspapers, the first question is your purpose in reading. With a ruthlessly clear idea of what you need, you will be able to select, to skip, to use to the full your ability to skim, to pre-read, and to question the value of everything your eye falls on. Indeed, nobody should *read* a newspaper. For example, the Sunday *New York Times* contains (excluding advertising) upwards of three quarters of a million words, equal to half a dozen sizable novels. You must skip in newspaper reading; you can do so easily and wisely if you remember several facts. First, since most newspapers appeal to a large, general readership, their coverage extends far beyond your particular interests. Second, most news stories follow a basic organizational pattern that is peculiar to newspaper journalism, which concentrates the most essential facts in the headline and the first several paragraphs of the article.

These special characteristics of newspaper writing require you to modify your techniques of pre-reading, skipping, and skimming. Let us consider first the *headline stories*, which make up the bulk of a paper's nonadvertising content. There are reasons why such stories are organized with the most important material at the top. . . . Readers are impatient, and want to get the gist of the story quickly. Also, newspaper articles must be written so that they can be shortened quickly and easily by cutting off the end paragraphs. For example, an article on the United Nations may be placed on the first page in an early edition. Then the story of a murder trial may replace it that same day in the next edition, with the United Nations story appearing on page 3 with its last paragraphs chopped off to make it fit the space available.

Thus, you will find that newspaper headline stories are already set up for pre-reading. Usually the headline will tell you whether you want to read further; if you do, you will then read the first several paragraphs thoroughly and skim the rest of the article until you are satisfied you have everything you need. . . . Much of the material after the first several paragraphs recapitulates in expanded form the topics of the opening paragraphs. The expansion is made by adding new details that the reporter and editor judge less important.

Newspapers try to increase circulation by attracting readers through the apparent urgency of their front page headline stories. Therefore, most stories are written from the point of view of what is happening right now — journalists call it the "today angle." . . . But regardless of what the screaming headlines insist, you can often save time by remembering that what today's story adds to yesterday's information may be very little indeed. Some readers even claim they miss surprisingly little by reading the paper fairly thoroughly only every other day!

Other kinds of reporting in newspapers include editorials, feature articles, and syndicated articles and columns. In contrast to headline stories, these other types are not so much required to look like "new" news. Instead, they may furnish you with background analysis for understanding current news; they may present political opinion; or they may treat subjects of more lasting interest, and thus be similar to magazine articles. Because these three kinds of articles are not often cut to make room for later news, they are unlike headline stories and may be organized similarly to other practical prose. That is, they are likely to show the familiar pattern of introduction, development, and conclusion. You should therefore pre-read and read them just as you would other practical prose. These articles, however, are also written at a level for general audiences; you read them at top speed.

Another newspaper category includes articles reviewing the theater, television, books, and music. Often these reviews are written regularly by the same critics; often, their approach to reviewing — within the limits of space, audience, and urgent deadlines — is highly individual. Regular reading of a reviewer, however, will quickly teach you both his habits and his quality, and therefore how you will read them. Does he habitually put his opinion in the first few paragraphs, or bury it at the end? How does he typically support his judgment with reasons? Are his judgment and his writing good enough so that you really want to read him thoroughly whenever he appears? Or can you skim most of his reviews?

A final category of newspaper article deserving separate consideration is the *national column*, the piece signed by the same author or team and appearing several times a week in perhaps hundreds of newspapers across the country. Some of these are humorous (like Art Buchwald), others are merely trivial (Hollywood or New York gossip, personal advice, and so on) — what you read of those is a matter of taste. The serious columnists range from James Reston of *The New York Times* (syndicated in many papers) to Joseph Alsop, Evans and Novak, William F. Buckley, Jr., and others. Almost all of these columns are about politics, which means first of all events, trends, and gossip in Washington, similar events of national importance elsewhere in the country, and international relations. The columnists sometimes offer a tidbit of inside information, but their chief claim is that they give you analysis and informed opinion about national and international affairs. Appropriately, they often appear on the editorial page of the papers that carry them. Acquaintance with such opinions and analyses is, arguably, an essential for responsible citizenship — but so is critical, highly selective reading of them. The views they offer are political, though in the best sense of the word, and indeed vary over a fairly wide political spectrum, so that an effective form of critical reading is simply to compare various columnists on the same topic. Beyond their differences, though, these columns share one bias which also makes critical and selective reading essential: the topics they treat are among the most important of the day, but their very topicality makes them liable to an exaggerated sense of urgency and a correspondingly short-term view.

1450 words

Write your ending time here: _____

Subtract your starting time: _____

Total time: _____

Check the Rate Chart in the back of the book to find out how many words per minute you have read, and then record your score on the Progress Chart.

ANSWERS TO SKIMMING QUESTIONS

1. Your answer should be similar to the correct answer for question 2 in the Comprehension Check.

2. Write the answers to your skimming questions here.

   a. _____

   b. _____

   c. _____

16

Newspapers

COMPREHENSION CHECK
Circle the letter before the best answer to each question below. Don't look back at the article.

Subject and Main Idea
1. The subject of the article is
   a. sources of information.
   b. famous newspaper columnists.
   c. types of newspaper columns.
   d. how to read the newspaper.

2. The main idea is that
   a. newspapers are not organized like books.
   b. efficient newspaper reading requires modifying your reading techniques.
   c. newspapers are easy to read.
   d. newspapers are a better source of information than television.

Details
3. A national column can
   a. be humorous, serious, or trivial.
   b. appear in hundreds of newspapers across the country.
   c. be written by one author or a team.
   d. be all of the above.

4. The most important step in reading a newspaper is
   a. knowing who wrote the articles.
   b. using prereading, skipping, and skimming.
   c. getting the gist quickly.
   d. determining your purpose.

5. A newspaper contains
   a. about as many words as an average novel.
   b. more types of stories than the average person wishes to read.
   c. only factual accounts of news events.
   d. only articles by local reporters.

6. Which of the following is written with the most important material at the top?
   a. syndicated columns
   b. editorials
   c. feature articles
   d. headline stories

Inferences

7. One advantage of a newspaper over a TV news program is that a newspaper
   a. can cover a last-minute news item better.
   b. is produced more times a day.
   c. allows you to read only what you want to.
   d. contains opinions.

8. The editorial page
   a. is more entertaining than the news.
   b. should be read every day.
   c. contains more facts than the rest of the newspaper does.
   d. demands more critical reading than news stories do.

9. The main purpose of reading a newspaper is to
   a. increase your reading speed.
   b. evaluate fact and opinion.
   c. gain information.
   d. improve your reading comprehension.

10. Judson implies that
    a. an independent thinker would get more out of a newspaper than from TV news.
    b. TV news is valuable only to lazy people.
    c. newspapers are too repetitious.
    d. a good reader reads only the headlines and the beginnings of articles.

QUESTIONS FOR ANALYSIS AND APPLICATION

1. How can you tell how biased a newspaper is? Why is it important to be able to tell?

2. Look at the editorial section of today's newspaper. Do you find it interesting or not? Why? Which writer do you like the best or least and why?

VOCABULARY IN CONTEXT
Fill-in

Write the best word from this list in the blank in each sentence below:

commentary   inescapable   gist   recapitulate   syndicated

prose   spectrum   ruthlessly   transient

1. Walter Cronkite became television's first news anchorman because

   he had the ability to _____ , analyze, and comment on important news events.

2. Although poetry is popular, _____ is more often read and heard.

3. The _____ of an entire hour's lecture can sometimes be written in one page of good notes.

4. When one person or group controls a market, a rise in prices is _____ .

5. Richard Cramer was awarded a Pulitzer Prize for his _____ on the effects of war on individuals in the Middle East.

6. The 13,500 known paintings of Pablo Picasso cover the entire _____ of styles, from realism to pure abstraction.

7. "Ann Landers" and "Dear Abby" are examples of _____ newspaper columns.

8. The landlord _____ evicted the unemployed tenant.

9. Gypsies have traditionally been _____ , often living in a dozen places in one year.

SKILLS EXERCISE:
CRITICAL READING
Inferences

For explanation see pp. 149–152

If you can draw any of the following conclusions from the article, write *yes* in the blank before the statement. If you cannot, write *no* in the blank.

_____ 1. Newspapers are harder to read than books.

_____ 2. Newspapers are more complete sources of information than television news programs.

_____ 3. Syndicated columnists express more personal opinions in print than newspaper reporters do.

_____ 4. Syndicated columns are not outdated so quickly as news stories are.

_____ 5. A good reader is equally interested in all parts of the paper.

_____ 6. The impatient reader finds it easier to read news stories than syndicated columns.

_____ 7. Newspapers take too long to read.

_____ 8. The fact that newspapers try to increase circulation with urgent headlines can lead to distortion of the news.

_____ 9. Headline stories give you analysis and informed opinion.

_____ 10. To give the paper a sense of urgency, a national column will often appear on the first page.

Author's Purpose: Titles

Whether writing for a newspaper, a magazine, or a book, authors write articles or chapters for a variety of purposes, such as to entertain, to inform, or to persuade.

1. Classify the following titles of articles in this book by writing them under the appropriate headings below.

   Some Questions and Answers About Sleep and Dreams
   Who Wins? Who Cares?
   Introduction to Computers
   Acting to End a Life Is Sometimes Justified
   How to Improve Your Vocabulary

To inform	To persuade

2. There are three basic purposes for newspaper articles: (1) News stories are to inform. (2) Entertainment is usually the purpose of feature articles, sports writing, advice and gossip columns, and so on. (3) Expressing opinions is the purpose of editorials, many national columns, and letters to the editor. Classify the following newspaper titles[1] by writing them under the appropriate headings below.

   Dear Abby
   Mistakes in Panama Could Fill a Book
   Spending: Yes on 71, No on 72
   The Difference Between a Hero and a Leader
   Hopes for Strategic Arms Treaty Told

To inform	To entertain	To express opinion or to persuade

[1]*Los Angeles Times*, May 29, 1988.

17

No-Win Situations

VOCABULARY PREVIEW

counterproductive (koun'tər prə duk'tiv):   bringing about effects or results that are contrary to those intended

benign (bi nīn'):   harmless

diminishing (də min'ish ŋ):   becoming smaller or less

devised (di vīzd'):   worked out or created

inherent (in hir'ənt):   existing in someone or something as a natural and inseparable quality

malicious (mə lish'əs):   spiteful; intentionally mischievous or harmful

camaraderie (käm'ə räd'ər ē; kam'-):   loyalty and warm, friendly feeling among comrades, comradeship

essence (es'əns):   that which makes something what it is, fundamental nature or most important quality (of something)

striving (strīv'ŋ):   making great efforts

gloat (glōt):   to express malicious pleasure or self satisfaction

toxic (täk'sik):   harmful, destructive, or deadly

epithet (ep'ə thet'):   a descriptive name or title, especially negative

collaborators (kə lab'ə rāt'ərz):   people cooperating with others

detest (di test'):   to dislike intensely; hate

conducive (kən dōo'siv):   that contributes; tending or leading (to)

aberration (ab'ər ā'shən):   a deviation from the normal or the typical

radical (rad'ik'l):   favoring fundamental or extreme change

fat, āpe, cär; ten, ēven; is, bīte; gō, hôrn, tōōl, look; oil, out; up, fʉr; chin, she; thin, *then*; zh, leisure; ŋ, ring; ə for *a* in *ago;* ' as in *able* (ā'b'l)

SKILLS EXERCISE:
SKIMMING AND SCANNING

For explanation see pp. 157–158

A. *Skimming.* Take one minute to skim the following article. Run your eyes over the article to get a general idea of what it is about.

   1. After you have skimmed the article, write its main idea in your own words. _____

     _____

   2. Without looking back at the article, write three questions that you think will be answered by reading it.

     a. _____

     b. _____

     c. _____

B. *Scanning.* First, underline the key words in the following questions. Next, scan the article to find the answers. Quickly underline each answer and move to the next question. It should take you no more than three minutes to answer all of the questions. After you finish scanning for all ten of the answers, write them in the spaces below.

   1. What is the title of the book that the author of the article wrote? _____

   2. The author found that competition holds us back from what?

     _____

   3. What do most people assume that competitive sports teach?

     _____

   4. What does recreation at its best not require? _____

   5. In games where people work together, an opponent becomes a what? _____

   6. To play tennis, you must try to make the other person do what?

     _____

   7. Cooperative games provide satisfaction and challenge without what? _____

   8. What fraction of the boys Orlick taught preferred noncompetitive games? _____

   9. Studies have shown that as a result of competition, our feelings of self-worth become dependent on what? _____

   10. What does the author feel is nothing more than an artificial way to try to limit the damage of competition? _____

Now read the article. Write your starting time here: _____

17

No-Win Situations

Alfie Kohn

I LEARNED MY FIRST GAME at a birthday party. You remember it: X players scramble for X-minus-one chairs each time the music stops. In every round a child is eliminated until at the end only one is left triumphantly seated while everyone else is standing on the sidelines, excluded from play, unhappy . . . losers.

This is how we learn to have a good time in America.

Several years ago I wrote a book called *No Contest*, which, based on the findings of several hundred studies, argued that competition undermines self-esteem, poisons relationships and holds us back from doing our best. I was mostly interested in the win/lose arrangement that defines our workplaces and classrooms, but I found myself nagged by the following question: If competition is so destructive and counterproductive during the week, why do we take for granted that it suddenly becomes benign and even desirable on the weekend?

This is a particularly unsettling line of inquiry for athletes or parents. Most of us, after all, assume that competitive sports teach all sorts of useful lessons and, indeed, that games by definition must produce a winner and a loser. But I've come to believe that recreation at its best does not require people to try to triumph over others. Quite to the contrary.

Terry Orlick, a sports psychologist at the University of Ottawa, took a look at musical chairs and proposed that we keep the basic format of removing chairs but change the goal; the point becomes to fit everyone on a diminishing number of seats. At the end, a group of giggling children tries to figure out how to squish onto a single chair. Everybody plays to the end; everybody has a good time.

Orlick and others have devised or collected hundreds of such games for children and adults alike. The underlying theory is simple: All games involve achieving a goal despite the presence of an obstacle, but nowhere is it written that the obstacle has to be someone else. The idea can be for each person on the field to make a specified contribution to the goal, or for all the players to reach a certain score, or for everyone to work with her partners against a time limit.

Note the significance of an "opponent" becoming a "partner." The entire dynamic of the game shifts, and one's attitude toward the other players changes with it. Even the friendliest game of tennis can't help but be affected by the game's inherent structure, which demands that each person try to hit the ball where the other can't get to it. You may not be a malicious person, but to play tennis means that you try to make the other person fail.

I've become convinced that not a single one of the advantages attributed to sports actually requires competition. Running, climbing, biking, swimming, aerobics — all offer a fine workout without any need to try to outdo someone else. Some people point to the camaraderie that results from teamwork, but that's precisely the benefit of cooperative activity, whose very essence is that *everyone* on the field is working together for a common goal. By contrast, the distinguishing feature of team competition is that a given player works with and is encouraged to feel warmly toward only half of those present. Worse, a we-versus-they dynamic is set up, which George Orwell once called "war minus the shooting."

The dependence on sports to provide a sense of accomplishment or to test one's wits is similarly misplaced. One can aim instead at an objective standard (How far did I throw? How many miles did we cover?) or attempt to do better than last week. Such individual and group striving — like cooperative games — provides satisfaction and challenge without competition.

If large numbers of people insist that we can't do without win/lose activities, the first question to ask is whether they've ever tasted the alternative. When Orlick taught a group of children noncompetitive games, two-thirds of the boys and all of the girls preferred them to the kind that require opponents. If our culture's idea of fun requires beating someone else, it may just be because we don't know any other way.

It may also be because we overlook the psychological costs of competition. Most people lose in most competitive encounters, and it's obvious why that causes self-doubt. But even winning doesn't build character: It just lets us gloat temporarily. Studies have shown that feelings of self-worth become dependent on external sources of evaluation as a result of competition; your value is defined by what you've done and who you've beaten. The whole affair soon becomes a vicious circle: The more you compete, the more you *need* to compete to feel good about yourself. It's like drinking salt water when you're thirsty. This process is bad enough for us; it's a disaster for our children.

While this is going on, competition is having an equally toxic effect on our relationships. By definition, not everyone can win a contest. That means that each child inevitably comes to regard others as obstacles to his or her own success. Competition leads children to envy winners, to dismiss losers (there's no nastier epithet in our language than "Loser!"), and to be suspicious of just about everyone. Competition makes it difficult to regard others as potential friends or collaborators; even if you're not my rival today, you could be tomorrow.

This is not to say that competitors will always detest one another. But trying to outdo someone is not conducive to trust — indeed it would be irrational to trust a person who gains from your failure. At best, competition leads one to look at others through narrowed eyes; at worst, it invites outright aggression.

But no matter how many bad feelings erupt during competition, we have a marvelous talent for blaming the individuals rather than focusing on the structure of the game itself, a structure that makes my success depend on your failure. Cheating may just represent the logical conclusion of this arrangement rather than an aberration. And sportsmanship is nothing more than an artificial way to try to limit the damage of competition. If we weren't set against each other on the court or the track, we wouldn't need to keep urging people to be good sports; they might well be working *with* each other in the first place.

As radical or surprising as it may sound, the problem isn't just that we compete the wrong way or that we push winning on our children too early. The problem is competition itself. What we need to be teaching our daughters and sons is that it's possible to have a good time — a better time — without turning the playing field into a battlefield.

1200 words

Write your ending time here: _____

Subtract your starting time: _____

Total time: _____

Check the Rate Chart in the back of the book to find out how many words per minute you have read and then record your score on the Progress Chart.

ANSWERS TO SKIMMING QUESTIONS

1. Your answer should be similar to the correct answer for question 2 in the Comprehension Check.

2. Write the answers to your skimming questions here.

    a. _____

    b. _____

    c. _____

17

No-Win Situations

COMPREHENSION CHECK
Circle the letter before the best answer to each of the following questions. Don't look back at the article.

Subject and Main Idea

1. The subject of the article is
   a. competition as a way of life.
   b. the dangers of competitive sports.
   c. children's problems with competition.
   d. that competition teaches you necessary skills for life.

2. The main idea is that
   a. sports competition is beneficial.
   b. competition is important.
   c. sports competition is harmful.
   d. sports are fun.

Details

3. The writer of the article wrote a book called
   a. *The Competitive Edge.*
   b. *No Context.*
   c. *No Contest.*
   d. *Don't Compete.*

4. The author believes competition
   a. undermines self-esteem.
   b. poisons relationships.
   c. holds us back from doing our best.
   d. does all of the above.

5. The author talks about Terry Orlick, who is
   a. a famous author.
   b. a sports psychologist.
   c. a professional athlete.
   d. a physical education teacher.

6. When Orlick taught a group of children noncompetitive games
   a. two-thirds of the girls liked them.
   b. two-thirds of all the children liked them.
   c. two-thirds of the boys liked them.
   d. none of the children enjoyed them.

Inferences

7. From the article we can infer that the author
   a. believes he is a "loser."
   b. is a coach of a sports team.
   c. believes physical activity is important.
   d. feels that periodic competition such as on the weekend is acceptable.

8. If the author were a member of a school board he would
   a. favor programs that would encourage women to participate in sports.
   b. eliminate all physical education.
   c. favor less competitive physical education programs.
   d. hire only female coaches for team sports.

9. Which activity would the author be most likely to participate in?
   a. volleyball
   b. recreational swimming
   c. tennis
   d. touch football

10. We can infer from the article that the author would
    a. rather play football than monopoly.
    b. enjoy working in sales.
    c. favor schools that don't have grades.
    d. enjoy being a professional athlete.

QUESTIONS FOR ANALYSIS AND APPLICATION

1. How do you think the author's childhood experiences affected his views on competition now? Do you think he won a lot? Do you think he was good at sports? Why or why not?
2. Decide if people in the following careers tend to be competitive. If they are competitive circle Y for yes; if they are not competitive circle N for no.

   A. 1. professional chess player   Y   N

       2. author   Y   N

       3. minister   Y   N

       4. professional football player Y   N

       5. firefighter   Y   N

       6. lifeguard   Y   N

   B. Choose one of the above or another career you might want and discuss why you think it will or will not be competitive.

VOCABULARY IN CONTEXT
Multiple Choice
Circle the letter before the definition of each underlined word
or phrase.

1. During the late 1960s at the University of California at Berkeley,
   many students had <u>radical</u> political ideas.
   a. amusing   b. extreme   c. important   d. varied

2. People should always <u>strive to do</u> their best.
   a. try not to do   b. avoid doing   c. plan to do
   d. attempt to do

3. It is extremely important to keep <u>toxic</u> chemicals out of the reach
   of children.
   a. sweet   b. irritating   c. poisonous   d. burning

4. Studies have shown that listening to classical music while studying can <u>be conducive to</u> higher productivity.
   a. lead to   b. be harmful to   c. distract from   d. limit

5. There is fear that the ozone layer is <u>diminishing</u>, which could result in dangerous changes in the environment.
   a. lessening   b. changing   c. thickening   d. evaporating

6. Children are often very <u>malicious</u> in their teasing of other
   children.
   a. friendly   b. harmful   c. harmless   d. angry

7. Little children often <u>detest</u> spinach, so parents are wise to let their
   children watch *Popeye* eat his spinach in the cartoons.
   a. love   b. eat   c. refuse   d. hate

8. Henry Ford <u>devised</u> a way to produce cars more quickly.
   a. believed in   b. created   c. supported   d. disproved

9. The offhand comment was meant to be <u>benign</u>, but it actually hurt
   the feelings of several people.
   a. informative   b. funny   c. harmless   d. persuasive

Fill-In

Write the best word from this list in the blank in each sentence below:

gloat   essence   epithets   camaraderie   inherent

collaborators   counterproductive   aberration

10. It is often _____ to work on a paper late into the night because you make more mistakes when you are tired.

11. It is poor sportsmanship to _____ after winning a game.

12. Sam expressed his displeasure with Bob's reckless driving by using rude _____ .

13. The _____ among the co-workers grew stronger after they formed a bowling team.

14. It can be easier for _____ to write a book than for one person to do it alone.

15. The _____ of being a good judge is being as fair as possible to all involved parties.

16. There is a(n) _____ assumption that a bank teller is honest.

17. Having six toes on one foot is a(n) _____ .

SKILLS EXERCISE:
CRITICAL READING
Argument and Support

For explanation
see pp. 152–156

A. Fill in the supporting statements for the following argument:

1. Competition is harmful.

   a. _____

   b. _____

   c. Holds us back from doing our best.

2. None of the advantages attributed to sports requires competition.

   a. Workout

   b. _____

   c. Sense of accomplishment or test of wits

3. Competition has a toxic effect on relationships.

   a. _____

   b. Leads one to envy winners, dismiss losers, be suspicious of everyone

   c. _____

   d. Difficult to regard others as potential friends or collaborators

B. In the following exercise, fill in the main argument:

1. _____

   a. Losing causes self-doubt.

   b. Feelings of self-worth become dependent on external sources of evaluation as a result of competition.

   c. Becomes a vicious circle: The more you compete, the more you *need* to compete to feel good about yourself.

Judging Support: Fact Versus Opinion

Write *F* in the space before each statement of fact; write *O* if the statement is someone's opinion.

_____ 1. "I learned my first game at a birthday party."

_____ 2. "Several years ago, I wrote a book called *No Contest* . . ."

_____ 3. "This is a particularly unsettling line of inquiry for athletes or parents."

_____ 4. "Orlick and others have devised or collected hundreds of such games for children and adults alike."

_____ 5. "The underlying theory is simple . . ."

_____ 6. "The dependence on sports to provide a sense of accomplishment or to test one's wits is similarly misplaced."

_____ 7. "When Orlick taught a group of children noncompetitive games, two-thirds of the boys and all of the girls preferred them to the kind that require opponents."

_____ 8. ". . . There's no nastier epithet in our language than 'Loser!'"

_____ 9. "And sportsmanship is nothing more than an artificial way to try to limit the damage of competition."

_____ 10. "The problem is competition itself."

Note: A Critical Reading exercise comparing Articles 17 and 18 appears following the exercises for Article 18.

18

Who Wins? Who Cares?

243

SKILLS EXERCISE:
SKIMMING AND SCANNING

For explanation see pp. 157–158

A. **Skimming.** Take one minute to skim the following article. Run your eyes over the article to get a general idea of what it is about.

 1. After you have skimmed the article, write its main idea in your own words. _____

 _____

 Without looking back at the article, write three questions that you think will be answered by reading it.

 a. _____

 b. _____

 c. _____

B. **Scanning.** First, underline the key words in the following questions. Next, scan the article to find the answers. Quickly underline each answer and move to the next question. It should take you no more than three minutes to answer all of the questions. After you finish scanning for all ten of the answers, write them in the spaces below.

 1. What are women more interested in than winning and losing?

 _____

 2. Female physical educators of what decade taught other skills than competition? _____

 3. What does the author call the mentality that the game is everything? _____

 4. Who were the two famous tennis stars who maintained a rapport as former rivals? _____

 5. The author states that sports are not about domination and defeat, but what? _____

 6. What tennis player said that she would like to become friends with Steffi Graf? _____

 7. How long has the author played sports competitively? _____

 8. What is an example of a game in which "losers" are no longer allowed to play? _____

 9. What do children naturally enjoy? _____

 10. Adults need to pay equal attention to what kinds of children?

 _____

Now read the article. Write your starting time here: _____

18

Who Wins? Who Cares?

Mariah Burton Nelson

C OMPETITION CAN DAMAGE self-esteem, create anxiety and lead to cheating and hurt feelings. But so can romantic love. No one suggests we do away with love; rather, we must perfect our understanding of what love means.

So too with competition. "To compete" is derived from the Latin *competere*, meaning "to seek together." Women seem to understand this. Maybe it's because we sat on the sidelines for so long, watching. Maybe it's because we were raised to be kind and nurturing. I'm not sure why it is. But I've noticed that it's not women who greet each other with a ritualistic, "Who won?"; not women who memorize scores and statistics; not women who pride themselves on "killer instincts." Passionate though we are, women don't take competition that seriously. Or rather, we take competition seriously, but we don't take winning and losing seriously. We've always been more interested in playing.

In fact, since the early part of this century, women have devised ways to make sport specifically inclusive and cooperative. Physical educators of the 1920s taught sportswomanship as well as sport skills, emphasizing health, vigor, high moral conduct, participation, respect for other players and friendship. So intent were these women on dodging the pitfalls of men's sports that many shied away from competition altogether.

Nowadays, many women compete wholeheartedly. But we don't buy into the "Super Bull" mentality that the game is everything. Like Martina Navratilova and Chris Evert, former "rivals" whose rapport has come to symbolize a classically female approach to competition, many women find ways to remain close while also reaching for victory. We understand that trying to win is not tantamount to trying to belittle; that winning is not wonderful if the process of play isn't challenging, fair or fun; and that losing, though at times disappointing, does not connote failure. For women, if sports are power plays, they're not about power over (power as dominance) but power to (power as competence). Sports are not about domination and defeat but caring and cooperation.

"The playing of a game has to do with your feelings, your emotions, how you care about the people you're involved with," says University of Iowa basketball coach C. Vivian Stringer.

Pam Shriver has said of Steffi Graf, "I hope in the next couple of years that I get to be friends with her because it's just easier. It's more fun. I don't think it affects the competitive side of things."

Friendship has been a major theme of my sporting life as well, along with physical competence, achievement and joy. Though I've competed in seven sports from the high school to the professional level, I have few memories of victories or losses. I don't think winning taught me to be a gracious winner. I don't think losing readied me for more serious losses in life. Rather, my nearly 30 years of competition have taught me how to *play*, with empathy, humor and honesty. If another player challenges me to row harder, swim faster or make more clever moves toward the basket, the games take on a special thrill. But the final score is nearly irrelevant. Chris Evert once said the joy of winning "lasts about an hour."

I'm choosy about whom I compete with, and how. I don't participate in games in which "losers" are no longer allowed to play. Monopoly, poker, musical chairs, and single-elimination tournaments are a few examples. If playing is the point, then exclusion never makes sense. I also eschew competitions that pit women against men; they only serve to antagonize and polarize. I no longer injure myself in the name of victory. Nor, as a coach, will I allow players to get that carried away.

Some women, scarred by childhood exclusion, shamed by early "defeats," or sickened by abuses such as cheating and steroid use, still avoid competition. They're right to be wary. Although these things are more visible in men's sports, female athletes and coaches can also succumb to the "winning is the only thing" myth, committing myriad ethical and personal offenses, from recruiting violations to bulimia, in the name of victory.

But once one understands the spirit of the game, it's not a matter of *believing* that winning and losing aren't important, it's a matter of noticing that they're not. Women seem to notice. Most women can play soccer, golf, or run competitively and enjoy themselves, regardless of outcome. They can play on a "losing" team but leave the court with little or no sense of loss. They can win without feeling superior.

I think it's the responsibility of these women — and the men who remain unblinded by the seductive glow of victory — to share this vision with young players. Children, it seems to me, naturally enjoy comparing their skills: "How far can you throw the ball? Farther than I can? How did you do it? Will you show me?" It's only when adults ascribe undue importance to victory that losing becomes devastating and children get hurt.

Adults must show children that what matters is how one plays the game. It's important that we not just parrot that cliché, but demonstrate our commitment to fair, participatory competition by paying equal attention to skilled and unskilled children; by allowing all children to participate fully in games, regardless of the score; and by caring more about process than results. This way, children can fully comprehend what they seem to intuit: that competition can be a way to get to know other people, to be challenged, and to have fun in a close and caring environment. To seek together.

Some of my best friends are the women and men who share a court or pool or field with me. Together we take risks, make mistakes, laugh, push ourselves and revel in the grace and beauty of sports. Who wins? Who cares? We're playing *with*, not *against* each other, using each other's accomplishments to inspire.

At its best, competition is not divisive but unifying, not hateful but loving. Like other expressions of love, it should not be avoided simply because it has been misunderstood.

1050 words

Write your ending time here: _____

Subtract your starting time: _____

Total time: _____

Check the Rate Chart in the back of the book to find out how many words per minute you have read and then record your score on the Progress Chart.

ANSWERS TO SKIMMING QUESTIONS

1. Your answer should be similar to the correct answer for question 2 in the Comprehension Check.

2. Write the answers to your skimming questions here.

   a. _____

   b. _____

   c. _____

18

Who Wins? Who Cares?

COMPREHENSION CHECK
Circle the letter before the answer to each of the following questions.
Don't look back at the article.

Subject and Main Idea
1. The subject of the article is
   a. dangers of competition.
   b. positive aspects of competition.
   c. superiority of women athletes.
   d. caring for others.

2. The main idea is that
   a. competition can be beneficial.
   b. anxiety leads to competition.
   c. being less competitive is better.
   d. caring people don't compete with each other.

Details
3. The author calls the highly competitive mentality
   a. "The Superbowl Mentality."
   b. "The Who Wins, Who Cares Mentality."
   c. "The Ends Justifies the Means Mentality."
   d. "The Super Bull Mentality."

4. The author says that
   a. losing does not mean you have failed.
   b. women would rather die than lose.
   c. trying to win is trying to upset the other person.
   d. women don't like to compete.

5. The author doesn't like
   a. losing to anyone when competing.
   b. games that require quick thinking.
   c. games that are not competitive.
   d. games in which "losers" are no longer allowed to play.

6. The author says she
   a. hates losing.
   b. has fond memories of every time she won a game.
   c. has few memories of victories or losses.
   d. thinks losing games as a child prepared her for more serious losses in life.

Inferences

7. From the article you can infer that women
   a. are becoming more like men as they enter the job market.
   b. are superior athletes compared to men.
   c. are not raised to enjoy athletic sports.
   d. are better "sports" than men when they lose.

8. From the article you can infer that most women
   a. would make good coaches of professional sports teams because they would emphasize playing for fun.
   b. would not be respected by male athletes because they are not as talented.
   c. would tend not to make good coaches of professional sports teams because they wouldn't play to win at all costs.
   d. have more difficulty than men trying to make friends with a competitor.

9. From the article you can infer that
   a. women are inferior athletes.
   b. women should be allowed to play in all professional sports.
   c. if you understand the meaning of competition, winning will not be so important.
   d. women are going to become more like men as time goes on.

10. Who would probably believe in the proverb "It's not whether you win or lose, it's how you play the game"?
    a. gamblers
    b. women
    c. coaches for varsity sports teams
    d. men

QUESTIONS FOR ANALYSIS AND APPLICATION

1. Based on the article, state how competition is good or bad for children.

2. Name two similarities between trying to win in sports and trying to get "A"s in school.

VOCABULARY IN CONTEXT
Multiple Choice
Circle the letter before the best definition of each underlined word or phrase.

1. She was so excited about going to Europe, she forgot to plan for the <u>pitfalls</u> of being a woman traveling alone.
   a. loneliness   b. needs   c. unanticipated dangers
   d. advantages

2. Couples in a good relationship develop a <u>rapport</u> that is the envy of their friends.
   a. language   b. game   c. schedule   d. harmony

3. Passing a friend without saying "hello" is <u>tantamount</u> to an insult.
   a. never   b. sometimes   c. equal to   d. rarely

4. The word *mother*, besides meaning your female parent, <u>connotes</u> feelings of warmth and caring.
   a. suggests   b. denies   c. forgives   d. destroys

5. The winner and loser had a certain <u>empathy</u> with each other because they had engaged in a hard-fought contest.
   a. rivalry   b. identification   c. argument
   d. friendliness

6. The alley cat <u>eschewed</u> all areas he knew were inhabited by dogs.
   a. hated   b. hurried   c. enjoyed   d. avoided

7. Jumping in puddles on a rainy day is <u>classically</u> childlike.
   a. occasionally   b. annoyingly   c. traditionally
   d. surprisingly

8. Failing a class can be a <u>devastating</u> experience.
   a. learning   b. disappointing   c. confusing
   d. destroying

9. Franklin D. Roosevelt's <u>competence</u> at speaking, especially in his "fireside chats," made him a popular president.
   a. awkwardness   b. skill   c. friendliness   d. pleasure

Fill-in

Write the best word from this list in the blank in each sentence below:

antagonize   polarize   steroid   succumb   myriad

ethical   ascribed   cliché   ritualistic   intuit   divisive

10. The student ⎯⎯⎯⎯⎯⎯⎯⎯⎯⎯⎯⎯⎯⎯⎯ his good grades to studying hard every night.

11. Many people ⎯⎯⎯⎯⎯⎯⎯⎯⎯⎯⎯⎯⎯ to the temptation of chocolate.

12. If you ⎯⎯⎯⎯⎯⎯⎯⎯⎯⎯⎯⎯⎯ a police officer you are likely to regret it.

13. A ⎯⎯⎯⎯⎯⎯⎯⎯⎯⎯⎯⎯⎯ is an overused expression.

14. Successful poker players ⎯⎯⎯⎯⎯⎯⎯⎯⎯⎯⎯ how good a hand their opponents have.

15. Taking sides on an issue can often ⎯⎯⎯⎯⎯⎯⎯⎯⎯⎯⎯ a community.

16. A ⎯⎯⎯⎯⎯⎯⎯⎯⎯⎯⎯⎯⎯ of animals can be found in any large zoo.

17. ⎯⎯⎯⎯⎯⎯⎯⎯⎯⎯⎯⎯⎯ statements can bring disagreement to an otherwise agreeable discussion.

18. Athletes can be disqualified from some competition if illegal

⎯⎯⎯⎯⎯⎯⎯⎯⎯⎯⎯⎯⎯ use is detected.

19. Lawyers must follow very strict ⎯⎯⎯⎯⎯⎯⎯⎯⎯⎯⎯ guidelines.

20. A handshake is a ⎯⎯⎯⎯⎯⎯⎯⎯⎯⎯⎯⎯⎯ greeting in many countries.

**SKILLS EXERCISE:
CRITICAL READING
Argument and Support**

*For explanation
see pp. 152–156*

A. Fill in the supporting statements for the following argument:

1. Women seem to understand that competition means "to seek together."

   a. _____

   b. _____

2. Women have different feelings than men have about competition.

   a. _____

   b. Don't memorize scores and statistics.

   c. _____

   d. _____

3. I'm choosy about whom I compete with, and how.

   a. _____

   1) _____

   2) _____

   3) _____

   4) Single-elimination tournaments

   b. _____

   c. _____

B. In the following exercise, fill in the main argument and the missing supporting statements:

1. _____

   a. Pay equal attention to skilled and unskilled children

   b. _____

   c. Care more about process than results

Judging Support: Fact Versus Opinion

Write *F* in the space before each statement of fact; write *O* if the statement is someone's opinion.

_____ 1. "Competition can damage self-esteem, create anxiety and lead to cheating and hurt feelings."

_____ 2. ". . . We must perfect our understanding of what love means."

_____ 3. "'To compete' is derived from the Latin competere, meaning 'to seek together.'"

_____ 4. "Maybe it's because we sat on the sidelines for so long, watching."

_____ 5. "Passionate though we are, women don't take competition that seriously."

_____ 6. "Physical educators of the 1920s taught sportswomanship as well as sports skills, emphasizing health, vigor, high moral conduct, participation, respect for other players and friendship."

_____ 7. "But we don't buy into the 'Super Bull' mentality that the game is everything."

_____ 8. "For women, if sports are power plays, they're not about power over (power as dominance) but power to (power as competence)."

_____ 9. "I don't participate in games in which 'losers' are no longer allowed to play."

_____ 10. "I also eschew competitions that pit women against men . . ."

COMPARISON OF ARTICLES 17 AND 18

SKILLS EXERCISE:
CRITICAL READING
Judging Support: Evaluating Evidence

Alfie Kohn's book *No Contest*, based on the findings of several hundred studies, concluded that competition undermines self-esteem, poisons relationships, and holds us back from doing our best. Whether or not these conclusions are justified depends on the validity of the research. Below are a few questions that should be answered before we can judge the value of any research.

1. Is the sample representative of the people about whom we want to draw conclusions? In this case, are the people in the studies similar to the whole population of the United States in terms of age, background, and types of competitive activities?

2. Is the sample large enough to draw the conclusions? In this case, is it big enough to predict the effects of competition on people all across the United States?

3. How were the people assigned to groups? For example, were they able to choose the type of competition? If not, could this have been a source of bias?

4. Was the method of measurement adequate? In this case, how could they measure the intensity of the competition, the self-esteem before and after, and the effect of competition in relationships and achievements?

5. Are the results significant? For example, were the differences in self-esteem, relationships, and achievement big enough to warrant the conclusion that competition makes a difference?

A. The following study measures the effect of competition on self-esteem. Two groups of Little League boys were selected. Team 1 had a coach who worked very hard to make the team win. He scheduled a great deal of difficult practice, praised and rewarded the boys who did well and ignored the boys who did not, and kept close track of batting averages and scores. Team 2's coach was more relaxed about practicing, stressed teamwork, and rewarded the entire team for playing, whether they won or lost. After one season, both groups of boys were given a questionnaire that rated their self-esteem in terms of how lovable, how good, how attractive, how intelligent, and how competent they considered themselves. There was a slight difference in that the average boy's score from team 1 was higher. Rate the study on the following scale.

	Yes	No	Can't tell
1. Is the sample representative?	✓		
2. Is the sample big enough?		✓	
3. How were people assigned to groups?	✓		✓
4. Was the measurement adequate?			
5. Are the results significant?			✓

B. The following study measures the effects of competitive games on physical aggression in preschoolers. Wadsworth Nursery School, which has ten locations throughout Los Angeles, did a pilot project using all 1,000 of its pupils. The children, who were between two and four years old, were randomly assigned to one of two groups within their home school for twenty minutes each day. Physical aggression, defined as hitting, pinching, biting, and pushing, was measured for each group, and no significant differences were found. Group A then played competitive games that had clear winners and losers. Group B played games that were participatory and cooperative, without winners and losers. After one month, incidents of physical aggression were again counted. It was found that Group A had twice as many incidents as Group B. Rate the study on the following scale:

	Yes	No	Can't tell
1. Is the sample representative?			
2. Is the sample big enough?			
3. How were people assigned to groups?			
4. Was the measurement adequate?			
5. Are the results significant?			

C. Author Mariah Burton Nelson believes that women engage in a healthier type of competition than men do. Using the preceding questions as a guide, design a research study to measure whether competition differs in women and in men. You want to be able to draw conclusions to apply to the general population of the United States.

1. How can you make sure your sample is representative?

   facts

2. How big a sample do you need?

   Large

3. Into what subgroups will you divide your people?

   men   women   Children

4. How will you decide which people go into which group?

   sex   age

5. How will you measure the differences between your groups concerning your topic?

   Competition

6. How will you decide whether the results are significant?

   _____

Author's Purpose:
Word Choice

Some authors use carefully chosen words to convince a reader of their ideas. For example, when Mariah Burton Nelson uses the phrase "killer instincts," it gives us a negative feeling. She could have chosen a less emotional phrase, such as "desire to win."

A. Below are ten words from the vocabulary previews of Articles 17 and 18. Each of these words makes you feel positive or negative. If the word is positive, circle *P*; if it is negative, circle *N*.

1.	competence	P	N
2.	gloat	P	N
3.	counterproductive	P	N
4.	ethical	P	N
5.	devastating	P	N
6.	antagonize	P	N
7.	conducive	P	N
8.	empathy	P	N
9.	toxic	P	N
10.	camaraderie	P	N

B. The sentences below contain quotations from Articles 17 and 18. Translate each underlined phrase into everyday language. In other words, write what you think the author means.

1. ". . . I've come to believe that recreation at its best does not require people to <u>triumph over others</u>."

   _____

2. "If large numbers of people insist that we can't do without win/lose activities, the first question to ask is whether they've ever <u>tasted the alternative</u>."

   _____

3. "It's <u>like drinking salt water when you're thirsty</u>."

   _____

4. "At best, competition leads one to <u>look at others through nar-</u><u>rowed eyes</u>."

_____

5. "What we need to be teaching our daughters and sons is that it's possible to have a good time — a better time — without <u>turning</u> <u>the playing field into a battlefield</u>."

_____

6. "I think it's the responsibility of these women — and the men who <u>remain unblinded by the seductive glow of victory</u> to share this vision with young players."

_____

7. "It's important that we not just <u>parrot that cliche</u> [what matters is how one plays the game] but demonstrate our commitment to fair, participatory competition. . . ."

_____

C. Now that you are familiar with how to identify how authors carefully choose phrases to promote positive or negative feelings, go back to Articles 17 and 18 and find four examples of words or phrases not used in previous exercises. Write the examples and translate them into less emotional language in the blanks below.

1. word or phrase _____

   meaning _____

2. word or phrase _____

   meaning _____

3. word or phrase _____

   meaning _____

4. word or phrase _____

   meaning _____

Application of Critical Skills
Practice your ability to read critically by comparing the two articles on competition.

1. How does each author feel about competition? On what do they agree? On what do they disagree?

2. Do you think Alfie Kohn would agree with Mariah Burton Nelson that women compete more constructively than men do? Why or why not?

3. Which author seems more supportive of professional sports? Give reasons for your opinions.

4. Which of the two authors seems more objective, less reliant on opinion as opposed to fact? Give evidence for your answer.

5. To what extent do you think each author would encourage his or her children's participation in competitive sports? What sports would each parent be likely to choose?

19

Acting to End a Life
Is Sometimes Justified

VOCABULARY PREVIEW

intercede (in'tər sēd'):   to make an appeal on behalf of another

welter (wel'tər):   confusion; turmoil

salient (sāl'yənt):   outstanding; striking

euthanasia (yōō'thə nā'zhə):   act of causing a painless death so as to end suffering

elicit (i lis'it):   to draw forth; to evoke (a response)

ultimate (ul'tə mit):   final; conclusive; greatest possible

refrain (ri frān'):   to hold back; to keep oneself (from doing something)

terminally (tur'mə nə lē):   incurably; finally

intervention (in'tər ven'shən):   interference in the affairs of others

restitution (res'tə tōō'shən):   return of something that has been lost or taken away; restoration

compos mentis (käm'pəs men'tis):   of sound mind; sane

squeamishness (skwēm'ish nəs):   ease with which one becomes nauseated or shocked

humanitarian (hyōō man'ə târ'ē ən):   person devoted to promoting the welfare of humanity, especially through the elimination of pain and suffering

hypocritical (hip'ə krit'i k'l):   pretending to feel what one does not

arbiter (är'bə tər):   judge

theological (thē'ə läj'i k'l):   having to do with the study of God or religion

compassion (kəm pash'ən):   deep sympathy; pity

glibly (glib'lē):   smoothly (spoken), often too smoothly to be convincing

bracket (brak'it):   to enclose; to classify together

deity (dē'ə tē):   God

fat, āpe, cär; ten, ēven; is, bīte; gō, hôrn, tōōl, look; oil, out; up, fur; chin, she; thin, *then*; zh, leisure; ŋ, ring; ə for *a* in *ago;* ' as in *able* (ā'b'l)

SKILLS EXERCISE: SKIMMING AND SCANNING

For explanation see pp. 157–158

A. *Skimming.* Take one minute to skim the following article. Run your eyes over the article to get a general idea of what it is about.

   1. After you have skimmed the article, write its main idea in your own words. _____

   _____

   Without looking back at the article, write three questions that you think will be answered by reading it.

   a. _____

   b. _____

   c. _____

B. *Scanning.* First, underline the key words in the following questions. Next, scan the article to find the answers. Quickly underline each answer and move to the next question. It should take you no more than three minutes to answer all of the questions. After you finish scanning for all ten of the answers, write them in the spaces below.

   1. At what conference did Dr. Joseph Fletcher deliver his paper?

   _____

   2. How many levels of attitudes and opinions did Fletcher describe? _____

   3. What did Fletcher cite as the ultimate human value in the first level listed? _____

   4. The second, third, fourth, and fifth situations cited by Fletcher are gradations of _____

   5. Active participation in euthanasia is described by which levels? _____

   6. How old was Dr. Christiaan Barnard's mother when she suffered her third stroke? _____

   7. Has Barnard ever practiced active euthanasia? _____

   8. According to Barnard, what is the greatest difficulty in practicing euthanasia? _____

   9. In what situation does Barnard feel that humans have totally accepted the right to kill and be killed? _____

   10. What kind of God does Barnard feel would approve of mercy killing? _____

Now read the article. Write your starting time here: _____

19

Acting to End a Life
Is Sometimes Justified

Christiaan Barnard

WHETHER LIFE ENDS with a bang or a whimper, the end is a private moment. No one can share the last fears or hopes at the bedside, and no one can intercede in a confrontation that concerns only the dying and the approach of death. Certainly, the concept of "death with dignity" has become an increasing focus of debate, not the least because of medical progress that has brought about demographic changes and a major increase in the number of retired and aged persons. The issue has generated a welter of legislation, much of which confuses rather than clarifies a salient question in euthanasia: Who will pull the plug?

Possibly one of the more useful outlines of the problem was put forward by Dr. Joseph Fletcher, a professor of medical ethics at the University of Virginia, in a paper given at a 1974 Euthanasia Conference in New York City. He listed eight levels of attitude and opinion on the human initiatives that can be exercised in the case of a patient dying of an incurable disease, as follows:

1. An absolute refusal to elicit any human initiative in the death or the dying. Life must always be considered as the ultimate human value.

2. A qualified refusal, in that the doctor can refrain from employing extraordinary means of preserving life but would nevertheless do whatever possible by ordinary means to keep life going.

3. Declining to start treatment in a patient who has an incurable disease and is suffering from a curable intercurrent illness (for example, the terminally ill cancer patient with pneumonia). The doctor refuses to initiate treatment for the lung infection that can be cured and in this way may actually hasten death.

4. Stoppage of treatment, with consent, where it is the patient's wish not to be treated any further.

5. Stoppage of treatment, without consent, when the attending physician feels that further treatment can only prolong suffering.

6. Leaving the patient with an overdose of narcotic or sedative, thus assisting the dying person to take his own life.

7. Prior permission is given by the patient to the doctor to administer an injection, under certain circumstances, from which the patient will not recover.

8. Without consent, and on his own authority, the doctor ends the patient's life with an overdose of drugs.

It is clear that the second, third, fourth and fifth situations are gradations of passive euthanasia. In none of these does the doctor take the initiative in ending the patient's life. The sixth, seventh and eighth describe grades of active participation.

There is thus a distinct difference between passive — or indirect — euthanasia, where death is induced by suspension of treatment, and the so-called active or direct euthanasia, where death is brought about by a definite act.

In general, the layman's view of euthanasia is one of "mercy killing," or active intervention to end life, with little or no concept of the possibility of a passive form.

I make no excuses and ask no forgiveness for admitting that I have practiced passive euthanasia for many years. In fact, I gave instructions to the doctor attending my own mother in her last illness that she should receive no antibiotics nor be tube fed. At that stage, she was in her 98th year, suffering from her third stroke and unconscious with pneumonia.

I have never practiced active euthanasia, a deed that in my country is regarded as murder and could merit the death penalty. But I do believe that in the clinical practice of medicine, active euthanasia has a definite place. I also believe that we should not be afraid to discuss its place in the scheme of things and to explore the possibilities in this approach to the terminally ill.

I cannot accept the simple statement that a doctor does not have the right to take life; furthermore, I believe the greatest difficulty is to define life. I myself have defined it as joy in living. Given the absence of this quality, without hope of restitution, the request of the suffering person — if conscious and compos mentis — and the satisfaction of other criteria such as good faith on the part of those caring for the person and the completion of legal requirements, there is no ethical reason why active medical euthanasia may not be administered.

Indeed, I have always wondered at the kind of person who would mercifully end the life of a suffering animal, yet would hesitate to extend the same privilege to a fellow being. It may be that in all of us there lurks a sense of guilt — and what more guilt-making burden can we assume than that of responsibility for another's death?

The error, perhaps, is one of category — that of regarding squeamishness as mercy.

As a scientist and a humanitarian, I find society's attitude toward the different ways of causing the death of an individual both hypocritical and illogical. Consider that, for as long as man has inhabited the earth, he has accepted with few reservations the right to kill and be killed on the battlefield, even when this leads to not only his own but multiple deaths.

I have talked to legal, ethical and medical authorities in many parts of the world on the need for active euthanasia, the problems that would confront the doctor in such situations and the safeguards required. Again and again the same questions came up:

Who will decide when a life is to be terminated and how can mistakes be avoided?

Would doctors perhaps misuse the right to take life by getting rid of the people they do not like?

Would the medical profession not lose a lot of the trust that is placed in it if doctors were given the right to take a life?

Does a doctor have the right to play God?

Must God be the final arbiter on the taking of life?

If it is feared that a doctor is playing God when he terminates a life, it can just as readily be argued that he is playing the same role when he prolongs the life of a terminally-ill patient. And surely, when the terminally-ill person develops an intercurrent infection that will cause death if not treated, are we not also interfering with God's will by instituting treatment and preventing the patient from dying of the infection?

Generally, these same questions can be raised about war, capital punishment and abortion. I maintain that if doctors are given the right to practice active euthanasia, and all the necessary safeguards are developed, then most of these objections would fall away.

And at the risk of finding myself out on a theological limb, I say that if it is playing God to reduce human suffering, then I do not believe that the God of mercy and compassion would mind if we mere mortals play God under such circumstances. When we glibly bracket talk of terminating life with mention of the Deity, what in fact do we know of God's interpretation of life?

1150 words

Write your ending time here: _____

Subtract your starting time: _____

Total time: _____

Check the Rate Chart in the back of the book to find out how many words per minute you have read, and then record your score on the Progress Chart.

ANSWERS TO SKIMMING QUESTIONS

1. Your answer should be similar to the correct answer for question 2 in the Comprehension Check.

2. Write the answers to your skimming questions here.

    a. _____

    b. _____

    c. _____

19

Acting to End a Life
Is Sometimes Justified

COMPREHENSION CHECK
Circle the letter before the best answer to each question below. Don't look back at the article.

Subject and Main Idea

1. The subject of the article is
   a. medicine.
   b. murder.
   c. euthanasia.
   d. religion.

2. The main idea is that
   a. euthanasia should be allowed under some circumstances.
   b. passive euthanasia is ethical.
   c. the decision about euthanasia should belong to the doctor.
   d. only God should decide on the taking of a life.

Details

3. An example of passive euthanasia is
   a. giving the patient an overdose of drugs.
   b. giving the patient an injection that will kill him or her.
   c. leaving an overdose of drugs with the patient, in case the patient wants to kill himself or herself.
   d. stopping treatment of the patient.

4. Barnard defines life as
   a. having a heartbeat.
   b. having brainwaves.
   c. breathing.
   d. having joy in living.

5. Barnard states that euthanasia has become an increasing focus of debate because
   a. more doctors are quietly practicing it.
   b. it has caused a large number of malpractice suits.
   c. there have been medical breakthroughs that can prolong life artificially.
   d. famous doctors like Barnard have been arrested for practicing it.

6. To those who believe that God is against euthanasia, Barnard says that
   a. a merciful God would approve of it.
   b. prolonging life artificially is also playing God.
   c. we do not know how God interprets life.
   d. all of the above are true.

Inferences

7. Barnard seems to believe that doctors
   a. cannot prolong life.
   b. never practice euthanasia now.
   c. should accept some responsibility for their patients' lives.
   d. should prolong life, hoping for new medical breakthroughs for the terminally ill.

8. Barnard suggests that people who are against euthanasia are really
   a. ethical.
   b. cowardly.
   c. vicious.
   d. brave.

9. After reading the article, one might conclude that Barnard
   a. has practiced active euthanasia without admitting it.
   b. would not practice passive euthanasia even if it were legal.
   c. wouldn't practice active euthanasia in any situation.
   d. would practice active euthanasia if it were legal.

10. Barnard feels that the public
    a. is naive about euthanasia.
    b. believes in active euthanasia.
    c. is convinced that active euthanasia occurs constantly.
    d. should sign statements telling their doctors not to administer life-prolonging treatment in terminal cases.

QUESTIONS FOR ANALYSIS AND APPLICATION

1. Why is capital punishment considered more acceptable than euthanasia?

2. What safeguards should be developed to prevent doctors from misusing euthanasia if they ever are given the right to take life?

VOCABULARY IN CONTEXT
Multiple Choice
Circle the letter before the best definition of each underlined word or phrase.

1. Veterinarians have been practicing underline euthanasia on people's pets for many years.
   a. mercy killing   b. giving drug overdoses   c. torture
   d. murder

2. The salient feature of the blue whale is its enormous length, which can equal three Greyhound buses.
   a. trivial   b. striking   c. boring   d. secondary

3. Discussions about sex, politics, and religion can be relied on to elicit strong feelings.
   a. call forth   b. stop   c. calm down   d. strengthen

4. Several illnesses that were often terminal in the past, such as tuberculosis, diphtheria, and smallpox, are no longer serious threats.
   a. mild   b. contagious   c. serious   d. leading to death

5. The intervention of the United States in the Vietnam conflict offered no solution.
   a. interference   b. defense   c. bombing   d. absence

6. A plea of insanity will not stand up if the court has ruled the accused compos mentis.
   a. guilty   b. sane   c. innocent
   d. not aware of what he is doing

7. A baseball umpire is the arbiter in all close decisions during a game.
   a. villain   b. victim   c. judge   d. hero

8. Becoming a clergyman takes many years of theological study.
   a. medical   b. legal   c. religious   d. difficult

9. Used-car salespeople often appear glib in TV commercials.
   a. awkward   b. crooked   c. slick   d. sincere

10. Hirohito, emperor of Japan during World War II, was considered a deity by the people he ruled.
    a. holy man   b. dictator   c. war lord   d. god

Fill-in

Write the best word from this list in the blank in each sentence below:

intercede   welter   ultimate   refrain   restitution

squeamishness   humanitarian   hypocritical

compassion   bracketed

11. An example of a great _____ is Albert Schweitzer.

12. It would be _____ of a TV repairman to take money to fix your set when he knows it's beyond repair.

13. The _____ of outdated laws includes one that makes it illegal to hunt camels in Arizona.

14. People who _____ between a husband and wife who are arguing often lose the friendship of both.

15. The _____ in bad taste is wearing white socks with a black tuxedo.

16. A word's etymology is _____ in the dictionary.

17. There are people who believe that it is actually beneficial to

    _____ from eating for 24 hours every few months.

18. _____ is not a desirable quality in a doctor or nurse.

19. Having _____ for your fellow humans is good.

20. In some cities, when a minor crime has been committed, the criminal is permitted to make _____ to the victim rather than go to jail.

SKILLS EXERCISE:
CRITICAL READING
Argument and Support

*For explanation
see pp. 152–156*

Fill in the supporting statements for the following argument:

A. Humans have played God all along.

    1. _____

        a. Animals

        b. _____

        c. _____

        d. Abortion

    2. We prolong life artificially in terminally ill patients.

B. In the following exercise, fill in the main argument:

    _____

    _____

    1. "Life" is more than just keeping organs functioning.
    2. It's wrong to make people suffer if they're going to die anyway.
    3. People who are compos mentis should be allowed to decide to die if they're terminally ill.
    4. The God of mercy would support euthanasia for the terminally ill.

Judging Support: Fact Versus Opinion

Write *F* in the space before each statement of fact; write *O* if the statement is someone's opinion.

_____ 1. ". . . I gave instructions to the doctor attending my own mother in her last illness that she should receive no antibiotics nor be tube fed."

_____ 2. "He [Fletcher] listed eight levels of attitude and opinion on the human initiatives that can be exercised in the case of a patient dying of an incurable disease . . ."

_____ 3. ". . . In the clinical practice of medicine, active euthanasia has a definite place."

_____ 4. "I have never practiced active euthanasia, a deed that in my country is regarded as murder and could merit the death penalty."

_____ 5. ". . . There is no ethical reason why active medical euthanasia may not be administered."

_____ 6. ". . . I find society's attitude toward the different ways of causing the death of an individual both hypocritical and illogical."

_____ 7. "I have talked to legal, ethical, and medical authorities in many parts of the world on the need for active euthanasia . . ."

_____ 8. ". . . If doctors are given the right to practice active euthanasia, and all the necessary safeguards are developed, then most of the objections would fall away."

_____ 9. The God of mercy and compassion wouldn't mind if we reduced human suffering through euthanasia.

_____ 10. In passive euthanasia the doctor does not take the initiative in ending the patient's life.

Note: A Critical Reading exercise comparing Articles 19 and 20 appears following the exercises for Article 20.

20

In Crisis, She Rejected Plea to Expedite Dying

VOCABULARY PREVIEW

expedite (ek'spə dīt'):   to speed up or make easy

impulsive (im pul'siv):   (done) without conscious thought

solemn (säl'əm):   sacred; formal; serious

hypothetical (hī'pə thet'i k'l):   speculative; not based on actual events

obliged (ə blījd'):   compelled by moral, legal, or physical force

affirmative (ə fʉr'mə tiv):   positive; confirming

objets d'art (äb'zhā där'):   small objects of artistic value

subsequent (sub'si kwənt):   coming after; following

salutary (sal'yo͞o ter'ē):   beneficial; healthful

recoiling (ri koil'iŋ):   drawing back, as in fear

stalk (stôk):   to pursue (for example, game) secretly

prime (prīm):   first in rank or importance

transition (tran zish'ən):   state of passing from one condition or state to another

commonweal (käm'ən wēl):   public good; general welfare

---

fat, āpe, cär; ten, ēven; is, bīte; gō, hôrn, to͞ol, look; oil, out; up, fʉr; chin, she; thin, *then*; zh, leisure; ŋ, ring; ə for *a* in *ago;* ' as in *able* (ā'b'l)

SKILLS EXERCISE:
SKIMMING AND SCANNING

For explanation see pp. 157–158

A. *Skimming.* Take one minute to skim the following article. Run your eyes over the article to get a general idea of what it is about.

   1. After you have skimmed the article, write its main idea in your own words. _____

   _____

   Without looking back at the article, write three questions that you think will be answered by reading it.

   a. _____
   b. _____
   c. _____

B. *Scanning.* First, underline the key words in the following questions. Next, scan the article to find the answers. Quickly underline each answer and move to the next question. It should take you no more than three minutes to answer all of the questions. After you finish scanning for all ten of the answers, write them in the spaces below.

   1. When did the Ross family move to Chicago? _____

   2. In what city did Mrs. Kubler live? _____

   3. When Elisabeth arrived, she discovered her mother had just completed _____

   4. What did Elisabeth's mother want her to promise? _____

   5. How many times had Elisabeth seen her mother cry? _____

   6. Erich Fromm stated that there was no such thing as medical ethics, only _____

   7. What was Elisabeth able to promise her mother? _____

   8. After her stroke, how was Elisabeth's mother able to communicate? _____

   9. How many stages of dying are there? _____

   10. How long did Mrs. Kubler live after her stroke? _____

Now read the article. Write your starting time here: _____

20

In Crisis, She Rejected Plea to Expedite Dying

Derek Gill

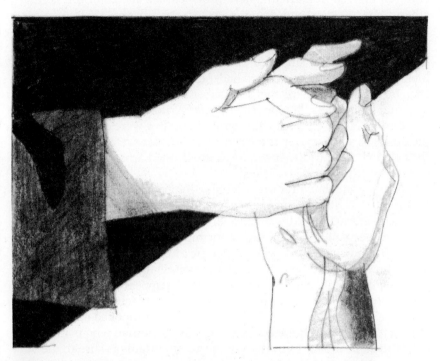

I N THE EARLY SUMMER OF 1967, Elisabeth and Manny Ross moved
for the fifth time. They now felt comfortably settled in Chicago
and, assuming they would be living and working there for the fore-
seeable future, they bought a home a few blocks away from the
house they had been renting.

Elisabeth and Manny had decided to postpone their annual summer
vacation and instead take a holiday at Christmas in order, as they had
just explained to their 7-year-old son, Kenneth, to give him and his little
sister, Barbara, "a real Swiss Christmas" with sleigh bells and festivals.

Suddenly, and apparently without stimulus or prompting, Elisabeth felt a deep and inexplicable concern about her mother's wellbeing. She turned to Manny and told him she had to fly to Switzerland immediately — tomorrow, if they could get plane reservations. She admitted that her impulsive decision sounded crazy, but there was some very important reason — a purpose she did not yet understand — why she should be with her mother as quickly as possible. A week later, she and the two children arrived in Zurich. There they boarded the train for Zermatt, where Mrs. Kubler and other members of Elisabeth's family were staying.

Zermatt was the ideal place for a restful vacation and for what Elisabeth called "a time for old-fashioned happiness." Mrs. Kubler looked in the pink of health and had, on the day the Ross family arrived, been on an eight-mile hike with Elisabeth's older brother, Ernst, and her fraternal triplet, Eva (her identical triplet, Erika, could not be there).

On the last evening at the resort where they were all staying, when the sun was setting over the peaks, Mrs. Kubler sat with Elisabeth on the balcony of her bedroom where Kenneth and Barbara, exhausted after the day's outing, were fast asleep.

Mother and daughter sat through a long silence and watched shadows move like ragged fingers across the green valleys far below. Then Mrs. Kubler turned to face Elisabeth and said, "I want your solemn promise that you'll do something for me. I want you to promise that, when I become incapable, when I become a human vegetable, you'll help me to die." She spoke with an uncharacteristic urgency.

Elisabeth was taken aback, both by the appeal and by its timing. She reacted not as an expert on dying, not as a teacher who instructed others to be alert for symbolic language, but as a shocked daughter. She replied too quickly, "What nonsense is this! A woman who is in her 70s and who can hike miles every day in the mountains is sure to die very suddenly. Mother, you're the last person to become a human vegetable."

Mrs. Kubler continued to speak as if she had not heard her. She again asked for a promise that, when she became incapable of caring for herself, Elisabeth would help her to die.

Elisabeth looked at her mother with astonishment and again protested that the question was purely hypothetical. In any case, she said firmly, she was totally opposed to mercy killing, if that was what her mother was talking about. In her opinion, no physician had the right to give a patient an overdose to relieve suffering. She could not promise her mother — or, for that matter, anyone else — to expedite dying. In the unlikely event that her mother did in fact become physically incapable, all that she could promise was that she would help her to live until she died.

Mrs. Kubler began to cry softly. It was only the second time in her life that Elisabeth had seen her mother shed tears.

Mrs. Kubler rose from her chair and went inside. For a while, Elisabeth sat alone and thought about her mother's request, her own response to it and her attitude toward euthanasia. It was tempting to avoid the issue. She remembered some lines of Erich Fromm, the psychiatrist-philosopher: "There is no such thing as medical ethics. There are only universal human ethics applied to specific human situations."

There were times, she was obliged to admit, when it was wrong to keep someone alive — but such a time would occur when a patient was clearly beyond medical help, when organs were kept functioning only with machines. So long as there was a meaningful life, so long as a patient could express and receive feelings, it had to be wrong to "play God" and decide arbitrarily whether a patient should live or die. Surely, though, it was not to answer this hypothetical question that she had changed the family's vacation plans and come to Switzerland.

Next day, when Mrs. Kubler accompanied Elisabeth and the children to the train station, both women were tense and uncomfortable. However, when the train came in, Elisabeth turned to her mother, hugged her and said, "All I can promise you is that I will do for you what I do for all my patients. I promise I will do my best to help you live until you die."

Mrs. Kubler appeared to understand now what Elisabeth was saying. She nodded, wiped her eyes, smiled and said, "Thank you."

Those were the last words Elisabeth heard her mother speak. Hardly had the family arrived back in Chicago when a cable came from Eva. It read, "Mother has had a massive stroke."

Three days later Elisabeth was back in Switzerland.

At the hospital Elisabeth found her mother unable to speak, unable to move anything except her eyelids and, very feebly, her left hand. It was obvious, however, from the expression in her eyes, that Mrs. Kubler understood what was said to her.

They devised a method of communicating. Her mother would use her eyelids and her slightly mobile left hand to indicate affirmative or negative answers to questions put to her. One blink of the eyelids or one squeeze of the hand would signify an affirmative and two blinks or two squeezes would mean a negative response.

Using this form of communication, Mrs. Kubler made it very clear that she did not want to remain in the hospital. Elisabeth confronted her mother with the impossibility of her returning home, where she would require round-the-clock nursing attention. It was Eva who came up with the solution.

She knew of an infirmary, more a rest home than a hospital, in Riehen, a few miles outside of Basel. Set in spacious well-tended grounds, it was run by a dedicated group of Protestant nuns.

Immediately after taking her mother to the infirmary, Elisabeth spent a couple of painful days quite alone at the Klosbachstrasse apartment. She sorted clothes, furniture and objets d'art; she took down pictures and curtains and labeled everything for subsequent distribution according to her mother's expressed wishes.

Elisabeth now believes that in closing down the family home in Zurich, she was given a new and important understanding about life and death. Life, she now sees, is a series of losses, and every loss is a "little death." In the hour or so before she finally left the home on Klosbachstrasse she had gone through the five identifiable stages of dying: denial, anger, bargaining, depression and acceptance.

Each "little death" — and this was one of hers — was a salutary and perhaps essential preparation for death itself. But every ending was also a new beginning.

Another lesson, long and difficult, now focused on the infirmary at Riehen. Mrs. Kubler, paralyzed and unable to speak, held on to life — not just for the few weeks that Elisabeth and her sisters had anticipated, not for months, but for four years. She had clearly foreseen the manner of her dying and, recoiling at the prospect, had pleaded with Elisabeth for mercy killing.

For Elisabeth, the issue of euthanasia was no longer a hypothetical one, no longer an intellectual debating point, but a question of the heart and conscience. There were times when she was ready to change her views, moments when she wondered agonizingly whether she should have given her mother the promise she had asked for; but these doubts stalked her only when she was far away from Switzerland.

For when she was with her mother, her conviction remained that neither she nor anyone else had the right to take the life of someone who could still express and receive feelings. Mrs. Kubler was not a human vegetable. She needed no machines to keep her heart beating or her lungs breathing.

Today, Elisabeth Kubler-Ross sees her prime task as helping people to live a full life without being burdened by their "negativities," helping people to take care of "unfinished business" before they die.

She claims that the evidence of patients who have had near-death encounters with spiritual guides and relatives who have predeceased them supports her belief that physical existence — with all its pain, stress, struggle and challenge — is, in effect, "a learning experience and a growth period" for an ongoing journey.

She is convinced that the only thing of value that man carries with him through the "transition" is the record of how much he contributed to the commonweal — "how much he cared and how much he loved."

1450 words

Write your ending time here: _____

Subtract your starting time: _____

Total time: _____

Check the Rate Chart in the back of the book to find out how many words per minute you have read, and then record your score on the Progress Chart.

ANSWERS TO SKIMMING QUESTIONS

1. Your answer should be similar to the correct answer for question 2 in the Comprehension Check.

2. Write the answers to your skimming questions here.

    a. _____

    b. _____

    c. _____

20

In Crisis, She Rejected Plea
to Expedite Dying

COMPREHENSION CHECK
Circle the letter before the best answer to each question below. Don't look back at the article.

Subject and Main Idea
1. The subject of the article is
   a. Elisabeth Kubler-Ross's life.
   b. Kubler-Ross's attitude toward euthanasia.
   c. the reasons that euthanasia is wrong.
   d. dealing with death.

2. The main idea is that
   a. euthanasia is always bad.
   b. euthanasia is bad unless the patient is a "vegetable."
   c. euthanasia is a sin against God.
   d. euthanasia is acceptable if the patient wants to die.

Details
3. Kubler-Ross went to Switzerland in early summer because
   a. her mother had sent a telegram saying she was ill.
   b. her mother hadn't seen her grandchildren in years.
   c. it was a planned vacation.
   d. she was concerned about her mother.

4. When Kubler-Ross arrived in Switzerland, she found that her mother was
   a. dying.
   b. dead.
   c. in fine health.
   d. depressed.

5. Closing down the family home made Kubler-Ross
   a. reconsider her mother's request.
   b. deny that her mother was dying.
   c. afraid of death.
   d. understand life and death better.

6. After Mrs. Kubler had her stroke, she could
   a. use sign language with her hands.
   b. talk with great difficulty.
   c. not communicate at all.
   d. blink her eyes and barely use her left hand.

Inferences

7. The article implies that Kubler-Ross
   a. is skeptical of extrasensory perception.
   b. believes in extrasensory perception.
   c. went to a psychic about her mother.
   d. saw a ghost.

8. Mrs. Kubler's relationship with Elisabeth seemed
   a. impersonal and cold.
   b. warm and close.
   c. not so warm as with her other daughters.
   d. abnormal for a mother and daughter.

9. The last time Kubler-Ross saw her mother before her mother's stroke she thought
   a. they were arguing.
   b. they parted on good terms.
   c. her mother was becoming senile.
   d. her mother was in poor health.

10. If Kubler-Ross were to develop an illness similar to her mother's, she would probably
    a. request euthanasia.
    b. change her mind about euthanasia.
    c. see her illness as a valuable experience.
    d. go to Switzerland, where euthanasia is legal.

QUESTIONS FOR ANALYSIS AND APPLICATION

1. Describe two incidents that imply Kubler-Ross believes in the supernatural.

2. What evidence does the article provide that Kubler-Ross thinks suffering is good for people?

VOCABULARY IN CONTEXT
Multiple Choice
Circle the letter before the best definition of each underlined word.

1. To underline{expedite} matters in criminal cases, the police look for
   eyewitnesses.
   a. speed up   b. slow down   c. confuse   d. clarify

2. No matter what happens, an undertaker should always maintain a
   underline{solemn} look.
   a. silly   b. frightened   c. sleepy   d. serious

3. A period of peace is always underline{subsequent to} a period of conflict.
   a. before   b. after   c. paralleled by   d. necessary to

4. A proper diet is underline{salutary}.
   a. healthful   b. unhealthy   c. boring   d. delicious

5. French poodles were once used to underline{stalk} wild birds.
   a. eat   b. frighten   c. hunt   d. hatch

6. Even though appearance is important, the underline{prime} concern of a chef
   is the way the food tastes.
   a. irrelevant   b. minor   c. first   d. last

7. The reduction of crime is a major factor affecting the
   underline{commonweal}.
   a. public welfare   b. average income
   c. history of the United States   d. future

Fill-in
Write in the best word from this list in the blank in each sentence
below:

impulsive   hypothetical   obliged   affirmative

objets d'art   recoiling   transition

8. _____ actions can often lead to long
   periods of regret.

9. _____ when someone startles you is a
   natural defense mechanism.

10. Priceless _____ are to be found in mu-
    seums around the world.

11. Before you give an _____ answer to a
    request for money, be sure you know all the facts.

12. The earth may be in _____ between two ice ages, according to some scientists.

13. A _____ point has no proof even though it may be true.

14. You may feel _____ to return it when somebody does you a favor.

SKILLS EXERCISE:
CRITICAL READING
Argument and Support

For explanation see pp. 152–156

A. Fill in the main argument supported by the statements below:

_____

_____

1. No one has the right to take the life of someone who can still express and receive feelings.
2. For people who are not vegetables, dying is a growth experience.
3. Watching a loved one die is a growth experience for the relatives and helps prepare them for their own deaths.

B. Fill in the supporting details for this argument: Mrs. Kubler was not a vegetable.

1. _____

2. _____

Judging Support: Fact Versus Opinion

Write *F* in the space before each statement of fact; write *O* if the statement is someone's opinion.

_____ 1. "There were times . . . when it was wrong to keep someone alive . . ."

_____ 2. "Three days later Elisabeth was back in Switzerland."

_____ 3. "Each 'little death' . . . was a salutary and perhaps essential preparation for death itself."

_____ 4. "They devised a method of communicating."

_____ 5. ". . . Physical existence . . . is . . . 'a learning experience and a growth period' for an ongoing journey."

_____ 6. ". . . The only thing of value that man carries with him through the 'transition' is the record of how much he contributed to the commonweal . . ."

_____ 7. "She needed no machines to keep her heart beating or her lungs breathing."

_____ 8. "She had clearly foreseen the manner of her dying . . ."

_____ 9. "So long as there was a meaningful life, so long as a patient could express and receive feelings, it had to be wrong to 'play God' and decide arbitrarily whether a patient should live or die."

_____ 10. "Those were the last words Elisabeth heard her mother speak."

COMPARISON OF ARTICLES 19 AND 20

SKILLS EXERCISE:
CRITICAL READING
Judging Support: Evaluating Evidence

| For explanation see pp. 155–156 |

Critical Judgments
Euthanasia ultimately involves a person's own moral sense. The authors' views can be summed up in the following quotations:

Barnard: ". . . I do believe that in the clinical practice of medicine, active euthanasia has a definite place."

Kubler-Ross: ". . . her conviction remained that neither she nor anyone else had the right to take the life of someone who could still express and receive feelings."

Under Dr. Barnard's and Dr. Kubler-Ross's names, write *yes* or *no* if you think they would agree or disagree with the decision in each case. Be prepared to support your decision with quotes from the articles. The third column is for you to write *yes* or *no* according to your own beliefs about euthanasia in each situation.

Situations	Barnard	Kubler-Ross	You
1. Patient is in extreme agony. Condition is terminal,but could drag on for months longer, painfully and very expensively. Patient begs to die and family agrees. Dr. gives patient a lethal overdose.	_____	_____	_____

Situations	Barnard	Kubler-Ross	You

2. Patient is a baby born missing a large part of her brain. She is being kept alive on machines; if the machines were turned off, she would slowly, and maybe painfully, die. Other babies need transplants of organs such as heart, lungs, kidneys, and liver in order to survive. These organs are healthy in our patient so long as the machine is on. If the machine were turned off so she could die, the organs would become unusable. Parents are eager to have her organs removed before her death so her death will give life to others rather than being completely meaningless. Dr. removes the organs while she is alive, causing the patient's death. _____ _____ _____

3. A soldier is fighting in a jungle area. His legs have been blown off and he is bleeding to death. There are no medics for miles around, no blood, no bandages, no painkillers. He screams and begs his buddy to put an end to his agony. His buddy shoots him in the head. _____ _____ _____

Judging Support: Evaluating Author's Credibility
Background and Reputation

When judging the credibility of a speaker or writer it is valuable to know the background of the person. At the beginning of some of the articles in this book, there is a short paragraph about the writer. For example, in Article 1, you find that Tony Randall is not only an actor; he is also a member of the *American Heritage Dictionary* usage panel. The latter fact makes him more an authority on vocabulary, although he is famous as an actor. Here are some facts about Dr. Christiaan Barnard and Dr. Elisabeth Kubler-Ross, whose opinions are key to the discussion of euthanasia in Articles 19 and 20.[1]

---

[1] The information on Christiaan Barnard is excerpted from *Current Biography Yearbook, 1968.* (New York: The H. W. Wilson Company, 1969), pp. 45–48. The information on Elisabeth Kubler-Ross is excerpted from *Current Biography Yearbook, 1980.* (New York: The H. W. Wilson Company, 1981), pp. 191–194.

A. Use this scale to rate each fact on whether it increases or decreases the person's credibility.

Greatly increases	Increases	Neither increases nor decreases	Decreases	Greatly decreases
1	2	3	4	5

Dr. Christiaan Barnard

_____ 1. Christiaan Barnard was born in 1923 and was raised in Cape Town, South Africa.

_____ 2. He conducted the first successful human heart transplant operation in medical history in December 1967.

_____ 3. Louis Washkansky, the first transplant recipient, died eighteen days after the transplant.

_____ 4. He teaches surgery at University of Cape Town Medical School and directs surgical research at the school's Groote Schuur Hospital.

_____ 5. His father was a Dutch Reformed minister.

_____ 6. Barnard and his three brothers grew up in conditions bordering on poverty.

_____ 7. He received his MD degree in 1953.

_____ 8. He did all his early research on animals.

_____ 9. He came to the United States and studied at the University of Minnesota Medical School under the renowned surgeon Dr. Owen H. Wangensteen.

_____ 10. At first he supported himself by mowing lawns, washing cars, and doing other odd jobs.

_____ 11. He was able to complete all the work for a PhD degree within two years.

_____ 12. In 1960 he attracted international attention in scientific circles by transplanting a second head onto a dog.

_____ 13. In the early 1970s, he retired from surgery because of severe arthritis in his hands.

_____ 14. He has two daughters.

_____ 15. His temper can be short and sharp.

Elisabeth Kubler-Ross

_____ 1. Elisabeth Kubler-Ross was born on July 8, 1926, in Zurich, Switzerland.

_____ 2. She weighed barely two pounds at birth.

_____ 3. During her own critical illness from pneumonia at the age of five, Elisabeth Kubler was taken to a children's hospital and kept in isolation for weeks.

_____ 4. Before going to medical school she worked as a cook, a mason, and a roofer.

_____ 5. She is a psychiatrist.

_____ 6. She is known for her pioneering work in counseling terminally ill patients.

_____ 7. She was the first doctor to describe the stages a terminally ill patient goes through: denial, anger, bargaining, acceptance.

_____ 8. Her books have brought generous praise from medical colleagues and laypeople and earned her a reputation as a scientist of courage and compassion.

_____ 9. Her later research has been directed toward verifying the existence of life after death.

_____ 10. She has said, "I know for a fact that there is life after death."

_____ 11. In recent years she has met with growing skepticism from the medical community.

_____ 12. She obtained her MD degree in 1957.

_____ 13. She became an assistant professor of psychiatry at the University of Chicago Medical School.

_____ 14. In 1973, she became the medical director of Family Services and Mental Health Center of South Cook County, Chicago Heights.

_____ 15. She has a son, Kenneth Lawrence, and a daughter, Barbara Lee.

B. Evaluating the Results

1. The arguments by Barnard and Kubler-Ross were both based on each author's opinions rather than on facts. Review Part A above and, based on the items you thought increased credibility (rated 1 or 2) or decreased credibility (rated 4 or 5), make a list of what kinds of information are important to know about the author's background and reputation when judging opinion.
2. When is age important?
3. In what kinds of cases does place of birth become important?
4. Does it make a difference that Barnard is a surgeon and Kubler-Ross is a psychiatrist?

What facts in Barnard's and Kubler-Ross's lives might have influenced their strong feelings about euthanasia?

Application of Critical Skills
Practice your ability to read critically by comparing the two articles on euthanasia.

1. Compare Barnard's and Kubler-Ross's definitions of life. How are they the same? How are they different?
2. Compare and contrast Barnard's and Kubler-Ross's implied attitudes about religion.
3. Which doctor allows the patient more freedom of choice? Which reserves the decision for himself or herself?
4. Do both doctors believe in an afterlife? How do you know?
5. Which type of euthanasia described in the Barnard article would Kubler-Ross be willing to practice? Support your argument.
6. Under what circumstances might you request euthanasia for yourself or for loved ones?

UNIT III

READING FOR STUDY

One reason students often have trouble remembering textbook information for tests is that they are reading the material the wrong way. If your purpose is to thoroughly comprehend and remember complex information, you cannot use the same reading techniques that you would use to read a popular magazine for relaxation. Special techniques for study reading must be used. Four such techniques are described below: SQ3R, outlining, mapping, and summarizing. All four techniques have one major feature in common: They all require you to select what you want to remember. This selection serves two purposes. First, it limits the amount you will have to memorize to what is really essential. Second, it prevents the aimless reading and lack of concentration that students complain of when they say they have "read" five pages and have no idea what was written on them.

SQ3R
SQ3R is especially useful as a study method in courses that require you to memorize a lot of detail, as many science courses do, for example. Here is an article that describes the method.

SQ3R*

Janet Maker and Minnette Lenier

The main difference between good students and poor students is the way they study. Poor students read their textbooks, underline, and hope that the significant points stick in their memories. Good students use a study system. A study system helps you choose the key ideas that are likely to be on a test, and it gives you a way to memorize them.

---

*Based on Francis P. Robinson, *Effective Study*, 4th ed. (New York, Harper & Row, 1970). From Minnette Lenier and Janet Maker, *College Reading, Book I*, 3rd ed. (Belmont, Calif.: Wadsworth Publishing Co., 1991), pp. 135–137.

There are many study systems. Some students outline chapters and memorize their outlines. Some students make chapter summaries. But the most efficient study system of all is SQ3R, which stands for Survey, Question, Read, Recite, and Review. SQ3R was designed for textbook reading, and it is guaranteed to increase your comprehension, memory, and speed.

Survey

Early in the academic term, you should survey each textbook before you begin to read it. First, survey the front matter (the title, the author, the date of publication, the table of contents, and the preface and/or the introduction). Second, survey the back matter (the index, the glossary, and the appendixes). Then thumb through the book, checking the organization within the chapters. Note whether there are chapter outlines, summaries, review questions, pictures, diagrams, and charts. This type of survey gives you an idea of the subjects in the book and the way they are organized. It also lets you know whether there are any study aids in the book.

When a chapter in the book is assigned to you, take a minute or two to survey it. Read the chapter outline (if there is one), the title, and all the headings and subheadings. Look at the pictures and diagrams and read the summary and review questions (if there are any). Surveying gives you a quick overview of all the main ideas, and it aids your comprehension.

Question

If the chapter is long, break it down into sections for the Question, Read, and Recite steps. First, using the headings you have surveyed, ask yourself questions about what you will be reading. Questioning gives direction to your reading, and it keeps you actively involved and prevents your mind from wandering.

Read

Now read the same section. Look for answers to your questions and note anything else that you think is important. During this step, don't try to memorize or underline — just try to comprehend. If there is anything you don't understand, write it down so you can ask about it in class or during the instructor's office hours.

Underlining   Don't underline until after you have finished reading. That way you can pick out the main ideas and the important details.

If you underline while you are reading, you will usually underline too much or not enough.

After you have finished reading, look back at what you have read. Underline only the material that you think is necessary to memorize for an exam. Try to underline as little as possible. Underline key words and phrases rather than whole sentences.

Marginal Notes   When you have finished underlining, write a note in the margin that you can use to test whether you remember what you have underlined. Don't write a summary. Write something you can use as a question. Look at this example.

> Human cells reproduce in two ways: *mitosis* and *meiosis*. *Mitosis*
> Mitosis is the process by which a cell and its twenty-three   *vs.*
> pairs of chromosomes splits into two identical cells. Each *Meiosis*
> new cell bears twenty-three identical pairs of chromo-
> somes. Body cells reproduce this way, so every cell in your
> body has the same genetic structure. Meiosis, however, is
> the process by which a cell splits into cells that are not
> identical. Sex cells reproduce this way, giving rise to cells
> that do not contain twenty-three *pairs* of chromosomes
> but instead contain twenty-three *single* chromosomes.

Notice that the marginal notes do not define the terms or discuss the differences between them. They merely let you test your memory of the terms.

Recite

After you have read and marked a section of a chapter, you can use the marginal notes to memorize the material. Cover up the page. Look at the notes in the margin to see whether you can remember what you underlined. For example, use the marginal note mitosis vs. meiosis to test your memory of the two terms. Uncover the page and check yourself. If you made any mistakes, repeat the process until you get the terms right. If you can't remember them now, you won't remember them for a test.

Repeat the Question, Read, and Recite steps for each section of the chapter until you reach the end.

Review

When you have finished a chapter, retest yourself on the marginal notes for the whole chapter. If there are any study questions, answer them. Check your answers by looking back at the chapter. Review again one week later, and then review occasionally throughout the term. That way you won't have to cram for the final exam.

The most efficient way of preparing for the Recite and Review steps is to write notes in the textbook margin to test your memory of what you underlined. You should be able to convert your notes into questions; therefore a summary is not appropriate. Here is the SQ3R article with sample underlining and marginal notes. Notice that the marginal notes do not summarize the five steps; they merely provide a basis for testing your memory of them.

SQ3R

good vs. poor students

The main difference between good students and poor students is the way they study. Poor students read their textbooks, underline, and hope that the significant points stick in their memories. Good students use a study system. A study system helps you choose the key ideas that are likely to be on a test, and it gives you a way to memorize them.

5 steps in SQ3R

advantages of SQ3R

There are many study systems. Some students outline chapters and memorize their outlines. Some students make chapter summaries. But the most efficient study system of all is SQ3R, which stands for Survey, Question, Read, Recite, and Review. SQ3R was designed for textbook reading, and it is guaranteed to increase your comprehension, memory, and speed.

Survey

3 steps to surveying a textbook

Early in the academic term, you should survey each textbook before you begin to read it. First, survey the front matter (the title, the author, the date of publication, the table of contents, and the preface and/or the introduction). Second, survey the back matter (the index, the glossary, and the appendixes). Then thumb through the book, checking the organization within the chapters. Note whether there are chapter outlines, summaries, review questions, pictures, diagrams, and charts. This type of survey gives you an idea of the subjects in the book and the way they are organized. It also lets you know whether there are any study aids in the book.

6 steps in surveying a chapter

When a chapter in the book is assigned to you, take a minute or two to survey it. Read the chapter outline (if there is one), the title, and all the headings and subheadings. Look at the pictures and diagrams and read the summary and review questions (if there are any). Surveying gives you a quick overview of all the main ideas, and it aids your comprehension.

Question

If the chapter is long, break it down into sections for the Question, Read, and Recite steps. First, using the headings you have surveyed, ask yourself questions about what you will be reading. Questioning gives direction to your reading, and it keeps you actively involved and prevents your mind from wandering.

how to question

Read

Now read the same section. Look for answers to your questions and note anything else that you think is important. During this step, don't try to memorize or underline — just try to comprehend. If there is anything you don't understand, write it down so you can ask about it in class or during the instructor's office hours.

3 parts of Read step

How to Read

Underlining   Don't underline until after you have finished reading. That way you can pick out the main ideas and the important details. If you underline while you are reading, you will usually underline too much or not enough.

After you have finished reading, look back at what you have read. Underline only the material that you think is necessary to memorize for an exam. Try to underline as little as possible. Underline key words and phrases rather than whole sentences.

What to underline

Marginal Notes   When you have finished underlining, write a note in the margin that you can use to test whether you remember what you have underlined. Don't write a summary. Write something you can use as a question. Look at this example.

What to write

> Human cells reproduce in two ways: *mitosis* and *meiosis*. Mitosis is the process by which a cell and its twenty-three pairs of chromosomes splits into two identical cells. Each new cell bears twenty-three identical pairs of chromosomes. Body cells reproduce this way, so every cell in your body has the same genetic structure. Meiosis, however, is the process by which a cell splits into cells that are not identical. Sex cells reproduce this way, giving rise to cells that do not contain twenty-three *pairs* of chromosomes but instead contain twenty-three *single* chromosomes.

Mitosis vs Meiosis

Notice that the marginal notes do not define the terms or discuss the differences between them. They merely let you test your memory of the terms.

Recite

how to recite

After you have read and marked a section of a chapter, you can use the marginal notes to memorize the material. Cover up the page. Look at the notes in the margin to see whether you can remember what you underlined. For example, use the marginal note mitosis vs. meiosis to test your memory of the two terms. Uncover the page and check yourself. If you made any mistakes, repeat the process until you get the terms right. If you can't remember them now, you won't remember them for a test.

Repeat the Question, Read, and Recite steps for each section of the chapter until you reach the end.

Review

how and when to review

When you have finished a chapter, retest yourself on the marginal notes for the whole chapter. If there are any study questions, answer them. Check your answers by looking back at the chapter. Review again one week later, and then review occasionally throughout the term. That way you won't have to cram for the final exam.

OUTLINING

Some people don't like to mark up their textbooks, so they may wish to use outlining instead of SQ3R. Outlining means organizing ideas in a visual form so that you can easily see the relationships between them. This makes the ideas easier to remember. Since virtually all textbook authors write from an outline, nearly all textbooks are very easy to outline. Compared to SQ3R, outlining is slower, but it can also be effective. Here is an outline of the article on SQ3R.

SQ3R

I. Most efficient study system
  A. Designed for textbook reading
  B. Increases comprehension, memory, and speed
II. Steps
  A. Survey
    1. Textbook
      a. Front matter
        (1) Title
        (2) Author
        (3) Date of publication

(4) Table of contents
(5) Preface and/or introduction
   b. Back matter
      (1) Index
      (2) Glossary
      (3) Appendixes
   c. Organization within chapters
  2. Each chapter
   a. Outline
   b. Title
   c. Headings and subheadings
   d. Pictures and diagrams
   e. Summary and review questions
B. Question
  1. Break chapters into subsections for Q, R, R
  2. Ask questions about headings
C. Read
  1. Find answers to questions and anything else important
  2. Don't memorize or underline until after
  3. Note anything you don't understand
  4. Underline
   a. After reading
   b. Only what is necessary: key words and phrases
  5. Make marginal notes
   a. To test memory
   b. Not summaries
D. Recite
  1. Use marginal notes to self-test
  2. Repeat until correct
  3. Repeat Q, R, R for each section
E. Review
  1. Retest on marginal notes for whole chapter
  2. Answer study questions and check answers
  3. Review one week later
  4. Review throughout the term

MAPPING

Mapping is a method of notemaking that some people prefer to outlining. Its supporters claim that it takes visual organization one step further than outlining does, providing a greater foothold for memory.

You should first survey the chapter as in SQ3R, then identify the main idea or topic. (This is often the title of the chapter.) This topic should be written toward the center of a piece of paper, with a shape, such as a circle, drawn around it.

The second step in making a study map can also be accomplished after the chapter survey. This step involves identifying the principal subdivisions of the topic. In a textbook, these usually correspond to headings. There should be no more than about seven of these, or the map will become too complicated. These secondary topics should be drawn on the map, working outward from the main topic near the center.

Before filling in the smaller details on the map, you should read the chapter as you would if you were using SQ3R. Then you should fill in the minor details, still working outward.

A drawback of mapping is that a map cannot hold as many details as marginal notes or an outline can. For example, in mapping the discussion of SQ3R on a page the size of this book, we would not comfortably be able to go beyond the third level on the outline. (Please refer to the outline in the section on outlining earlier in this chapter.) The title of the outline appears in the center circle on the map. The two Roman numeral headings appear on the map in squares. The capital letter headings appear on the map as triangles.

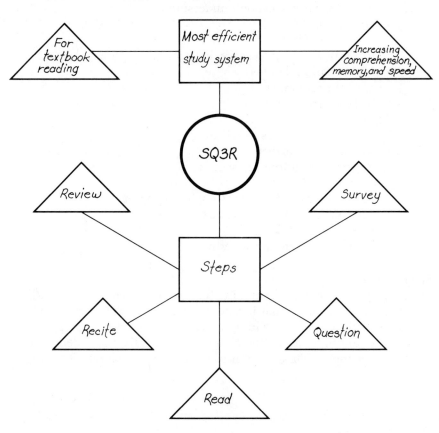

The final step is to memorize the map. Since nearly all maps look different, especially if you put different ideas in different colors, they are said to be easier to memorize than outlines, which tend to look alike.

SUMMARIZING

Summarizing allows you to put ideas "in a nutshell," making them easier to memorize. It is most useful when you have to learn only the main ideas rather than a lot of detail. You can easily summarize by writing out in complete sentences the same topics you would have used for marginal notes in SQ3R or as topics on an outline or a map. Here is a summary of the discussion of SQ3R.

SQ3R

SQ3R is the most efficient of study systems. It is designed for textbook reading and will increase comprehension, memory, and speed. It has five steps: Survey, Question, Read, Recite, and Review. The Survey step should be done on whole textbooks: front matter (title, author, date of publication, table of contents, preface and/or introduction), back matter (index, glossary, appendixes), and chapter organization. It should also be done on individual chapters, with close attention paid to chapter outlines, headings, pictures and diagrams, summary, and review questions. The Question step, along with the Read and Recite steps, should be done on only one section of a chapter at a time if the chapter is long. You should convert the headings into questions. In the Read step, you look for the answers to your questions and other important information, noting anything you don't understand. Underlining comes after the reading. Underline only what is necessary: key words and phrases. Marginal notes are used to test memory in the Recite step, so they should not be summaries. In the Recite step, you use the marginal notes to test your memory, repeating the self-testing until your answers are correct. The Question, Read, and Recite steps are repeated for each section of the chapter. The Review step involves retesting yourself on the whole chapter and answering any study questions. The Review step should be repeated one week later and then occasionally throughout the term.

21

Music Formats

VOCABULARY PREVIEW

constraint (kən strānt'):   confinement; restriction

innovative (in'ə vā'tiv):   new; changed, inventive

contended (kən tend'id):   argued; asserted

irrepressible (ir'i pres'ə b'l):   unstoppable; unrestrainable

esoteric (es'ə ter'ik):   meant for or understood by only a chosen few

counterculture (koun'tər kul'chər):   the culture of those young people whose life style is opposed to the prevailing culture

predominantly (pri däm'ə nənt lē):   largely; most frequently

alienating (āl'y ən āt' iŋ):   making unfriendly; causing a feeling of not belonging

raucous (rô'kəs):   loud and rowdy

closed-circuit (klōzd' sʉr'kit):   a system for broadcasting by cable only to receivers connected in the circuit

ethnic (eth'nik):   having to do with cultural or racial groups

subsidized (sub'sə dīzd):   granted or given money for support

discern (di sʉrn'):   recognize clearly; perceive

capitalizes (kap'ət 'l īz'əz):   uses to one's advantage (with *on*)

fat, āpe, cär; ten, ēven; is, bīte; gō, hôrn, to͞ol, look; oil, out; up, fʉr; chin, she; thin, *th*en; zh, leisure; ŋ, ring; ə for *a* in *ago;* ' as in *able* (ā'b'l)

**SKILLS EXERCISE:
SQ3R**

For explanation
see pp. 291–296

A. *Survey.* Survey the following article by reading the author's name, the title, the headings, and the first sentence of every paragraph. This should take no longer than thirty seconds. (The marginal notes are for a later exercise, so you can ignore them at this time.)

B. *Question.* Without looking back at the article, write three questions that you think will be answered by reading it.

    1. _____

    2. _____

    3. _____

C. *Read.* Now read the article. Write your starting time here: _____

21

Music Formats

Edward Jay Whetmore

LTHOUGH NO TWO RADIO STATIONS are exactly alike, a number of basic formulas exist. These formulas, or *formats*, involve a specific blend of certain types of music and talk designed to attract the largest possible audience to the station. Radio formats are not permanent things but are constantly shifting as audience needs evolve.

1. formats : def.

Because of the constraints on its programming, commercial radio is seldom at the forefront of musical trends. It always takes some time for new styles to catch on with the mass audience. When they do, you can be sure some innovative radio programmers somewhere will find a way to fit them into current programming. For example, disco music was quite popular in the mid-1970s, but it took several years before disco formats began to appear. Ironically, by the time "all-disco" radio had gotten under way, the disco craze had cooled. Today only a handful of disco stations are left.

2. new formats in comm. radio

A more current example is punk and new-wave music. Punk pioneers like the Sex Pistols and the Ramones were played little, if at all, by established rock stations in the mid- and late 1970s. In fact, some resistance to the "new music" in mainstream rock formats remains.

Occasionally, a commercial station will follow the lead of a college station. KUSF-FM, the station licensed to the University of San Francisco, offered punk and new-wave music in the late 1970s. By 1982, a new-wave format had emerged along with a large and loyal audience. Finally the city's commercial KQAK adopted a similar format, and soon several other commercial rock stations began adding more new music to their playlists. However, KQAK ultimately failed, as did many commercial "new music" format stations across the coun-

3. College station's influence on comm. radio

303

try. Nevertheless, the tremendous success of rock videos — coupled with increased record sales by new-wave groups (such as the Clash, whose *Combat Rock* was one of the best-selling albums of 1983) — have forced virtually all rock stations to finally respond to obvious shifts in the public's musical tastes and include some new wave on their playlists.

The basic formats of radio cover a wide spectrum of listener needs and tastes. Some, like classical, are tried and true and have been around since the beginning of broadcasting. Others, like new age, are relatively recent and experimental. In each case, the goal is to get and hold as many listeners as possible, particularly those with desirable demographics, or audience characteristics. Contemporary hit radio (CHR), album-oriented rock, middle of the road, adult contemporary, urban contemporary, country and western, and "beautiful music" are some formats reflecting radio trends of the 1980s.

4. *goal of formats*

CHR: CONTEMPORARY HIT RADIO

5. *CHR history*

Hot hits, CHR, Top 40 — by any name this jukebox method of radio programming has seen its ups and downs over the years. Top 40, as it was called in the beginning, reigned supreme on the airwaves from the mid-1950s until the emergence of album-oriented rock in the early 1970s. It appeared that Top 40 would die with the decrease in AM listeners in the 1970s, but a new, less cluttered version appeared on FM in the early 1980s. Dubbed CHR or hot hits, this "new" format became the rage on the FM dial and by the mid-1980s was enjoying healthy ratings in New York (WPLJ), Los Angeles (KIIS), Chicago (WLS), and many other markets.

The Top 40 genre spawned some giants. Bill Drake's success came in the early 1960s with KHJ, a Los Angeles Top 40 station. While sitting by his pool at Malibu Beach, he picked the songs that were to be played on his station. His method was simple: Play only the very top singles and play them more often than anyone else.

Another giant was Casey Kasem, who helped form Watermark Productions to begin his syndicated *American Top 40*. Kasem got his hits from the number one authority in the industry, *Billboard* magazine. Every week he counted 'em down in order for thousands of

listeners in hundreds of cities from New York to New-
berg, Oregon. Kasem's show was also heard in Europe
and Asia. His trademark was airing little-known facts
about the group or star:

> A certain singer sold his guitar and then decided he had
> to get it back and spent three weeks wandering around
> the streets of Columbus, Ohio, until one day, tired and
> discouraged, he stopped in Winchell's to have a dough-
> nut and there, lo and behold, was the man to whom he
> had sold it! He went on to form a new singing group and
> this week they have the number one song on *American
> Top 40*. Who is it? . . . Well, we'll find out right after this
> message. . . .

ALBUM-ORIENTED ROCK
Album-oriented rock emerged in the late 1960s when it
became evident that a growing number of rock enthusi-
asts were tired of Top 40's limitations. Rebellious deejays contended that innovative rock music was not
getting on the air because songs were often too long or
too controversial to fit into the tight Top 40 format.

6. *AOR history*

The founding father of AOR is generally acknowl-
edged to be Tom "Big Daddy" Donahue, a dissatisfied
Top 40 deejay who left a successful job at San Francisco's
KYA to start a new kind of radio, first at that city's
KMPX-FM and later at KSAN-FM. Donahue and his irrepressible deejays would play anything on the air that
struck their fancy. In the early days, it was not unusual
to hear a 15-minute live recording of the Grateful Dead
sandwiched between an esoteric sitar piece by Ravi
Shankar and a song by the Jefferson Airplane, praising
the merits of an illegal drug. Because the music and the
deejays' "rap" often centered on counterculture themes,
the format was initially dubbed "underground radio."

Most stations using this format were found on the
FM dial. Also called "progressive" radio for a time, the
form evolved into AOR in the 1970s. Many AOR stations
still feature heavy-duty rock, but as the counterculture
aged, their musical tastes mellowed. Thus "mellow
rock," a derivative of AOR, began making inroads in the
mid-1970s. Mellow-rock stations feature music from the
softer side of the rock spectrum by artists like Lionel
Richie, Dan Fogelberg, the Beatles, James Taylor, and
Carly Simon.

7. *mellow rock*

URBAN CONTEMPORARY

8. urban
    contemp.

In the early 1980s the term *urban contemporary* became commonplace in many markets around the country. The format is often found on CHR-type stations on the AM dial that program a large amount of dance music and upbeat hits to appeal to the black and "inner-city" audience. Often this audience is heavily populated with teens and young adults.

Many urban contemporary formats evolved from the "soul" stations of the 1960s, which appealed predominantly to the black audience, though they were often owned and listened to by nonblacks. San Francisco's KSOL is so successful with urban contemporary that it is now the city's top-rated music station, and there are numerous examples on the East Coast as well. Groups like Run-DMC currently dominate their playlists.

"Urbancontemp" is also responsible for introducing rap music into the popular music mainstream. From Tone Loc's humorous accounts of the dating scene to 2 Live Crew's sexually explicit lyrics, rap is hotter than ever. In the 1950s black music was instrumental in forging what was to become rock and roll. Now, a radio format aimed primarily at the black audience is once again on the cutting edge of what rock and roll is all about.

MIDDLE OF THE ROAD

9. MOR

MOR radio began as "chicken rock" in the 1950s. Stations afraid of playing the hard-driving sounds of upstarts like Elvis Presley would lean toward the softer love ballads of contemporary artists and blend them with songs by the standard crooners like Bing Crosby and Frank Sinatra. As MOR evolved, the idea was to get some young listeners without alienating the older crowd who found the more raucous rock tunes unacceptable. Unlike Top 40 deejays, MOR personalities feature a continual patter between songs in an effort to entertain the audience with their words as well as the music.

ADULT CONTEMPORARY

Adult contemporary is really a blend of MOR and AOR programming. In the 1970s, MOR programmers found their audience growing older and thus less desirable to many advertisers. They spiced up their playlist with soft-rock songs, particularly those that had been popular in the late 1960s and early 1970s, in an attempt to reach the 18- to 34-year-old audience. Most major markets have several stations that call themselves adult contemporary.

10. adult contemp.

COUNTRY AND WESTERN

Country and western programming is probably America's most commercially successful radio format. Though there are more rock-oriented stations than country, the latter tend to be more profitable. More than 50 percent of all popular-music radio stations play some country music. Every major metropolitan market has at least one C&W station. C&W is common in the rural Western states. In the Deep South, it competes with Top 40 for the highest ratings.

11. C & W

For years, it was easy to separate country music from Top 40, but the recent country influence on rock groups has made the distinction less clear. In addition, many country singers have found success on the Top 40 charts. The result has been an introduction to country music for many listeners. Several stations now follow a "pop-corn" formula, alternating rock and country hits, hoping to attract listeners from both camps.

12. pop-corn formula

BEAUTIFUL MUSIC

Originally called "easy listening" or "good music" by its fans, beautiful music is one of the most popular of today's radio formats. The music of artists like Henry Mancini and Mantovani forms the basis for this format, but more adventurous beautiful-music stations may occasionally program a soft vocal track by the Carpenters or Neil Diamond. This trend has become more noticeable of late, because beautiful music, like MOR, appeals to an audience that is growing older.

13. beautiful music

The secret of the success of beautiful music lies in the nature of radio itself. Often, radio is something we listen to while we're doing something else. It provides a sound backdrop for our daily activities. Beautiful-music programming is perfectly suited to this background function.

Beautiful-music fans see their stations as an oasis amid the "noise" of the other stations. The announcers display little emotion or personality, but simply and softly announce the songs. News and commercials (when possible) are done in the same soft-spoken way. The idea is never to violate the listener's trust by starting to sound like "those other stations." Beautiful-music formats are usually automated or prerecorded, with the computer selecting programming elements according to a formula (three instrumentals, one vocal, two commercials, and so on).

The competition among beautiful-music stations is fiercer than the name might suggest. Although fans are as devoted to their format as any radio listeners, they also tend to be less tolerant of commercials. Typically, a new beautiful-music station will enter a market with few sponsors. As the ratings grow, so do the number of commercials. Soon, listeners are turning elsewhere.

14. *Muzak*

The more conservative strains of beautiful music are often piped into dentists' and doctors' offices. Sometimes these offices pay to receive a closed-circuit broadcast of such music, such as the one called Muzak. The Muzak format is the easy listener's dream — no commercials, no disc jockey, no interruptions, just music. Critics contend that Muzak isn't music at all, but simply a pleasant, mindless noise.

JAZZ

15. *Jazz*

In a few urban markets, the jazz format receives a comfortable chunk of the ratings. Jazz stations were once quite popular, but enthusiasm dwindled in the 1960s. Those fans that remained were hard-core, however, and went to great lengths to find a station that offered what they wanted. Now there is some indication that young people are becoming interested in jazz again. Pop performers like Joni Mitchell and Sting are combining traditional and experimental jazz sounds with rock.

NEW AGE

New age is radio's newest format, featuring light jazz and classical-like instrumentals from labels such as Windham Hall and ECM. Artists like George Benson, Michael Franks, Pat Metheny and Kitaro are new-age favorites. Critics often refer to this format as "Muzak for yuppies" and the much sought-after 18–39 young urban professionals do indeed form the core of its audience. New-age stations have not enjoyed overpowering ratings to date, but the desirable demographics of those listeners they do attract have helped them keep their heads above water while attempting to build a larger audience.

16. New age

ETHNIC

Ethnic stations are so labeled because their programming tends to be targeted largely to one ethnic group. Many offer programs in foreign languages. Of these, the Spanish-speaking stations are most numerous, particularly in New York City and the Sunbelt.

17. ethnic

Because ethnic programming tends to appeal to a small, specialized audience, its impact is often overlooked. Yet it is important to recognize the cultural contributions made by various ethnic formats over the years. For many Americans, native language programming and music formats offer a lifeline. Often ethnic programming can be found on noncommercial outlets, because the smaller audience cannot support a commercial station.

CLASSICAL

The commercial classical station, once a firmly established format, is now virtually extinct. About 20 full-time commercial classical stations are operating today, down from more than 50 in 1965. Classical music may be alive and well, but teaming it with the financial realities of commercial radio seems an impossible task. Often classical stations are subsidized by listeners or survive because a wealthy owner writes off station losses at income-tax time.

18. classical

Classical fans now find themselves drawn primarily to noncommercial stations found between 88 and 92 on the FM dial. Many noncommercial stations offer classical music along with other fine-arts programming.

BIG BAND

19. big band

One solution for some struggling AM stations has been to switch to a nostalgia — big band format. Such a format appeals to older demographic groups, of course, but often will entice some listeners who would not otherwise listen to music radio.

NEW MUSIC/ROCK OF THE 1980S AND 1990S

20. new music

A recent and innovative rock format is *new music*, generally found on FM. The distinctions between these and AOR stations are sometimes difficult to discern. However, the emergence of punk, new-wave, and new-music songs in the late 1970s and early 1980s generated a tremendous interest and enthusiasm for rock that had not been seen since the 1960s. A few stations, mostly in major markets, responded to this interest by featuring what they call "new music" exclusively. KROQ in Los Angeles calls its format "Rock of the '80s and '90s" and features only what are considered to be innovative contemporary songs. The playlist includes mainstream acts like U2 and Billy Idol, as well as more esoteric music by groups like R.E.M.

Noting the connection between experimental music of the 1980s and the more innovative music of the 1960s by groups like the Doors and the Jimi Hendrix Experience, Lee Abrams, a renowned radio consultant, created his "Superstars II" format. Currently syndicated around the country, this format capitalizes on both new-music trends and the desirability of reaching the older listeners who identify with the 1960s. Listeners hear everything from Neil Young to U2. If a station in your market has a daily feature known as the "Psychedelic Supper," you can bet it is an Abrams-programmed station.

These are the basic music formats that make up the constructed mediated reality of radio today. Many stations offer a combination of two or more formats in an attempt to "fine tune" the station's audience demographics. Thus it is difficult to know exactly where the boundaries of CHR end and urban contemporary begin, for example. Even those stations that do admit to following an established format trend have program directors who claim their sound is different from established norms in order to convince advertisers that they are offering something unique.

Yet the truth is most stations stay pretty well within the boundaries of established formats. These boundaries, initially set up in the 1950s, have spelled success for many stations. Although station programmers always think they should be allowed to experiment, station owners are usually more concerned with the bottom line. If the station is making money, let's keep it the way it is; if it's not, *then* we can talk about change.

21. bottom line

According to *Broadcasting* magazine, more commercial music stations report losses than profits each year, but those figures can be misleading. Owners often pay excessive salaries to themselves or their top executives to avoid heavy profit taxes at the end of the year. Actually, as soon as a station is a real money-loser, it will change formats, go up for sale, or both.

2800 words

Write your ending time here: _____

Subtract your starting time: _____

Total time: _____

Check the Rate Chart in the back of the book to find out how many words per minute you have read and then record your score on the Progress Chart.

SQ3R

C. *Read.* Without looking back at the article, write the answers to your SQ3R questions here:

1. _____

2. _____

3. _____

Underline the main ideas and supporting details in the article that you believe will be tested in the Comprehension Check.

D. *Recite.* Now cover up the text of the article and use the marginal notes to test your memory of it. Check your underlining to see whether you forgot anything. Repeat this step until you are able to remember everything you underlined.

E. *Review.* This article is organized like a short textbook chapter. It is too short to break into sections, but if it were a long article, you might have had to divide it into sections. In that case, you would have done your major review immediately after you finished each section, again one week later, and then as often as needed to maintain your memory.

MAIN IDEA

Before going on to the Comprehension Check, and without looking back at the article, write one complete sentence stating the main idea of this article.

_____

_____

Your answer should be similar to the correct answer for question 2 in the Comprehension Check.

21

Music Formats

COMPREHENSION CHECK
Circle the letter before the best answer to each of the following questions. Don't look back at the article.

Subject and Main Idea
1. The subject is
   a. types of music.
   b. radio.
   c. types of music and talk in radio.
   d. how to attract the largest possible audience.

2. The main idea is that
   a. commercial stations compete with noncommercial FM stations.
   b. stations change what they play according to what their sponsors demand.
   c. the most successful format is Top 40.
   d. most stations can be grouped into certain formats.

Details
3. "Underground radio" refers to
   a. contemporary hit radio.
   b. album-oriented rock.
   c. middle of the road.
   d. big band.

4. The most commercially successful format is
   a. urban contemporary.
   b. adult contemporary.
   c. country and western.
   d. new age.

5. Muzak is a type of
   a. beautiful music.
   b. jazz.
   c. ethnic music.
   d. classical music.

6. Rap music is a type of
   a. new-age music.
   b. album-oriented rock.
   c. urban contemporary.
   d. adult contemporary.

Inferences

7. Radio stations vary their formats to
   a. keep in the forefront of musical trends.
   b. attract the largest audience they can.
   c. provide the highest quality music.
   d. appear noncommercial.

8. Compared with commercial stations, college stations usually play
   a. newer music.
   b. more news.
   c. more oldies.
   d. all of the above.

9. Generally, the "newer" the music is, the more it appeals to
   a. youth.
   b. middle-aged people.
   c. yuppies.
   d. ethnic groups.

10. Commercial radio stations make money by
    a. attracting donations.
    b. attracting sponsors.
    c. receiving payoffs from record companies.
    d. selling records and tapes.

QUESTIONS FOR ANALYSIS AND APPLICATION

1. Write the call letters of your favorite radio station and label the format it uses according to the categories in the article.

2. Find a commercial and a noncommercial station in your area. Write their call letters, and describe the differences between the two.

VOCABULARY IN CONTEXT
Multiple Choice
Circle the letter before the best definition of each underlined word or phrase.

1. Innovative people are usually successful.
   a. constructive   b. inventive   c. sterile   d. pleasant

2. Executives in large corporations in the United States are predominantly college graduates.
   a. largely   b. completely   c. often   d. rarely

3. In his trial for murder his lawyer contended that he was innocent.
   a. said   b. believed   c. denied   d. lied

4. His feeling of loyalty to the company that gave him his first job acted as a constraint to career advancement with other companies.
   a. restriction   b. boost   c. catalyst   d. stepping stone

5. Grammar school students are often raucous when a substitute teacher comes.
   a. polite   b. rowdy   c. disorderly   d. helpful

6. From the facts she had gathered, the private investigator was able to discern that certain individuals could not have been involved in the crime.
   a. guess   b. prove   c. disprove   d. perceive

7. Because humans have an irrepressible need to breathe, a child holding his breath may turn blue but will pass out before he dies.
   a. unstoppable   b. unusual   c. unfortunate
   d. surprising

Fill-in
Write the best word from this list in the blank in each sentence below:

subsidize   capitalizes   counterculture   ethnic

closed-circuit   alienating   esoteric

8. Employers cannot legally discriminate based on one's

    _____ background.

9. Some words are so _____ they can only
   be found in an unabridged dictionary.

10. The hippie movement in the late 1960s was an example

    of a _____ .

11. Special television programs that have very limited transmission

    are _____ .

12. Fund raisers are often held because groups need money to

    _____ various programs.

13. When an individual invests money and makes a profit, she

    _____ on her investment.

14. When the coffee shop started raising prices, the owners found they

    were _____ their regular customers.

SKILLS EXERCISE: OUTLINING

For explanation see pp. 292–297

Fill in the missing parts of the following outline, which is based on the reading selection.

Music Formats

I. Specific blends of music and talk

   A. Largest possible audience
   B. Seldom at forefront — behind college stations
   C. Wide spectrum

II. _____

   A. CHR

      1. Jukebox method. Started with Top 40 in 1950s
      2. New, less cluttered

   B. _____

      1. Late 60s
      2. "Underground" radio, "progressive" radio
      3. Usually FM
      4. "Mellow-rock" derivation in 1970s

   C. _____

      1. Early 1980s

      2. _____

      3. Appeal to black and inner-city audiences

      4. _____

      5. Introduced rap music

   D. _____

      1. Began as "chicken rock" in 1950s
      2. Continuous patter

   E. _____

      1. Blend of AOR and MOR
      2. Attempt to reach 18–34-year-old audience

F. _____

1. Most commercially successful (profitable) format
2. Pop-corn format alternates rock and country

G. _____

1. Background
2. Example: Muzak

H. _____

1. Dwindled in 1960s

2. _____

I. _____

1. Light jazz and classical-like instrumentals
2. "Muzak for yuppies"

J. _____

1. Foreign language, especially Spanish
2. Often a noncommercial station

K. _____

1. Commercial dwindled
2. Now mostly noncommercial

L. _____

1. Nostalgia
2. Older audience

M. _____

1. Usually FM
2. Innovative contemporary

III. Combinations/Changes

A. Sometimes combine formats
B. Must stay within boundaries
C. Changes or quits when loses money

22

Women: The War and After

319

SURVEY

Survey the following article by reading the author's name, the title, the headings, and the last sentence. This should take no longer than thirty seconds. After your survey, and without looking back at the article, write three questions that you think will be answered by reading it.

1. _____

2. _____

3. _____

Now read the article. Write your starting time here: _____

22

Women: The War and After

Jackson Wilson et al.

I N 1945, *HOUSE BEAUTIFUL* MAGAZINE addressed its female readers in an article on returning soldiers entitled "Home Should Be Even More Wonderful Than He Remembers It." As the author put it, "He's head man again. . . . Your part in the remaking of this man is to fit his home to him, understanding why he wants it this way, forgetting your own preferences."

As this article suggests, the postwar years left women with an ambiguous experience that touched their identity and particularly their social image. During the war, they had been welcomed — and even encouraged — to enter the labor force to take the place of men drafted into the armed forces. Now they were encouraged — and sometimes forced — to leave. Many of them, however, did not leave. They simply could not afford to stop working. But most of these women took up jobs that were traditionally labeled "women's work," such as waiting on tables or nursing. Married women who remained in the work force found themselves shouldering a double burden; they had a job from nine to five and housework and cooking afterward. Statistics demonstrate that the percentage of working women shrank after 1945, but did not fall as low as prewar levels. In fact, after the initial drop, the number and percentage of working women resumed a steady increase.

These abrupt changes in women's activities gave rise to contradictory and conflicting pictures of the proper role of women in American society. During the war, the popular press, newspapers, and government publications stressed the contributions of women to the war effort. Of course, there were exceptions. In 1943, government and the press alike lamented the fate of "latch-key" children, working mothers' unsupervised progeny who returned from school to an empty house and "unfilled hours of loneliness." Generally, however, when women enlisted to work for the duration of the war, they were well received. Indeed, during the war, both major political parties endorsed an Equal Rights Amendment, which would have improved wages and job opportunities for women. However, both Secretary of Labor Frances Perkins and Eleanor Roosevelt, the president's wife, declined to support it.

Women's Participation in the Labor Force

Married, with Children Under 6		With Children Under Age 1	
1950	11.9%	1976	31.0%
1955	16.2	1978	25.3
1960	18.6	1980	38.0
1965	23.3	1982	43.9
1970	30.3	1983	43.1
1975	36.6	1984	46.7
1980	41.5	1985	48.4
1985	53.4	1986	49.8
1987	56.8	1987	50.8

Source: *The New York Times*

After the war, government, business, and labor unions pressured women to return home. Women's magazines were filled with articles urging meticulous housekeeping, giving suggestions for improving domestic skills, or showering readers with new beauty and fashion tips. Eventually this pressure — and the desire of many women to live up to ideals of femininity derived from novels and movies — affected a wide range of behavior. It also led to a "family first" ideology that dominated American culture during the 1950s, giving that period a tone of orthodoxy and conservatism. According to the new domestic philosophy, women — whatever else they did — should put family above all else. As girls, their goal was marriage. As women, their duties revolved around caring for children and maintaining a home.

Statistics suggest that the revived ideology of domesticity was linked to changes in family-related behavior. From 1945 to the end of the 1950s, family stability increased. After a momentary postwar rise, the divorce rate in the United States fell until about 1960. Thereafter, it increased sharply and then zoomed upward in the 1970s. After the war, the marriage rate also increased. Not only were more persons of eligible age actually married, but the average age for marriage had also dropped. For women, this meant that about half married before the age of twenty. Most significant, the birth rate rose sharply after the war, reaching a peak in 1956. Simply put, more women were having more babies — thus reversing, temporarily, a twentieth-century American trend toward smaller families.

By the end of the 1950s, most of these trends began to shift. The marriage and birth rates declined, the divorce rate increased, the family appeared less stable, and the role of women was no longer clearly defined. Pressure to appear a model mother remained, but women increasingly found the role irrelevant. The suburban home, touted as the ideal environment in the 1950s, could be a barren place. Boring and empty days drove many women to various addictions (alcohol, barbiturates) in an effort to disguise their aimlessness. Perhaps more important, lifestyles were changing. Increasing accessibility of the means for birth control ("the pill" and intrauterine devices) made it easier for women to control reproduction. And economic necessity — the need to pay for the affluent lifestyles that modern families sought — often required women to work.

Women in the Labor Force as a Percentage of Total Female Population, 1945–80*

1945	38.1
1950	33.0
1955	34.8
1960	37.7
1965	39.3
1970	43.4
1975	46.3
1980	51.6
1984	53.7

*Male participation in the labor force ranges from about 77 to 80 percent in this same period.

As women increasingly entered the job market in the 1960s, they encountered discrimination, the effects of inferior education, and sexism. Learning from the civil rights movement of the late 1950s and 1960s, some women organized to advance their cause. By 1966 the National Organization for Women (NOW) began to concentrate its efforts on passage of the Equal Rights Amendment (ERA) to the Constitution; the amendment passed Congress on March 22, 1972, but failed to win the necessary ratification by two-thirds of the states. In 1973, the Supreme Court in *Roe* v. *Wade* assured the right of women to secure abortions.

Enormous counterpressures developed despite these rulings. Many women did not wish to be "liberated" from traditional roles centering on the family; housewives often felt slighted by the career-oriented rhetoric of the women's movement. Many men resented the attack on their dominant position in the workplace. By 1982 the ERA had been blocked and its life as a proposed constitutional amendment ended. National agitation to end abortions, control contraception, and regulate sexual behavior of teenage girls grew quickly. As even more women entered the labor force, the conflict over their roles remained unsettled. New issues like child care and dual-track careers emerged. And in July, 1989, the Supreme Court, in *Webster* v. *Reproductive Health Services*, returned power to limit abortions to the states.

1000 words

Write your ending time here: _____

Subtract your starting time: _____

Total time: _____

Check the Rate Chart in the back of the book to find how many words per minute you have read, and then record your score on the Progress Chart.

ANSWERS TO SURVEY QUESTIONS
Without looking back at the article, write the answers to your survey questions here.

1. _____

2. _____

3. _____

22

Women: The War and After

COMPREHENSION CHECK
Circle the letter before the best answer to each question below. Don't look back at the article.

Subject and Main Idea

1. The subject is American women's
   a. employment history.
   b. struggle for equal rights.
   c. roles from World War II to the present.
   d. strengths and weaknesses.

2. The main idea is that postwar women
   a. emerged with stronger roles.
   b. emerged with weaker roles.
   c. couldn't agree on which roles they wanted.
   d. had an ambiguous experience.

Details

3. The right to abortion
   a. can be limited by each state.
   b. is guaranteed by a Supreme Court decision.
   c. exists only in cases of incest or rape.
   d. is guaranteed only when it will save the mother's life.

4. The Equal Rights Amendment was
   a. passed by Congress.
   b. not ratified by enough states.
   c. supported by the National Organization for Women.
   d. all of the above.

5. In the 1950s
   a. the birth rate increased.
   b. divorce increased.
   c. family stability decreased.
   d. most people married later.

6. Since World War II, the percentage of women who work has
   a. increased.
   b. decreased.
   c. remained the same.
   d. varied without any pattern.

Inferences

7. The author implies that the percentage of suburban housewives
   a. has increased since the 1950s.
   b. has decreased since the 1950s.
   c. has remained the same.
   d. cannot be determined.

8. The forces determining women's roles are probably primarily
   a. hereditary.
   b. religious.
   c. traditional.
   d. economic.

9. The author implies that in the history of American women
   a. World War II continued the trends begun in World War I.
   b. the most important changes occurred before the war.
   c. World War II was an important turning point.
   d. the most important changes occurred in the 1960s.

10. Current trends indicate efforts to control women's
    a. sexual behavior.
    b. access to jobs.
    c. right to equal pay.
    d. access to affirmative action programs.

QUESTIONS FOR ANALYSIS AND APPLICATION

1. Describe the major features of the conservative view of women's roles.

2. What are some reasons why some women might work against equal rights for women?

VOCABULARY IN CONTEXT
Multiple Choice
Circle the letter before the best definition of each underlined word.

1. Beverly Hills is one of the most <u>affluent</u> areas of Los Angeles County.
   a. attractive   b. desirable   c. wealthy   d. snobbish

2. The <u>ratification</u> of the Nineteenth Amendment to the Constitution in 1920 gave women in the United States the right to vote.
   a. implication   b. approval   c. idea   d. importance

3. When a scientist is <u>meticulous</u> during an experiment, her results are more often accurate.
   a. careful   b. creative   c. interested   d. involved

4. Liberal and conservative political groups have opposing <u>ideologies</u>.
   a. leaderships   b. doctrines   c. allies   d. names

5. The <u>accessibility</u> of library books to students is crucial for their success in college.
   a. location   b. danger   c. interesting aspects
   d. availability

Fill-in
Write the best word from this list in the blank in each sentence below:

progeny   **rhetoric**   **lamented**   **orthodoxy**   **duration**

6. He _____ his carelessness for years after killing the woman in a car accident.

7. Since she failed many classes in high school, for the

   _____ of her college years she worked much harder.

8. A speech writer for the president uses the art of

   _____ .

9. Adults often hope that their _____ will take care of them when they get old.

10. During the Inquisition, suspects were tested to establish their

    religious _____ .

SKILLS EXERCISE: OUTLINING

For explanation, see pp. 296–297

Fill in the missing parts of the following outline, which is based on the reading selection.

Women: The War and After

I. Ambiguous experience — affected women's identity and social image

II. Labor force

    A. _During WWII_

        1. Many women worked
        2. Generally well received — parties endorsed the Equal Rights Amendment

    B. After World War II

        1. Initial drop in number of working women, then a steady increase
        2. _incourage to stay home_

III. Family–related behaviors

    A. _Family first_

        1. Women put family first.
        2. Family stability increased.
            a. _more marriages_
            b. ~~more babies~~ _birth rate increased_
            c. _less devorce_
            d. _average age of marriage dropped_

    B. 1960s shift in trends

        1. _devorce increased_
        2. _brith rate + marriage dropped_
        3. Family less stable
        4. Women's role not so clear
        5. Change in life styles
            a. Better birth control
            b. Economic necessity for more women to work

6. Working women encountered discrimination, effects of inferior education, and sexism.

   a. Organized (NOW)

   b. Supported ERA

C. Counterpressures

  1. <u>*Support for EQUAL Rights*</u>

  2. Agitation to end abortion, control contraception, and regulate sexual behavior of teenage girls

  3. Role of women unclear

  4. <u>*Roe vs wade*</u>

SKILLS EXERCISE: STUDY MAPPING

For explanation see pp. 297–299

Use the first three levels of the preceding outline in this chapter to fill in the blank spaces in the following study map.

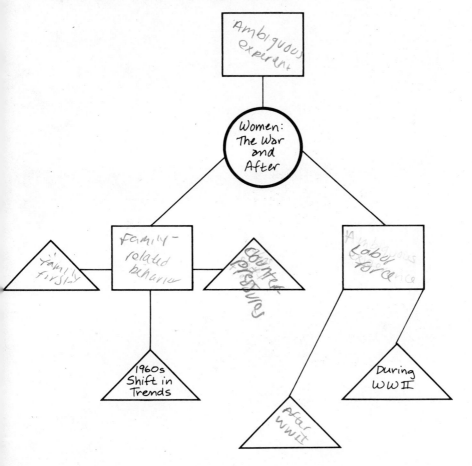

SKILLS EXERCISE:
TEXTBOOK GRAPHICS
Look at the table, "Women's Participation in the Labor Force," and answer the following questions.

1. What percentage of married working women had children under 6

   in 1950? _____

   In 1987? _____

2. What percentage of working women had children under age 1 in

   1985? _____

   1987? _____

23

Shared Characteristics of Life

SKILLS EXERCISE:
SQ3R

For explanation
see pp. 291–296

A. *Survey.* Survey the following article by reading the author's name, the title, and the headings. This should take no longer than thirty seconds. (The numbered blanks in the margin are for a later exercise, so you can ignore them at this time.)

B. *Question.* Without looking back at the article, write three questions that you think will be answered by reading it.

1. _____

2. _____

3. _____

C. *Read.* Now read the article. Write your starting time here: _____

23

Shared Characteristics of Life

Cecie Starr

DNA AND BIOLOGICAL ORGANIZATION

Picture a croaking frog squatting on a rock. Without even thinking about it, you know that the frog is alive and the rock is not. At a much deeper level, however, the difference between them blurs. They and all other things are composed of the same particles (protons, electrons, and neutrons). The particles have become organized into atoms, according to the same physical laws. At the heart of those laws is something called **energy** — a capacity to make things happen, to do work. Energetic interactions bind atom to atom in predictable patterns, giving rise to what we call molecules. Energetic interactions among molecules hold a rock together — and they hold a frog together.

It takes a special type of molecule called deoxyribonucleic acid, or DNA, to set living things apart from the nonliving world. DNA molecules contain the instructions for assembling each new organism from a few kinds of "lifeless" molecules. By analogy, think of what you can do with a little effort and a pile of just two kinds of ceramic tiles. When you glue the tiles together according to certain blueprints, different patterns of organization emerge (Figure 1). Similarly, life emerges from lifeless matter with a DNA "blueprint," some raw materials, and energy.

Look carefully at Figure 2, which outlines the levels of organization in nature. The quality of "life" actually emerges at the level of cells. A **cell** is the basic living unit. This means it has the capacity to maintain itself as an independent unit and to reproduce, given appropriate sources of energy and raw materials. Amoebas

333

and many other single-celled organisms lead independent lives. A **multicelled organism** has specialized cells arranged into tissues, organs, and often organ systems. Although each cell depends on the integrated activities of other cells in the body, it still has the capacity for independent existence. (Such cells can be removed from the body and kept alive under controlled conditions.)

At a more inclusive level of organization we find the **population**: a group of single-celled or multicelled organisms of the same kind — that is, of the same *species* — occupying a given area. A flock of penguins is an example. The populations of whales, seals, fishes, and all other organisms living in the same area as the penguins make up a **community**. The next level includes the community *and* its physical and chemical environment; this is the **ecosystem**. The most inclusive level of organization is the **biosphere**: those regions of the earth's waters, crust, and atmosphere in which organisms live.

INTERDEPENDENCY AMONG ORGANISMS

With few exceptions, a flow of energy from the sun maintains the great pattern of organization in nature. Some single-celled and multicelled organisms (plants, mostly) trap and convert sunlight energy to chemical energy that can be used to build sugars, starch, and other biological molecules from simple raw materials in the environment. This process is called **photosynthesis**. In another process, called **aerobic respiration**, cells release

4. _____

5. _____

6. _____

7. _____

8. _____

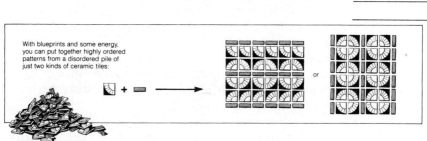

Figure 1.   Emergence of organized patterns from disorganized beginnings. Two ceramic tile patterns are shown here. (Can you visualize other possible patterns using the same two kinds of tiles?) Similarly, the organization characteristic of life emerges from simple pools of building blocks, given energy sources, and specific DNA "blueprints."

Biosphere
Those regions of the earth's waters, crust, and
atmosphere in which organisms can exist

↑ ↓

Ecosystem
A complex of organisms and their physical environment,
linked by a one-way flow of energy and a cycling of materials

↑ ↓

Community
An association of populations, tied together directly
or indirectly by competition for resources, predation,
and other interactions

↑ ↓

Population
Group of individuals of the same kind (that is, the same
species) occupying a given area in a given interval of time

↑ ↓

Multicellular Organism
Individual composed of specialized, interdependent cells
arrayed in tissues, organs, and often organ systems

↑ ↓

Organ System
Two or more organs whose separate functions
are integrated in the performance of a specific task

↑ ↓

Organ
One or more types of tissues
interacting as a structural, functional unit

↑ ↓

Tissue
A group of cells and intercellular substances
functioning together in a specialized activity

↑ ↓

Cell
Smallest *living* unit; may live independently or
may be part of a multicellular organism

↑ ↓

Organelle
Membranous sacs or other compartments that
separate different metabolic reactions inside the cell

↑ ↓

Molecule
A unit of two or more atoms of the same or
different elements bonded together

↑ ↓

Atom
Smallest unit of an element that still retains
the properties of that element

↑ ↓

Subatomic Particle
An electron, proton, or neutron; one of the three
major particles of which atoms are composed

Figure 2. Levels of organization in nature.

energy stored in molecules — energy that can be used to drive cellular activities.

Think of plants as being food "producers" for the world of life. Animals are "consumers." Directly or indirectly, they feed on energy stored in plant parts. Bacteria and fungi are "decomposers." When they feed on tissues or remains of other organisms, they break down complex molecules to simple raw materials — which can be recycled back to producers (Figure 3).

9. _____

_____

_____

Energy flows to, within, and from single cells and multicelled organisms; it flows within and among populations, communities, and ecosystems. As you will see, interactions among organisms even influence the cycling of carbon and other substances on a global scale, and they influence the earth's energy "budget." Understand the extent of these interactions and you will gain insight into the greenhouse effect, acid rain, and many other modern-day problems.

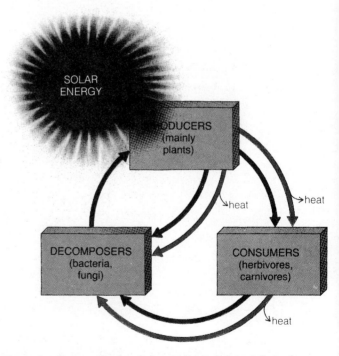

Figure 3.   Energy flow and the cycling of materials in the biosphere. Here, grasses of the African savanna are producers that provide energy directly for zebras (herbivores) and indirectly for lions and vultures (carnivores). The wastes and remains of all these organisms are energy sources for decomposers, which cycle nutrients back to the producers.

METABOLISM

Photosynthesis and aerobic respiration are examples of metabolic activity, which occurs only in living things. **Metabolism** refers to the cell's capacity to (1) extract and transform energy from its surroundings and (2) use energy in ways that ensure its maintenance, growth, and reproduction. In essence, metabolism means "energy transfers." In photosynthesis, for example, energy is transferred from the sun to a molecule called ATP, then ATP transfers energy to molecules that the cell uses as building blocks or tucks away as energy reserves.

10. _____
_____
_____

HOMEOSTASIS

It is often said that organisms alone "respond" to the environment. Yet a rock also responds to the environment, as when it yields to gravity and tumbles downhill or changes shape slowly under the battering of wind, rain, or tides. The real difference is this: Organisms show *controlled* responses to change.

Life happens to be maintained within narrow limits. Your body, for example, can withstand only so much heat or cold. Your body also must rid itself of harmful substances. Certain foods must be available to it, in certain amounts. Yet temperatures shift, harmful substances may be encountered, and food is sometimes plentiful and sometimes scarce.

You and all other organisms have built-in means of adjusting to change. These internal adjustments help maintain operating conditions within some tolerable range. The capacity for maintaining the "internal environment" is called **homeostasis**. Single cells and multicelled organisms both have homeostatic controls. For example, your cells rapidly take up energy-rich sugar when their metabolic activity increases. Birds fluff their feathers and so retain body heat when the outside temperature drops.

11. _____
_____
_____

Homeostasis implies constancy, a sort of perpetual bouncing back to a limited set of operating conditions. In some respects, constancy is indeed vital. Your red blood cells will not function unless they are bathed in water that contains fairly exact amounts of dissolved components. Your body works so that this fluid is always much the same. Yet organisms also adjust to certain irreversible changes. We might call this *dynamic*

12. _____
_____
_____

homeostasis, for the adjustments actually shift the body's form and function over time.

A simple example will do here. In humans, irreversible chemical changes trigger *puberty*, the age at which sexual reproductive structures mature and become functional. At puberty, the body steps up its secretions of hormones (including testosterone in males and estrogen in females). The increased secretions call for new events such as the menstrual cycle. This cycle includes a rhythmic buildup of substances that prepare the female body for pregnancy, then disposal of substances when pregnancy does not occur. Homeostasis is still operating, but developmental events now demand new kinds of adjustments in the body.

REPRODUCTION
We humans tend to think that we enter the world rather abruptly and are destined to leave it the same way. Yet we and all other organisms are more than this. We are part of an immense, ongoing journey that began billions of years ago. Even before birth, the sperm and egg destined to form a new human being are developing according to instructions passed on through countless generations. Each new human body proceeds through many stages of development that prepare it, ultimately, for *reproduction*. With reproduction, the journey of life continues.

13. _____
_____
_____

What comes to mind when you think of a moth? Do you think simply of a winged insect? What about the tiny egg deposited on a branch by a female moth? The egg contains all the instructions necessary to become an adult moth. By those instructions, the egg develops into a caterpillar — a larval form adapted for rapid feeding and growth. The caterpillar eats and increases in size until an internal alarm clock goes off. Then the body enters a pupal stage of wholesale remodeling. Some cells die, and other cells multiply and become organized in different patterns that lead to the adult moth. The adult has organs in which egg or sperm develop. And its wings are brightly colored and move at a frequency that can attract a potential mate. In short, the adult is adapted for reproduction.

None of these stages is "the insect." The insect is a series of organized stages — and the instructions for each stage were written long before the formation of that moth egg.

MUTATION AND ADAPTING TO CHANGE

The word **inheritance** refers to the transmission, from parents to offspring, of structural and functional patterns characteristic of each species. In living cells, hereditary instructions are encoded in molecules of DNA. Hereditary instructions assure that offspring will resemble their parents, but they also permit *variations* on the basic plan. (For example, some humans are born with six fingers on each hand instead of five.) The variations arise through **mutations**, which are changes in the structure or number of DNA molecules.

14. _____

_____

_____

Most mutations are harmful, for the separate bits of information in DNA are part of a coordinated whole. For example, a single mutation in a tiny bit of human DNA may lead to hemophilia or some other genetic disorder.

Yet some mutations may prove to be harmless, even beneficial, under prevailing conditions. One type of mutation in light-colored moths leads to dark-colored offspring. When a dark moth rests on a soot-covered tree, bird predators do not see it. Where most trees are soot-covered, as in industrial regions, light moths are more likely to be seen and eaten — so the dark form has a better chance of surviving and reproducing. Under such conditions, the mutant form is more adaptive.

1450 words

Write your ending time here: _____

Subtract your starting time: _____

Total time: _____

Check the Rate Chart in the back of the book to find out how many words per minute you have read and then record your score on the Progress Chart.

SQ3R

C. *Read.* Without looking back at the article, write the answers to your SQ3R questions here:

1. _____

2. _____

3. _____

Underline the main ideas and supporting details in the article that you believe will be tested in the Comprehension Check.

For this article, the notes have been left blank for you to fill in with your own *marginal notes.*

D. *Recite.* Now cover up the text of the article and use the marginal notes to test your memory of it. Check your underlining to see whether you forgot anything. Repeat this step until you are able to remember everything you underlined.

E. *Review.* This article is organized like a short textbook chapter. It is too short to break into sections, but if it were a long article, you might have had to divide it into sections. In that case, you would have done your major review immediately after you finished each section, again one week later, and then as often as needed to maintain your memory.

MAIN IDEA

Before going on to the the Comprehension Check, and without looking back at the article, write a complete sentence stating the main idea of this article.

_____

_____

Your answer should be similar to the correct answer for question 2 in the Comprehension Check.

23

Shared Characteristics of Life

COMPREHENSION CHECK
Circle the letter before the best answer to each question below. Don't look back at the article.

Subject and Main Idea

1. The subject of the article is
   a. cells.
   b. plants.
   c. animals.
   d. living things.

2. The main idea is that all living things
   a. have certain characteristics in common.
   b. live in order to reproduce.
   c. are made of DNA.
   d. are interdependent.

Details

3. Only living things have
   a. molecules.
   b. atoms.
   c. particles.
   d. DNA.

4. A population is a group of
   a. cells.
   b. molecules.
   c. organs.
   d. organisms.

5. Living things can be categorized as
   a. molecules or mutations.
   b. metabolic or homeostatic.
   c. populations, communities, or biosystems.
   d. producers, consumers, or decomposers.

6. Photosynthesis is accomplished mainly by
    a. atoms.
    b. cells.
    c. plants.
    d. animals.

Inferences
7. Animals shedding their winter fur is an example of
    a. metabolism.
    b. homeostasis.
    c. mutation.
    d. photosynthesis.

8. A group of lions, zebras, and rhinos living in the African plains comprises
    a. a population.
    b. a community.
    c. an ecosystem.
    d. a biosphere.

9. The advantage of mutation is that it
    a. weeds out the weaker organisms.
    b. is a creative energy.
    c. may lead to better adaptations.
    d. prevents defective organisms from reproducing.

10. Animals that require a great deal of energy to live must have a high rate of
    a. homeostasis.
    b. metabolism.
    c. reproduction.
    d. all of the above.

QUESTIONS FOR ANALYSIS AND APPLICATION
1. Describe at least three characteristics common to all living things.

2. Discuss interdependency among organisms.

VOCABULARY IN CONTEXT
Fill-in
Write the best word from this list in the blank in each sentence below:

secretion   **larval**   **pupal**   **adaptive**   **transmission**

integrated   **perpetual**

1. _____ species are able to adjust to their environment, and therefore don't become extinct.

2. The earliest stage for insects that go through metamorphosis is the

   _____ stage.

3. The _____ of perspiration is the function of our body's sweat glands.

4. Immediately before reaching maturation, many insects go through a

   _____ stage.

5. Satellite _____ has allowed billions of people to simultaneously view programs such as the Olympics or the Academy Awards.

6. To get a touchdown in a football game, it takes the

   _____ effort of all the players on a team.

7. I'm tired of your _____ complaints.

SKILLS EXERCISE: STUDY MAPPING

For explanation see pp. 297–299

Use the SQ3R marginal notes in this chapter to fill in the blank spaces in the following study map.

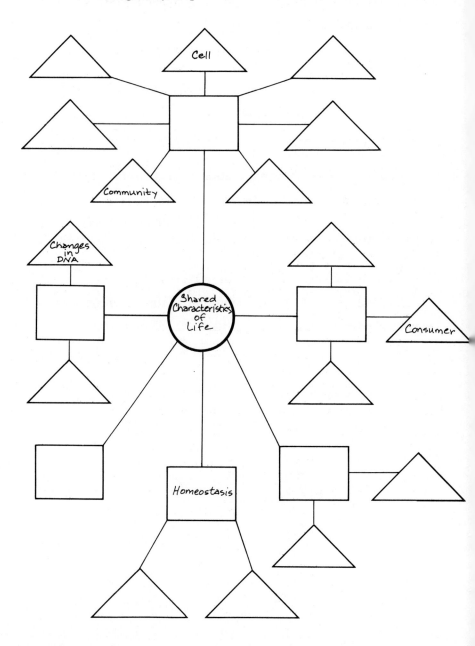

24

Measuring the Costs of Economic Decisions

345

SKILLS EXERCISE:
SQ3R

For explanation
see pp. 291–296

A. *Survey.* Survey the following article by reading the author's name, the title, the headings, and the first sentence of every paragraph. This should take no longer than thirty seconds.

B. *Question.* Without looking back at the article, write three questions that you think will be answered by reading it.

1. _____

2. _____

3. _____

C. *Read.* Now read the article. Write your starting time here: _____

24

Measuring the Costs of Economic Decisions

Philip C. Starr

EVERY ECONOMIC DECISION HAS A cost. The cost can be evaluated from the viewpoint of the buyers or sellers and from the viewpoint of the buying and selling that takes place at different levels. For example, think about a movie. When the movie is being made, the producers have to buy all of the resources they need to produce the movie from the owners of those resources. At that level, the resource owners are the sellers; the producers are the buyers. Then, when the movie is produced, your local theater is at first the buyer when it buys (or rents) the movie from the producer, and then the theater becomes the seller when you buy a ticket.

Thus we see that there are costs at various levels to obtain the use of resources. All of these costs arise because resources are to some extent scarce and because it takes time and effort to obtain them. One way to appreciate this fact of life is to consider what economists mean by a free good. A **free good** (or service) is one that exists in such abundance that people can take or use as much of it as they please without any effort or cost, and there will still be enough left to satisfy the wants of everyone else.

We used to call air and water free goods, but many of us who live in or near cities realize that clean air and water do not exist in unlimited quantities; that there is a cost connected with obtaining sterilized, piped, purified, or bottled water and occasionally a cost connected with filtering air in our homes. And so, sad but true, everything is to some extent scarce. When something is scarce, someone has to be paid to provide it; the price covers the costs borne by the supplier for supplying the scarce good or service, and the price helps determine which buyers will be able to obtain it.

_1._ Back to the movie example. When you go to see the movie, two different kinds of costs are involved. The first is the time and effort involved in getting to the theater (and possibly standing in line) plus the price of the movie. The second is the cost of having to choose among alternatives. You could have done something else with the time, effort, and money it took to see the movie. Because of the scarcity of resources and money, we can't do everything at once. Choices have to be made. Thus, the second meaning of cost involves the sacrifice we make every time it is necessary to choose among alternatives. As the next section illustrates, economists prefer this second meaning of cost.

OPPORTUNITY COST
How should we measure the cost of anything — of a new motorcycle, a new freeway, or a rapid transit system? Economists use a concept called opportunity cost.

_2._ To determine **opportunity cost**, we measure the value of the *next most* desirable opportunity we must sacrifice in order to take the course of action we have selected. When you decide to study in the library, you give up the opportunity to watch television at home. The opportunity cost of studying in the library is the value you place on the television program or movie you miss.

What is the opportunity cost of the $1,000 motor-cycle you want? It is not the price. The opportunity cost to you if you buy it is not $1,000 but the next most desirable product or service you might have bought with that $1,000. Notice that the money (price) is *not* the cost itself. The cost is your evaluation of the real things sacrificed.

So, money is a *means* of getting the things we want, price is a *measure* of how much money is required, and the real cost is the value of what we *forego*. The question economists ask is how much in actual products and services must be sacrificed to build whatever is being considered — a dam, hospital, school, rocket, weather satellite, and so on.

3. _____
_____
_____

We can look at the opportunity cost of any decision, but one of the most frequently underestimated costs is the cost of war. The obvious costs are lost lives, destroyed property, and interrupted careers, as well as wasted resources in the form of helicopters, guns, bullets, uniforms, trucks, and all the rest of the military paraphernalia. Less obvious costs are the things we might otherwise have undertaken — slum clearance, antipollution measures, and public health and welfare projects. Consider also the costs in hospitals, doctors, medicine, and equipment devoted to veterans' care long after the war is over, as well as the costs of the benefits paid to dependents. For instance, in 1967 more than 1,300 dependents of veterans of the American Civil War — a war that ended 102 years before — received *annual* benefits totaling more than $1 million. Total veterans' benefits for the Spanish-American War amounted to $5.3 billion, or twelve times the original cost of that war. World War II benefits are not expected to decline until the year 2000. Benefits to dependents of Vietnam veterans are expected to continue beyond 2100.

Every personal decision involves many calculations, but you should consider, at least briefly, the idea of opportunity cost when you make a decision. Because you are a student, the opportunity cost of doing your

homework may be the sacrifice of a tennis game, party
ing with your friends, or just goofing off, while the
opportunity cost of marriage, children, or social activ
ities may be poor grades. The idea of opportunity cost is
probably the most important one; unfortunately, few
people, businesses, or governments stop to think deeply
about it.

Perhaps the reason the idea is so often neglected is
that money tends to make us forget opportunity cost.
Suppose you have $250 in a bank account, and, at that
time, you notice an advertisement extolling the merits
of a compact disk player for $249.95. You are immedi-
ately attracted to buying the player. You have the
money — you can *afford* it. You become so entranced
with the idea of having a new toy that you rush to buy
it — despite heavy-handed admonitions by your economics instructor against doing just that.

The problem is that we all love to buy things, but
when we do, we tend to focus only on the fact that we
can afford the new purchase and how much fun it will
be to have it. We forget to consider all the other things
we could buy with $250 — perhaps a new suit, a 1,000-
mile airplane trip, a pair of new loudspeakers, a VCR,
a microwave oven, an air conditioning unit, and so on.
We forget to think about whether or not we want the
compact disk player badly enough to sacrifice the opportunity to buy these alternative products. We forget
opportunity cost. Notice also that having the money —
being able to afford something — does tend to confuse
the issue. Opportunity cost is measured by the value to
us of the real things sacrificed, a point to remember in
making individual buying decisions or when evaluating
the spending projects of businesses or of government
agencies.

COSTS OF WORK, STUDY, OR PLAY

4. _____ The opportunity costs of choosing a job are especially
_____ important to college students. There is a kind of trian-
_____ gular relationship among (1) part-time work or work in
a secondary job market, (2) work in a primary job market, and (3) a college education.

In a **secondary job market** are jobs with low pay,
high turnover, little required skill, and little training by
employers, such as waiting on tables, pumping gas, or

clerking in stores. In the **primary job market**, jobs involve skills, investment by employers in training, higher pay, avenues for promotion, career possibilities for employees, and low turnover.

Frequently, college students take jobs in secondary markets because primary market jobs require more time than commitment to a college education will permit. One college student (we'll call him Kirk) took a night job as a security guard in a manufacturing plant so that he could spend some of the time studying. The job required little skill or training. The company's executives knew Kirk, realized that he was management material, and were ready to promote him to a primary job. Kirk preferred to stay where he was in order to finish college.

The opportunity cost of Kirk's going to college can therefore be estimated as the sum of his college expenses, plus the extra income he lost by staying in his security guard job (rather than taking a better paying job), plus the chances of promotion he may also have lost. Economists have estimated that half of the cost of going to college is in the form of lost earnings, often called **foregone income**. Or, to put it another way, the true cost of going to college is double the money costs to students, parents, or taxpayers. Most economists believe that the college degree *is* worth it, and that investing in one's education has a higher return than putting money into savings accounts or stocks and bonds.

SOCIAL COSTS OF INDIVIDUAL DECISIONS

A personal decision may impose costs, not just on oneself, but also on others. Consequently, the total cost to society — **social cost** — is measured by the opportunity costs borne by individuals for their own decisions *plus* additional costs that may be borne by others. Examples are the purchase of a car that pollutes the atmosphere or a powerful stereo that keeps the neighbors awake, the noise and smoke trails from jet planes, and disease-producing waste from industrial production. Economists try to uncover the additional costs that may not be part of a buyer-seller transaction in order to estimate the total social costs of decisions to produce, buy, sell, or discard products or services.

5. _____

COST-BENEFIT ANALYSIS

The preceding section has emphasized the costs of every decision. This view of economics is, as you might guess, only one side of the coin. Usually, there are both gains (benefits) and losses (costs) in most decisions. Consequently, economists are faced with the job of measuring the benefits as well as the costs to society of business and government decisions.

A simple example may help. You are trying to decide about spending an evening with an attractive member of the opposite sex. There are, inevitably, both actual (monetary) and opportunity costs involved. On the other hand, the evening promises benefits in the form of an improved relationship. So, as a budding economist, you compare the expected costs with the expected benefits of the decision to go out with Mr. or Ms. Z. This comparison of costs and benefits is called **cost-benefit analysis**. It is an extremely important approach to problems in economics. Obviously, one only has to make sure that the benefits exceed the costs and then make an affirmative decision. But, in the real world there are many, many complications.

Difficulties with Cost-Benefit Analysis

The first difficulty, and undoubtedly the toughest, is that any measurement of costs and benefits is necessarily an estimate, because decisions made now affect future courses of action, and the future, as economists are fond of saying, is full of risk and uncertainty. The second difficulty is that there may be more than one alternative wherein the benefit exceeds the cost. In such a case accurate measurement becomes important, and accuracy about future events may be impossible.

Another difficulty is that costs may be relatively easy to estimate but the measurement of benefits, next to impossible. Some examples of these situations are projects like bridges, dams, and sewage disposal plants. Consider the latter.

The cost of building a sewage disposal plant can be estimated in dollars and cents. Now, let's assume that one benefit of the sewage disposal plant will be a future reduction of diseases like dysentery. Precise calculation of such a benefit in dollars and cents will be impossible. We will never know for sure if the sewage disposal plant is really the cause of a reduction in the disease. And there is no good way to measure the benefit anyhow. The disease affects different people in different ways depending on their age and previous health condition.

This difference between the ease of cost estimation and the difficulty of benefit estimation makes public acceptance of projects like this very difficult to obtain. The taxes (costs) the project will require are easy for individuals to visualize; the private benefit to taxpayers of a sewage disposal plant is extremely difficult for them to visualize. Consequently, taxpayers are reluctant to vote for such projects.

External Costs and Benefits
Usually, when any decision is made, people other than those directly involved receive some benefit or bear some cost. If I buy and use a cold remedy, the companies that made and sold the remedy and I are "directly" involved in that transaction. Economists will say that other people whom I know are "external" to the transaction of producing, selling, and using the product. Yet, these other people, who are external to the transaction, may be affected by my decision to buy the remedy — if, for example, the remedy helps cure my cold and reduces the chance of their getting it. Consequently, if we want 8. _____ to measure the costs and benefits to society as a whole _____ of any decision, we should take into account the effects of decisions on people who are external to the direct _____ impact of the decision. We mention this problem because it further demonstrates the difficulties facing economists who attempt cost-benefit analysis. What follows is an example of costs and benefits to people who are external to the original decision.

Suppose that a local lumber company dumps paper pulp into a nearby stream thereby killing the fish, making swimming impossible, and requiring much more expensive purification of the water for household use. A regulatory agency tells the company to quit polluting the stream. Now the company loses the benefit of cheap waste disposal, but the townspeople get the benefit of cleaner water. But, the additional cost to the company of disposing of its waste in some less convenient way forces it to raise the price of its lumber. The result of the price increase causes some customers to cancel orders. The company is forced to reduce production and lay off employees. Business in the town suffers. Some store employees are laid off. Here we have costs borne by people external to the original decision to regulate the waste.

Now we have the difficult problem of comparing the costs and benefits as they affect at least two groups of people: the townspeople and the owners of the lumber company. We say "at least" because there are other, external people who will be affected by a regulation forcing the company to quit polluting the stream. What about firms located in other towns that supply the local stores and the future generations of people who might or might not decide to live in our town?

What we have here is a classic case of what economists call a trade-off. It's a trade-off because, at least in the short run, we can have cleaner water, but we have to trade jobs to get it. In the long run, we don't know what will happen; the company might have to close its doors or it might find a way of solving the problem economically (by finding by-products for the paper pulp that would eliminate the waste problem completely).

9. ———————— The term *trade-off* is a popular synonym for the term *opportunity cost*. We could just as well have said that the opportunity cost of cleaner water was the loss of jobs. Either reference to the problem is correct. *Trade-off* is the term more generally used in the popular press.

2600 words

Write your ending time here: ————————————————

Subtract your starting time: ————————————————

Total time: ————————————————

Check the Rate Chart in the back of the book to find out how many words per minute you have read, and then record your score on the Progress Chart.

SQ3R
C. *Read.* Without looking back at the article, write the answers to your SQ3R questions here:

1. _____

2. _____

3. _____

Underline the main ideas and supporting details in the article that you believe will be tested in the Comprehension Check.

For this article, the notes have been left blank for you to fill in your own *marginal notes.*

D. *Recite.* Now cover up the text of the article and use the marginal notes to test your memory of it. Check your underlining to see whether you forgot anything. Repeat this step until you are able to remember everything you underlined.

E. *Review.* This article is organized like a short textbook chapter. It is too short to break into sections, but if it were a long article, you might have had to divide it into sections. In that case, you would have done your major review immediately after you finished each section, again one week later, and then as often as needed to maintain your memory.

MAIN IDEA
Before going on to the Comprehension Check, and without looking back at the article, write a complete sentence stating the main idea of this article.

_____

_____

Your answer should be similar to the correct answer for question 2 in the Comprehension Check.

24

Measuring the Costs of Economic Decisions

COMPREHENSION CHECK
Circle the letter before the best answer to each question below. Don't look back at the article.

Subject and Main Idea
1. The subject of the article is
   a. decision making.
   b. measurement of the costs and benefits of decisions.
   c. measuring social costs.
   d. primary and secondary job markets.

2. The main idea is that
   a. the costs of decisions can't be measured.
   b. it is difficult to assess social costs of decisions.
   c. the costs and benefits of decisions should be weighed.
   d. there is a triangular relationship among primary and secondary job markets and opportunity cost.

Details
3. Cost is
   a. a measure of how much money is required.
   b. the value of what we forego.
   c. how long it takes to earn the money.
   d. all of the above.

4. Another term for opportunity cost is
   a. price.
   b. value.
   c. sacrifice.
   d. trade-off.

5. The primary job market includes
   a. high pay.
   b. high turnover.
   c. few avenues for promotion.
   d. little skill.

6. The true cost of going to college is
    a. half the money cost.
    b. double the money cost.
    c. triple the money cost.
    d. equal to the money cost.

Inferences
7. An example of a decision with no social costs or benefits is
    a. mowing your lawn.
    b. going out to dinner.
    c. starting a business.
    d. none of the above.

8. The author implies that
    a. economists' cost-benefit analyses are usually accurate.
    b. most people never consider the costs of their decisions.
    c. the government does not do enough cost-benefit analysis.
    d. most of our decisions are made with an incomplete understanding of costs and benefits.

9. The author seems to be
    a. antiwar.
    b. militaristic.
    c. a veteran.
    d. a conscientious objector.

10. The author implies that opportunity costs are usually
    a. accurately predicted.
    b. never considered.
    c. overestimated.
    d. underestimated.

QUESTIONS FOR ANALYSIS AND APPLICATION
1. Explain why the true cost of going to college is double the money cost.

2. In light of your current financial situation, do a cost-benefit analysis of buying a new car.

VOCABULARY IN CONTEXT
Multiple Choice
Circle the letter before the best definition of each underlined word.

1. Some young children can still be <u>entranced</u> by a movie such as *The Wizard of Oz,* which they might have seen a hundred times.
   a. bored   b. frightened   c. fascinated   d. encouraged

2. A city inspector can give a homeowner an <u>admonition</u> or a citation if there is an illegally installed light outside a window.
   a. an award   b. a warning   c. a compliment
   d. a court suit

3. The new automated tellers outside banks make <u>transactions</u> possible at any time of the day or night.
   a. robberies   b. business   c. reactions   d. entering

4. The federal <u>regulatory</u> commissions are supposed to protect us against bad food and drugs, air traffic problems, and pollution. However, most of the agencies are understaffed, so unnecessary problems still occur.
   a. controlling   b. safety   c. numerous   d. helpful

5. In the Bible, Joseph told the Egyptian king that there would be seven years of <u>abundance</u> and seven years of famine. His dream saved the Egyptian people, who were able to store enough food and water to survive the drought.
   a. poverty   b. little water   c. plenty   d. starvation

6. Although people on diets often <u>forego</u> potatoes, one has to eat eleven potatoes to put on one pound of weight.
   a. include   b. look forward to   c. restrict   d. give up

7. The <u>monetary</u> units in the nineteenth century in Siberia were blocks of tea.
   a. dietary   b. official   c. military   d. money

Fill-in

Write the best word from this list in the blank in each sentence below.

economic   purified   extolling   commitment   borne

paraphernalia

8. _____ the virtues of your teacher will probably not get you a better grade in a college class.

9. _____ decisions are faced by everyone no matter how much or little money he or she makes.

10. _____ water has chemicals and some minerals removed, which some people think makes it taste better.

11. The graduated income tax is an attempt to make sure that social costs are _____ fairly.

12. Gambling _____ includes slot machines, roulette wheels, dice, cards, and chips.

13. Dressing fashionably involves a _____ of time and money.

SKILLS EXERCISE: SUMMARIZING

For explanation see p. 299

Use your marginal self-test notes to write a brief summary of the article in sentence form.

25

Choosing an Occupation or Career

SKILLS EXERCISE:
SURVEY

Survey the following article by reading the author's name, the title, and the headings. This should take no longer than thirty seconds. After your survey, and without looking back at the article, write three questions that you think will be answered by reading it.

1. _____

2. _____

3. _____

Now read the article. Write your starting time here: _____

25

Choosing an Occupation or Career

Gerald Corey

WHAT DO YOU EXPECT FROM WORK? What factors do you stress in selecting a career or an occupation? In working with college students, we find that many of them haven't really thought seriously about why they are choosing a given vocation. For some, parental pressure or encouragement is the major reason for their choice. Others have idealized views of what it would be like to be a lawyer, engineer, or doctor. Many of these people haven't looked at what they value the most and whether these values can be attained in their chosen vocation. John Holland's (1985) theory of career decision making is based on the assumption that career choices are an expression of personality: "The choice of an occupation is an expressive act that reflects the person's motivation, knowledge, personality, and ability. Occupations represent a way of life, an environment rather than a set of isolated work functions or skills."

BEING ACTIVE IN CAREER PLANNING

One of the major factors that might prevent you from becoming active in planning for a career is the temptation to put off doing what needs to be done to *choose* your work. If you merely "fall into" a job, you will probably be disappointed with the outcome.

A reviewer of this book called our attention to predictions that typical workers will make five to seven occupational changes in their life. Thus, it could well be a mistake to think about selecting *one* occupation that will last a lifetime. Instead, it may be more fruitful to think about choosing a general type of work or a broad field of endeavor that appeals to you. You can consider your present job or field of study as a means of gaining experience and opening doors to new possibilities, and you can focus on what *you* want to learn from this experience. It can be liberating to realize that your decisions about work can be part of a developmental process and that your jobs can change as you change.

THE DANGERS OF CHOOSING AN OCCUPATION TOO SOON

So much emphasis is placed on what you will do "for a living" that there is a real danger of feeling compelled to choose an occupation or a career before you're really ready to do so. In our society there is pressure from an early age to grow up. The encouragement to identify with some occupation begins in childhood with the often-heard question "What are you going to be when you grow up?" (Part of the implication of this question is that we're not grown up until we've decided to *be* something.) If freshman year in high school isn't too early to start worrying about acceptance to college, then no grade is too early to start worrying about acceptance to the right high school! Carney and Wells (1987) write that society expects young people to identify their values, choose a vocation and a lifestyle, and then settle down. The implication is that once young people make the "right decision," they should be set for life. Yet deciding on a career is not that simple.

One of the dangers in focusing on a particular occupation too soon is that students' interest patterns are often not sufficiently reliable or stable in high school or, sometimes, even the college years to predict job success and satisfaction. Furthermore, the typical student does not have enough self-knowledge or knowledge of educational offerings and vocational opportunities to make realistic decisions. The pressure to make premature vocational decisions often results in choosing an occupation in which one does not have the interests and abilities required for success.

FACTORS IN VOCATIONAL DECISION MAKING

Making vocational choices is a process spanning a considerable period rather than an isolated event. Researchers in career development have found that most people go through a series of stages in choosing the occupation or, more typically, occupations that they will follow. . . . Various factors emerge or become influential during each phase of development. The following factors have been shown to be important in determining a person's occupational decision-making process: self-concept, interests, abilities, values, occupational attitudes, socioeconomic level, parental influence, ethnic identity, gender, and physical, mental, emotional, and social handicaps. In choosing your vocation (or evaluating the choices you've made previously), you may want to consider which factors really mean the most to you. Let's consider some of these factors, keeping in mind that vocational choice is a process, not an event.

Self-Concept

Some writers in career development contend that a vocational choice is an attempt to fulfill one's self-concept. People with a poor self-concept, for example, are not likely to envision themselves in a meaningful or important job. They are likely to keep their aspirations low, and thus their achievements will probably be low. They may select and remain in a job that they do not enjoy or derive satisfaction from, based on their conviction that such a job is all they are worthy of. In this regard choosing a vocation can be thought of as a public declaration of the kind of person we see ourselves as being.

Occupational Attitudes

Research indicates that the higher the educational requirements for an occupation, the higher its status, or prestige (Isaacson, 1986). We develop our attitudes toward the status of occupations by learning from the people in our environment. Typical first-graders are not aware of the differential status of occupations, yet in a few years these children begin to rank occupations in a manner similar to that of adults. Some research has shown that positive attitudes toward most occupations are common among first-graders but that these preferences narrow steadily with each year of school (Nelson, 1963). As students advance to higher grades, they reject more and more occupations as unacceptable. Unfortunately, they rule out some of the very jobs from which they may have to choose if they are to find employment as adults. It is difficult for people to feel positively about themselves if they have to accept an occupation they perceive as low in status.

Abilities

Ability or aptitude has received as much attention as any of the factors deemed significant in the career decision-making process, and it is probably used more often than any other factor. *Ability* refers to your competence in an activity; *aptitude* is your ability to learn. There are both general and specific abilities. Scholastic aptitude, often called general intelligence or IQ, is a general ability typically considered to consist of both verbal and numerical aptitudes. Included among the specific abilities are mechanical, clerical, and spatial aptitudes, abstract reasoning ability, and eye/hand/foot coordination. Scholastic aptitude is particularly significant, because it largely determines who will be able to obtain the levels of education required for entrance into the higher-status occupations.

Interestingly, most studies show little direct relationship between measured aptitudes and occupational performance and satisfaction (Drummond, 1988; Herr & Cramer, 1988). This does not mean that ability is unimportant, but it does indicate that we must consider other factors in career planning.

Interests

Interest measurement has become popular and is used extensively in career planning. Interests, unlike abilities, have been found to be moderately effective as predictors of vocational success, satisfaction, and persistence (Super & Bohn, 1970). Therefore, vocational planning should give primary consideration to interests. It is important to first determine your areas of vocational interest, then to identify occupations for which these interests are appropriate, and then to determine those occupations for which you have the abilities required for satisfactory job performance. Research evidence indicates only a slight relationship between interests and abilities (Tolbert, 1980). In other words, simply because you are interested in a job does not necessarily mean that you have the ability needed for it.

Values

It is important for you to assess, identify, and clarify your values so that you will be able to match them with your career. There is some merit to following the combination of your interests and abilities as primary reliable guides for a general occupational area. After you have considered how your interests and abilities match with possible career choices, it is then helpful to explore your values. For purposes of this discussion, values can be classified in three general areas: (1) spiritual/religious, (2) family/interpersonal, and (3) money/material possessions. Refer to the "Activities and Exercises" in this chapter for a self-assessment of your work-related values.

Your *work values* pertain to what you hope to accomplish through your role in an occupation. Work values are an important aspect of your total value system, and knowing those things that bring meaning to your life is crucial if you hope to find a career that has personal value for you. Most career-guidance centers in colleges and universities now offer one or more computer-based programs to help students decide on a career. One popular program is known as the System of Interactive Guidance and Information, or more commonly referred to as SIGI. This program assesses and categorizes your work values. Taking it will aid you in identifying specific occupations that you might want to explore.

You might consider scheduling an appointment in the career-counseling center at your college to participate in a computer-based occupational guidance program. In addition to SIGI, other programs are the Career Information System (CIS), the Guidance Information System (GIS), Choices, and Discover. Each of these programs develops lists of occupations to explore. As you will see, it is both realistic and useful to think of an occupation that is consistent with your *personal orientation to life*, which is described below.

2200 words

Write your ending time here: _____

Subtract your starting time: _____

Total time: _____

Check the Rate Chart in the back of the book to find how many words per minute you have read, and then record your score on the Progress Chart.

ANSWERS TO SURVEY QUESTIONS
Without looking back at the article, write the answers to your survey questions here.

1. _____

2. _____

3. _____

MAIN IDEA

Before going on to the Comprehension Check, and without looking back at the article, write a complete sentence stating the main idea of this article.

_____

_____

Your answer should be similar to the correct answer for question 2 in the Comprehension Check.

25

Choosing an Occupation or Career

COMPREHENSION CHECK
Circle the letter before the best answer to each question below. Don't
look back at the article.

Subject and Main Idea

1. The subject of the article is
   a. how professionals can help you choose a good career.
   b. when to choose a career.
   c. problems in career planning.
   d. guidelines in choosing an occupation or career.

2. The main idea is that
   a. career planning should be done with a professional counselor.
   b. choosing a career is difficult.
   c. self-concept is a key factor in choosing a career.
   d. choosing a career takes thought and knowledge.

Details

3. Which is *not* a factor in choosing a career mentioned in the article?
   a. abilities
   b. self-concept
   c. attitudes
   d. availability of jobs

4. The author says that choosing a career is
   a. an event that should take place as early as possible.
   b. an ongoing process that takes time.
   c. something that must be done while in college.
   d. the goal of any good college program.

5. How many career changes will a typical worker make in his or
   her life?
   a. one to three
   b. three to five
   c. five to seven
   d. seven to ten

6. Our attitudes toward certain occupations
   a. are formed before we enter school.
   b. narrow as we grow older.
   c. broaden as we grow older.
   d. are inborn.

Inferences

7. The author is probably a
   a. high school counselor.
   b. college dean.
   c. college career counselor.
   d. researcher.

8. A student seeing the author as a career counselor would
   a. not be given any tests but would talk with him extensively about interests.
   b. be given many tests of aptitude.
   c. be given a general battery of tests but also interviewed.
   d. feel uncomfortable taking so many tests.

9. The author would probably
   a. prefer students to get career guidance in high school.
   b. not believe in tests as a way to help in career planning.
   c. like to see more guidance counselors hired at the college level.
   d. encourage students to make a decision and stick to it.

10. The author implies that
    a. most career counselors do a poor job of helping students choose an occupation.
    b. parents, teachers, and counselors are wrong to pressure high school students into choosing a career.
    c. students are more than willing to change majors in college.
    d. students change majors too many times in college.

QUESTIONS FOR ANALYSIS AND APPLICATION

1. Go to your college career center and make a list of the methods the counselors use to help you choose a career.

2. If you have chosen a career, use the questions below to analyze how you went about doing so. If you have not chosen a career, use the questions to help decide how you should go about doing so.

   A. Rating important factors:

   Indicate how important each of the following would be for you using the scale below.

Essential	Important	No opinion	Somewhat important	Unimportant
1	2	3	4	5

   Free time (short hours) _____

   Light work load _____

   Money _____

   Status _____

   Being your own boss _____

   Having responsibility for others _____

   Opportunity for advancement _____

   Creativity _____

   Variety _____

   Mental challenge _____

   Travel _____

   Opportunity to work with others _____

   Social importance _____

   B. Finding the career:

   Did you (will you)

   Go to the career center to take tests? _____

   Ask people in the field? _____

   Go to the library to look up books on occupations? _____

   Do other things? _____ If so, what? _____

VOCABULARY IN CONTEXT
Multiple Choice
Circle the letter before the best definition of each underlined word or phrase.

1. It is important that you set some goals you can <u>attain</u> quickly, so that you don't get discouraged.
   a. abandon   b. find   c. reach   d. invent

2. If you have no <u>aspirations</u>, you will never have anything to look forward to.
   a. goals   b. ideas   c. money   d. failures

3. Some people <u>derive</u> great pleasure out of drinking a $50 bottle of wine, while others see it as a waste of money.
   a. deny   b. get   c. discover   d. avoid

4. Born-again Christians have strong <u>convictions</u> about the role of God in their lives.
   a. doubts   b. imaginations   c. beliefs   d. proof

5. Although he hasn't received an Oscar, Steven Spielberg established his <u>status</u> as a top director with the success of *E.T.* and *Jaws*.
   a. finances   b. position   c. feelings   d. unimportance

6. It is too bad when you have no <u>aptitude</u> for things that deeply interest you because you have little chance of succeeding at them.
   a. interest   b. judgment   c. desire   d. talent

7. It is difficult to <u>assess</u> a situation when you are emotionally involved. Sometimes it is best to get someone else's opinion.
   a. evaluate   b. avoid   c. find   d. solve

Fill-in

Write the best word from this list in the blank in each sentence below:

idealized   socioeconomic   deemed   spatial

envision   fruitful   stable   gender

8. The _____ relationship between the size
   of a room and the furniture in it can make the room look large
   or small.

9. It is usually _____ unwise to take twenty
   units in college while working full time.

10. During the 1940s, Judy Garland was the _____
    image of the wholesome girl, so she could never play a villain or
    sex symbol in a movie.

11. The _____ status of people in India once
    varied widely because of their caste.

12. Many people who are not mentally _____
    have been released from institutions only to become homeless
    wanderers on public streets.

13. Everyone who invests in the stock market hopes to have a

    _____ year.

14. It is illegal to do hiring based on _____ .
    Whether a person is male or female should not make a difference.

15. Some writers have the ability to _____
    beautiful scenes, while others must write about what they have
    experienced.

SKILLS EXERCISE: STUDY MAPPING

For explanation
see pp. 297–299

Fill in the blank spaces on the following map.

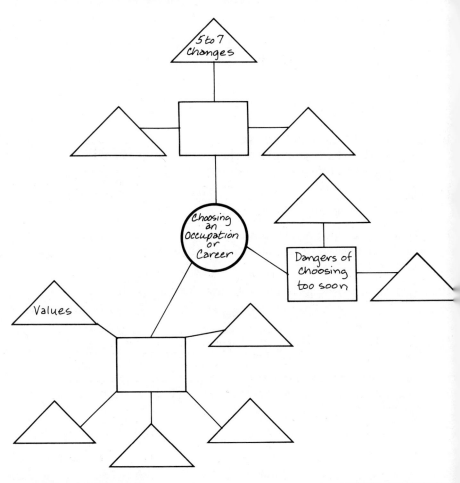

SKILLS EXERCISE: SUMMARIZING

For explanation
see pp. 299

Use the study map to make a brief summary of the article in sentence form.

26

Problem Solving

VOCABULARY PREVIEW

generating (jen'ə rāt iŋ):   originating or producing

hypotheses (hī päth'ə sēz):   possibilities that can be tested; theories or propositions

phenomenon (fi näm'ə nän', -nən):   a scientific fact; an unusual occurrence

heuristics (hyoo ris'tiks):   strategies for simplifying a problem

strategies (strat'ə jēz):   methods or means to an end

replicable (rep'li kə b'l):   able to be duplicated; reproducible

plausible (plô'zə b'l):   seemingly true, acceptable: often implying disbelief

probability (präb'ə bil'ə tē):   the number of times something will probably occur over the range of possible occurrences, expressed as a ratio

statistical (stə tis'tik'l):   of or having to do with, consisting of or based on facts or data of a numerical kind which has been assembled and classified

novel (näv''l):   new; unusual

disproportionate (dis'prə pôr'shən it):   imbalanced; lopsided; unequal

fat, āpe, cär; ten, ēven; is, bīte; gō, hôrn, tōōl, look; oil, out; up, fur; chin, she; thin, then; zh, leisure; ŋ, ring; ə for a in ago; ' as in able (ā'b'l)

SKILLS EXERCISE:
SQ3R

For explanation see pp. 291–296

A. *Survey.* Survey the following article by reading the author's name, the title, and the headings and subheadings. This should take no longer than thirty seconds.

B. *Question.* Without looking back at the article, write three questions that you think will be answered by reading it.

1. _____

2. _____

3. _____

C. *Read.* Now read the article. Write your starting time here: _____

26

Problem Solving

James W. Kalat

O N A COLLEGE PHYSICS EXAM, a student was once asked how to use a barometer to determine the height of a building. He answered that he would tie a long string to the barometer, go to the top of the building, and carefully lower the barometer until it reached the ground. Then he would cut the string and measure its length.

When the professor marked this answer incorrect, the student asked why. "Well," said the professor, "your method would work, but it's not the method I wanted you to use." The student protested that he had no way of reading the professor's mind. The professor then offered, as a compromise, to let the student try again.

"All right," the student said. "Take the barometer to the top of the building, drop it, and measure the time it takes to hit the ground. Then from the formula for the speed of a falling object, using the gravitational constant, calculate the height of the building."

"Hmmm," replied the professor. "That too would work. And it does make use of physical principles. But it still isn't the answer I had in mind. Can you think of another way to use the barometer to determine the height of the building?"

"Another way? Sure," replied the student. "Place the barometer next to the building on a sunny day. Measure the height of the barometer and the length of its shadow. Also measure the length of the building's shadow. Then use the formula

$$\frac{\text{height of barometer}}{\text{length of barometer's shadow}} = \frac{\text{height of building}}{\text{length of building's shadow}}$$

The professor was becoming more and more impressed with the student, but he was still reluctant to give credit for the answer. He asked for yet another way.

The student suggested, "Measure the barometer's height. Then walk up the stairs of the building, marking it off in units of the barometer's height. At the top, take the number of barometer units and multiply by the height of the barometer to get the height of the building."

The professor sighed. "Just give me one more way — any other way — and I'll give you credit, even if it's not the answer I wanted."

"Really?" asked the student with a smile. "Any other way?"

"Yes, any other way."

"All right," said the student. "Go to the man who owns the building and say, 'Hey, buddy, if you tell me how tall this building is, I'll give you this neat barometer!'"

We sometimes face a logical or practical problem that we have never tried to solve before. Perhaps no one has ever dealt with it before. In any case, we have to devise a new solution; we cannot rely on a memorized or practiced solution. Sometimes people develop creative, imaginative solutions, like the ones the physics student proposed. Sometimes they offer less imaginative, but still reasonable, solutions. Sometimes they suggest something quite illogical, and sometimes they cannot think of any solution at all. Psychologists study problem-solving behavior partly to understand the thought processes behind it and partly to look for ways to help people reason more effectively.

Generally we go through four phases when we set about solving a problem. . . . (1) understanding the problem, (2) generating one or more hypotheses, (3) testing the hypotheses, and (4) checking the result. A scientist goes through those four phases in approaching a new, complex phenomenon, and you would probably go through them in trying to assemble a bicycle that came with garbled instructions. To at least a small extent, people can be trained to solve problems more successfully. We shall go through the four phases of problem solving, with advice on how to handle each phase.

UNDERSTANDING AND SIMPLIFYING
A DIFFICULT PROBLEM

You are facing a question or a problem, and you have no idea how to begin. You may even think the problem is unsolvable. Then someone shows you how to solve it and you realize, "I could have done that, if I had only thought of trying it that way."

When you do not see how to solve a problem, try starting with a simpler version of it. For example, here is what may appear to be a difficult, even an impossible, problem: A professor hands back students' test papers at random. On the average, how many students will accidentally receive their own paper? (Note that the problem fails to specify how many students are in the class.)

At first the problem sounds impossible, but see what happens if we start with simpler cases: How many students will get their own paper back if there is only one student in the class? One, of course. What if there are two students? There is a 50% chance that both will get their own paper back and a 50% chance that neither will. On the average, one student will get the correct paper. What if there are three students? Each student has one chance in three of getting his or her own paper. One-third chance times three students means that, on the average, one student will get the correct paper. We begin to see a pattern. Having worked through a few simple examples, we realize that the number of students in the class does not matter; on the average, one student will get his or her own paper back.

Here is another way to approach a seemingly impossible problem: *If you do not see how to answer the question, answer a related question.* For example, try the following problem (Figure 1): Train A goes from Baltimore to Washington at 25 miles per hour. Train B travels from Washington to Baltimore at the same speed. Baltimore and Washington are 50 miles apart. A bird leaves Baltimore at the same time as the trains, flying 60 miles per hour. It flies until it reaches train B and then instantly reverses direction and flies back until it reaches train A. Then it flies back to train B, and so forth. By the

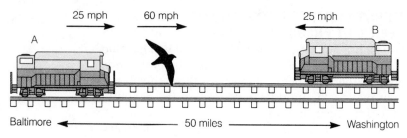

Figure 1. As the crow flies: A bird flies back and forth between two trains traveling at the speeds indicated. When
it meets one train, it reverses direction instantaneously and
flies toward the other. How far will the bird have traveled
when the two trains meet at the halfway point?

time the two trains and the bird meet at the center, how
far will the bird have traveled?

If you start by calculating how far the bird will
travel by the time it meets train B for the first time, then
how far it travels to meet train A again, you quickly
become discouraged. A better solution is to begin by
answering an easier question: How much time will it
take for the two trains to meet? That is the same period
of time the bird will fly. At 60 miles per hour, how far
will the bird have flown during that time? Note how the
answer to the easy question enabled us to answer the
difficult question.

Finally, *if you do not know the answer to a factual
question, see whether you know enough to make a decent estimate.* The physicist Enrico Fermi posed questions to his students that they could answer in this
manner. For example, what is the circumference of the
Earth? Even if you do not know the answer, you might
know the distance from New York to Los Angeles —
about 3,000 miles (4,800 km). The distance from New
York to Los Angeles is also a change of three time zones.
How many time zones would a traveler cross in going
completely around the Earth? Twenty-four. So the distance from New York is ³⁄₂₄ (or one eighth) of the distance
around the Earth. Eight times the distance from New
York to Los Angeles is 8 × 3,000 miles (4,800 km) =
24,000 miles (38,400 km). That is a decent approxima-
tion of the actual circumference of the Earth, 24,902.4
miles (40,068 km).

GENERATING HYPOTHESES

Suppose that after simplifying a problem as well as we can, we realize that many answers are possible. At that point we need to generate hypotheses — preliminary interpretations that we can evaluate or test.

In some cases, we can generate more hypotheses than we can test. Consider the traveling salesperson problem in Figure 2. Starting and finishing at the place marked HOME, how could you travel through each of the marked cities while keeping your total travel distance to a minimum? We could set up an algorithm to solve the problem. An algorithm is a mechanical, repetitive mathematical procedure for solving a problem such as "Calculate the distance from HOME to a first city, then to a second city, and so on through all cities and back to HOME again. Repeat the same procedure for all possible orders of the cities. Compare the distances of all the possible routes."

That algorithm tests all the possible hypotheses (routes) and is sure to lead us to the best. But even with just 10 cities to visit there are nearly 2 million possible routes (10 factorial divided by 2). As the number of cities

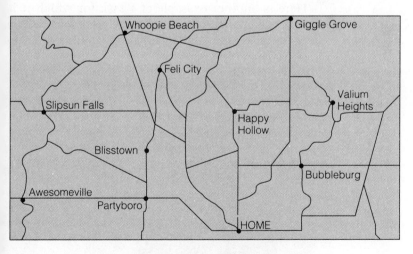

Figure 2.   What is the shortest route from home through each of the other cities and back again? In this problem, we can generate more hypotheses than we can easily test.

increases, the task becomes unmanageable even for large computers. To make the problem manageable, we must narrow the number of hypotheses. We do so by resorting to heuristics, strategies for simplifying a problem or for guiding an investigation. For instance, we might decide to test only those routes in which each move takes us to one of the four closest cities or only those routes that do not cross an earlier route.

For other problems, we find that we have too few hypotheses rather than too many. Consider the following: Take any 3-digit number, such as 427, and then repeat it: 427427. Whatever number you choose, the resulting 6-digit number will be evenly divisible by 13. Why?

You might begin by testing several such numbers to see whether they are in fact evenly divisible by 13, but that would not be the same as testing a hypothesis. The difficulty here is generating *any* hypothesis at all. Try for a while. Sometimes people who cannot generate a hypothesis, or who find themselves generating the same few hypotheses again and again, find it helpful to do something else for a while and then return to the problem afresh.

Here is another example of a task for which it is difficult to generate a hypothesis. Figure 3 shows an object that was made by cutting and bending an ordi-

Figure 3.   An object made by cutting and folding an ordinary piece of cardboard. How was it done?

nary piece of cardboard. How was it made? If you think you know, take a piece of paper and try to make it yourself.

People react to this problem in different ways. Some see the solution almost at once; others take a long time before insight suddenly strikes them; still others never figure it out. Some people have looked at this illustration and told me that it was impossible, that I must have pasted two pieces together or bought a custom-made piece of "trick" cardboard.

Give it a try. When you discover the answer, you will see how your thinking was at first limited by certain habits and assumptions.

Solving problems of this type differs from solving, say, algebra problems. Most people can look at an algebra problem and reasonably predict whether or not they will be able to solve it. As they work on it, they can estimate how close they are to reaching a solution. On insight problems, however, such as the cardboard-folding problem, the answer comes either suddenly and unpredictably ("Aha!") or not at all.

TESTING HYPOTHESES

If you think you have solved a problem, test your idea to see whether it will work. Many people who think they have a great idea never bother to try it out, even on a small scale. One inventor applied for a patent on the "perpetual motion machine" shown in Figure 4. Rubber balls, being lighter than water, rise in a column of water and overflow the top. Being heavier than air, they fall, moving a belt and thereby generating energy. At the bottom, they reenter the water column. Do you see why this system could never work? You would if you tried to build it.

CHECKING THE RESULTS

The final step in solving a problem is to check the results. You think you have the solution; you think your hypothesis works. Fine, but to make sure, check it again.

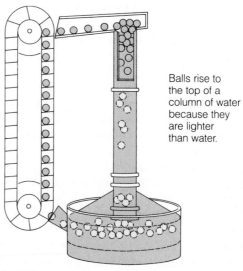

Balls overflow onto conveyor belt and pull it down because they are heavier than air.

Balls rise to the top of a column of water because they are lighter than water.

Balls reenter column of water.

Figure 4. What is wrong with this perpetual motion machine?

In scientific research, checking may mean repeating an experiment to see whether the results are replicable. In mathematics, checking may be a matter of repeating the calculations or at least of thinking about whether the answer you calculated is plausible. For example, if you have calculated that the answer to some question is "40 square IQ points per cubic second," you might realize that the answer is inherently meaningless and that something must have gone wrong.

GENERALIZING SOLUTIONS TO SIMILAR PROBLEMS

After laboriously solving one problem, can people then solve a related problem more easily? Can they at least recognize that the new problem is related to the old problem, so they know where to start?

Sometimes yes, but all too frequently no. For example: You just flipped a coin 10 times and got *heads* all

0 times. You are going to flip it 10 more times. How many heads should you *expect* to get?

Most people know that, according to probability theory, the answer is 5. Getting 10 heads in the first 10 tries was a matter of chance. There is no reason to expect that the next 10 tries will be mostly heads or that they will be mostly tails to "make up for" the string of heads.

Now consider a related question: Your basketball team has won its first 10 games. How many of its next 10 games is it likely to win? Here 5 may be the wrong answer, but 10 is also a wrong answer. A 10-game winning streak is partly a matter of skill but also partly a matter of chance. In its first 10 games, your team probably enjoyed some good breaks and some helpful calls by the referees on close plays. It may not be so lucky with the next 10. A reasonable prediction is that your team will win 7 or 8 of its next 10 games, even if it plays as well as it did before.

Most people who apply the laws of probability to the first question fail to apply them to the second question. They understand statistical reasoning, but they fail to see its relevance to familiar situations.

In other situations as well, people who have solved one problem correctly fail to solve a second problem that is basically similar. Figure 5a shows a coiled garden hose. When the water spurts out, what path will it take? (Draw it.) Figure 5b shows a curved gun barrel. When the bullet comes out, what path will it take? (Draw it.)

Almost everyone draws the water coming out of the garden hose in a straight path. Even after doing so, however, many people draw a bullet coming out of the gun in a curved path, as if the bullet remembered the curved path it had just taken. The physics is the same in both situations: Both the water and the bullet will follow a straight path (except for the effects of gravity).

Sometimes we recognize similar problems and use our solution to an old problem as a guide to solving a new one; sometimes we do not. What accounts for the difference? One reason is it is easier to generalize a solution after we have seen several examples of it; if we have seen only a single example, we may think of the

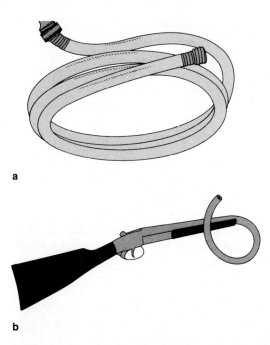

a

b

Figure 5.   Around the bend? (a) Draw the trajectory of water as it flows out of a coiled garden hose. (b) Draw the trajectory of a bullet as it leaves a coiled gun barrel.

solution in only that one context. For example, one group of high school students had learned to solve arithmetic-progression problems in algebra, practicing on a variety of problems. When they were given a fundamentally similar problem in physics, they recognized the similarity and solved it. A different group of students had been taught to solve the physics problem; when they were given the related problem in algebra, most of them failed to recognize the similarity. Apparently the physics students associated the solution entirely with physics, and they failed to see it as a general principle that could be applied more widely.

Let's try a series of problems that are fundamentally similar and see whether after solving one or more of them you can transfer the solution to other problems.

First: Last summer Lisa traveled from Toronto to Miami. David traveled from New York to Los Angeles (see Figure 6). Both took a route that was approximately, but not exactly, straight. Lisa says, "There must be some point on the map that we both passed through last sum-

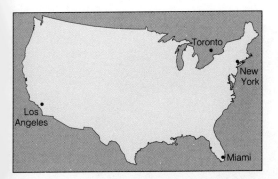

Figure 6.   Going my way? Lisa traveled from Toronto to Miami. David traveled from New York to Los Angeles. Both must have traveled through at least one point in common on the map — though not necessarily at the same time. How do we know that?

mer." She does not know *where* that point was, and Lisa and David need not have passed through it at the same time. Still, there must be some point that they both passed through. How does Lisa know that?

Second problem: This summer Lisa traveled from Anchorage, Alaska, to Miami. David traveled across the South Pacific from Madagascar to New Zealand (see Figure 7). Both followed paths that were only approximately straight. David says, "You must have passed through some point on the globe that is *exactly* opposite to some point I passed through." Again, there is no way to know which points those were. How does David know he's right?

Third problem: Joan says, "I have been at two points on the Earth's surface that are *exactly* opposite each other. I know I am right about that, even though I do not know which points they were." How does she know that?

Almost no one who *begins* with the third problem gets the right answer. But after working through the first two problems, you may have succeeded in transferring your solution to the third problem.

CREATIVITY AND PROBLEM SOLVING
Solving a problem is always to some extent a creative activity. The problem solver must come up with a solu-

Figure 7.   Down south and down under: Lisa traveled from Anchorage to Miami; David traveled from Madagascar to New Zealand. Lisa must have passed through at least one point that was exactly on the opposite side of the world from a point that David passed through (not necessarily at the same time). How do we know that?

tion which is, at least for that person, new and unfamiliar. A higher degree of creativity is represented when someone finds a solution or makes a product that no one has ever achieved before. Psychologists define creativity as the development of novel, socially valued products. Note that the product must be "socially valued." I once watched the premiere performance of a new ballet that I could describe only as "odd." At the end, I joined a few others in the audience in polite applause, but no one seemed to enjoy the performance. Even though the ballet was novel, most people would not consider it creative.

Some people consistently produce more creative ideas and products than others, although they may be more creative in one situation than in another. That is, someone who thinks of creative solutions to mathematical or engineering problems may show little creativity as a poet or painter.

Still, psychologists have tried to identify whatever it is that all forms of creativity have in common. The

Torrance Tests of Creative Thinking use items similar to the one shown in Figure 8 to measure creativity. Scores on these tests provide a reasonably good prediction of long-term creative performance. Children who score high are more likely than others to make creative achievements as adults, including inventions, publications, artistic and musical compositions, and clothing designs.

Although psychologists can measure creativity, they have made little progress in explaining what causes it or why some people are more creative than others. The causes of "major" creative contributions may differ from those of "minor" contributions. Major contributions are those that reorganize a body of information; minor contributions are those that apply known methods to new examples. For example, Pavlov's theory of classical conditioning is a major contribution, whereas a new study of the classical conditioning of fears is a minor contribution. In fields ranging from science to the arts, young adults make a disproportionate number of major contributions, while middle-age adults are responsible for the greatest share of minor (though still important) contributions.

2800 words

Figure 8.   A "what-is-it?" picture similar to those in one part of the Torrance Tests of Creative Thinking.

Write your ending time here: _____

Subtract your starting time: _____

Total time: _____

Check the Rate Chart in the back of the book to find how many words per minute you have read, and then record your score on the Progress Chart.

SQ3R

C. *Read.* Without looking back at the article, write the answers to your SQ3R questions here:

1. _____

2. _____

3. _____

Underline the main ideas and supporting details in the article that you believe will be tested in the Comprehension Check.

Write in the *margin* short *notes* that will remind you of the *main ideas* and details you want to remember.

D. *Recite.* Now cover up the text of the article and use the marginal notes to test your memory of it. Check your underlining to see whether you forgot anything. Repeat this step until you are able to remember everything you underlined.

E. *Review.* This article is organized like a short textbook chapter. It is too short to break into sections, but if it were a long article, you might have had to divide it into sections. In that case, you would have done your major review immediately after you finished each section, again one week later, and then as often as needed to maintain your memory.

MAIN IDEA

Before going on to the Comprehension Check, and without looking back at the article, write one complete sentence stating the main idea of this article.

_____

_____

Your answer should be similar to the correct answer for question 2 in the Comprehension Check.

26

Problem Solving

COMPREHENSION CHECK
Circle the letter before the best answer to each question below. Don't look back at the article.

Subject and Main Idea
1. The subject is
   a. testing hypotheses.
   b. dealing with uncertainty.
   c. reasoning.
   d. problem solving.

2. The main idea is that
   a. problem solving is a four-step process.
   b. decision making involves probabilities.
   c. people are not always logical.
   d. computers make problem solving easier.

Details
3. Which of the following is *not* one of the four phases of problem solving?
   a. generating hypotheses.
   b. checking the result.
   c. dealing with uncertainty.
   d. understanding the problem.

4. To simplify a problem, we use
   a. probabilities.
   b. hypotheses.
   c. heuristics.
   d. generalizing.

5. Most major creative contributions come from
   a. children and teenagers.
   b. young adults.
   c. middle-aged adults.
   d. elderly adults.

6. Solutions to insight problems
   a. come suddenly.
   b. come from testing several hypotheses.
   c. are based on mathematical algorithms.
   d. come after the problem is simplified.

Inferences
7. People who enter state lotteries probably
   a. don't really understand the probability of their winning.
   b. are gamblers at heart.
   c. make good investments.
   d. always follow their hunches.

8. Which of the following statements is a provable hypothesis?
   a. Shakespeare is the greatest writer in English.
   b. Mary is better looking than Jean.
   c. Math classes are harder than English classes.
   d. The cost of living has increased.

9. The most successful gamblers probably
   a. are just luckier than other people.
   b. are those most willing to take risks.
   c. make choices based on probabilities.
   d. get the most practice.

10. Logical errors in our thinking cause us to
    a. be manipulated by advertisers.
    b. make poor choices of elected officials.
    c. make poor financial decisions.
    d. do all of the above.

QUESTIONS FOR ANALYSIS AND APPLICATION
1. Female students at your school have been complaining that they are failing Mr. Smith's auto-shop class, while the males are passing. When asked why they believe this is so, they have said that the grade in the class depends on performing a tune-up, and that the males have opportunities during the class to practice tune-ups, while the females only observe. According to the article, the way to solve a problem is to generate a hypothesis, test the hypothesis, and check the result. Follow these steps to solve the female students' problem.

2. Look at the problem in the section "Generating Hypotheses" concerning why six-digit numbers are divisible by 13. Test the following hypothesis and determine whether or not it works: All numbers of the form XYZXYZ are integral multiples of 1001. You can get any of these numbers by multiplying 1001 times XYZ. Because 1001 is evenly divisible by 13, every number that is evenly divisible by 1001 is also evenly divisible by 13.

VOCABULARY IN CONTEXT
Multiple Choice
Circle the letter before the best definition of each underlined word.

1. There are many <u>hypotheses</u> about the causes of mental illness, including everything from chemical to environmental factors, but none has been proven.
   a. books   b. arguments   c. theories   d. lectures

2. If an experiment's procedures are <u>replicable</u>, then its results can be considered legitimate.
   a. copied   b. followed   c. reproducible   d. easy

3. Perhaps only a <u>novel</u> idea will provide an answer to the growing problem.
   a. familiar   b. new   c. usual   d. foreign

4. Though his excuse for speeding on the freeway seemed <u>plausible</u>, the highway patrolman gave him a citation.
   a. believable   b. improbable   c. unlikely   d. miserable

5. Brainstorming is a technique for <u>generating</u> possible solutions to problems.
   a. rejecting   b. selecting   c. producing   d. judging

Fill-in

Write the best word from this list in the blank in each sentence below.

heuristic   strategies   probability   disproportionate

statistical   phenomenon

6. The earthquake of 1906 in San Francisco was a devastating

    _____ .

7. _____ for problem solving are taught in
    math classes.

8. The letter of the alphabet with the highest _____
    of occurring in any given word is *e*.

9. Focusing on only one aspect of a problem at a time is a

    _____ strategy.

10. The Nielsen Ratings use _____ methods
    to determine how popular various television programs are.

11. Overcrowded schools have a _____
    number of students.

SKILLS EXERCISE:
SUMMARIZING

For explanation
see p. 299

Use your marginal self-test notes to write a brief summary of the
article in sentence form.

27

Violence in the Family

SKILLS EXERCISE:
SQ3R

For explanation
see pp. 291–296

A. *Survey.* Survey the following article by reading the author's name, the title, and the first sentence of every paragraph. This should take no longer than thirty seconds.

B. *Question.* Without looking back at the article, write three questions that you think will be answered by reading it.

1. _____

2. _____

3. _____

C. *Read.* Now read the article. Write your starting time here: _____

27

Violence in the Family

Guy Le François

P ROPHETS AND OTHERS WHO SPECIALIZE IN
GLOOM and related states have been warning us
for some time that violence is rapidly becoming
a way of life in modern societies. And perhaps
they are correct. Certainly, police reports indicate that
violent crimes in Western industrialized nations have
increased sharply during recent decades, as has international terrorism. However, wife abuse, defined in terms
of physical violence by the husband, appears to have
decreased by about 27 percent between 1975 and 1985
(Figure 1).

Although it might be tempting to assume that violence typically involves strangers and that surrounding
ourselves with friends and family will therefore protect
us, that, sadly, does not appear to be the case. Indeed,
more than 25 percent of all assaults and homicides that
are reported to police involve members of the same *family*. And a large percentage of the rest involve friends or
at least acquaintances. More than half of all rapes,
crimes that most of us attribute to disturbed strangers
in dark parking lots, are committed by acquaintances or
relatives — or "dates." One third of all female murder
victims are killed by boyfriends or husbands. As Gelles
puts it: "We have discovered that violence between family members, rather than being a minor pattern of behavior, or a behavior that is rare and dysfunctional, is a
patterned and normal aspect of interaction between
family members."

Violence in the family takes a variety of forms. It is
perhaps most evident in the observation that more than
9 out of 10 parents admit to using physical force to punish children. It is even more dramatically apparent in

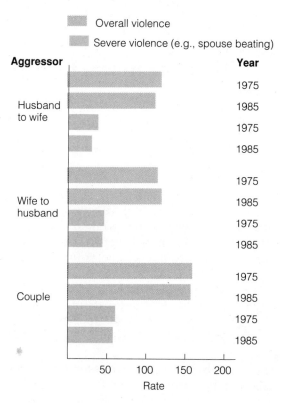

Figure 1. Rate of marital violence per 1,000 couples. (From Straus & Gelles, 1986.)

instances of child abuse. And it is present, as well, in countless episodes of violence among siblings. Indeed, violence among siblings seems to be common among young children, although it diminishes rapidly with increasing age. In a sample of 2,143 families, Straus found that 74 percent of all 3- to 4-year-old children who had siblings occasionally resorted to some form of physical aggression in their interactions. Only 36 percent of those aged 15 to 17 behaved in similar fashion.

Violence in the family is also apparent in instances of wife and husband beating. And surprisingly, husband beating is almost as common as wife beating. In Straus and Gelles's investigation of American families, 3.8 percent of all husbands admitted to activities that the authors define as wife beating. These activities include

Minor violence

Threw something

Pushed, grabbed, shoved

Slapped

Severe violence

Kicked, bit, hit with fist

Hit, tried to hit with something

Beat up

Threatened with gun or knife

Used gun or knife

Year
1975
1985

■ Husband-to-wife violence
■ Wife-to-husband violence

25   50   75   100   125
Rate

Figure 2. Comparison of interspouse violence rates per 1,000 couples, 1975–1985. (From Straus & Gelles, 1986.)

Interspouse Violence. Two large-scale surveys of domestic violence conducted 10 years apart show little change in violent acts between husband and wife during this period, although Straus and Gelles note a trend toward a reduction in the incidence of family violence. They speculate this reduction may result from (1) differences in the two studies, (2) a greater reluctance to report violence in 1985, or (3) an actual reduction in family violence, perhaps because of programs designed to combat child and wife abuse, or because of social changes that make such behavior less acceptable and less likely. Still, overall incidence of family violence is shockingly high. Projections of these figures led to an estimate of some 1.6 million battered wives in the United States in 1985. A surprising finding, first reported in 1975 and confirmed again in 1985, is that as many wives beat their husbands as vice versa.

kicking, biting, hitting with the fist or some other object, threatening with a knife or a gun, or actually using a knife or a gun. And an amazing 4.6 percent of all wives admitted to similar activities with respect to their husbands. However, Straus cautions that wife beating tends to be hidden and secretive more often than is husband beating and that wives are, in fact, far more often *victims* than are husbands.

The picture presented by surveys such as these is probably only a partial sketch, given the privacy of the family. Its affairs are not open to social science or to law-enforcement agencies. In addition, we have attitudes concerning the *right* of parents to punish their children physically, the normality of siblings fighting, and, yes, even the right of a husband to beat his wife. These tend to cloud the prevalence and seriousness of violence in the family. Thus, when Shotland and Straw staged a series of events where one individual attacked another, bystanders almost always tried to assist the victim unless the attack involved a man and a woman. When a man attacked a woman, bystanders usually assumed that the couple was married and that they should therefore not interfere. It is perhaps the same sort of reasoning that generally makes it legally impossible for a husband to rape his wife.

In most jurisdictions, rape is defined as forcible sexual intercourse with someone *other* than a spouse. This same implicit acceptance of a husband's right to use physical force on his wife explains why many law-enforcement agencies are reluctant to charge husbands with assault when wives are the victims — unless the results of the assault are obvious and serious. English common law maintains that a man is still king in his castle — however humble that castle might be.

But winds of change have begun to blow more strongly over our kingdoms. There are now increasing numbers of shelters for battered and abused women and children. And there are some reasons to think that these may sometimes reduce family violence. Also, legal systems have become more forceful in their recognition and treatment of the problem.

Why do some husbands beat their wives? There is no simple answer. Some, probably a minority, might be classified as suffering from a psychological disorder. In one study involving 100 battered wives, 25 percent of the husbands had received psychiatric help in the past. And, according to the wives, many more were in need of such help. A great many of these husbands came to their marriages with a history of violence. Many had been abused and beaten as children. And compared with the general population, more of them were chronically unemployed and poorly educated.

Other factors that contribute to violence in the family include the high incidence of violence in society, cultural attitudes that accept violence as a legitimate reaction in certain situations, and our predominantly sexist attitudes toward the roles of husband and wife in contemporary marriage.

1050 words

Write your ending time here: _____

Subtract your starting time: _____

Total time: _____

Check the Rate Chart in the back of the book to find how many words per minute you have read, and then record your score on the Progress Chart.

SQ3R

C. *Read.* Without looking back at the article, write the answers to your SQ3R questions here:

1. _____

2. _____

3. _____

Underline the main ideas and supporting details in the article that you believe will be tested in the Comprehension Check.

Write in the *margin* short *notes* that will remind you of the *main ideas* and details you want to remember.

D. *Recite.* Now cover up the text of the article and use the marginal notes to test your memory of it. Check your underlining to see whether you forgot anything. Repeat this step until you are able to remember everything you underlined.

E. *Review.* This article is organized like a short textbook chapter. It is too short to break into sections, but if it were a long article, you might have had to divide it into sections. In that case, you would have done your major review immediately after you finished each section, again one week later, and then as often as needed to maintain your memory.

MAIN IDEA

Before going on to the Comprehension Check, and without looking back at the article, write one complete sentence stating the main idea of this article.

_____

_____

Your answer should be similar to the correct answer for question 2 in the Comprehension Check.

27

Violence in the Family

COMPREHENSION CHECK
Circle the letter before the best answer to each question below. Don't
look back at the article.

Subject and Main Idea
1. The subject of the article is
    a. violent crimes.
    b. family violence.
    c. wife beating.
    d. child abuse.

2. The main idea is that
    a. we need to understand family violence.
    b. child abuse has increased.
    c. we think some family violence is normal.
    d. family violence is hard to study because it's so private.

Details
3. Between 1975 and 1985, wife abuse appears to have
    a. increased.
    b. decreased.
    c. remained the same.
    d. changed its form.

4. Bystanders will be least likely to help when a
    a. man is attacked by a man.
    b. child is attacked by an adult.
    c. woman is attacked by a woman.
    d. woman is attacked by a man.

5. Factors contributing to family violence include
    a. a high incidence of violence in society.
    b. cultural attitudes that accept violence in certain situations.
    c. sexist attitudes about husbands and wives.
    d. all of the above.

403

6. In most places, rape of a wife by a husband is
   a. legal.
   b. illegal.
   c. unknown.
   d. common.

Inferences

7. Police may be reluctant to interfere in family violence because
   a. they don't think it's a serious crime.
   b. they think the husband has a right to beat his wife.
   c. they can't believe the victim will press charges.
   d. all of the above.

8. Children should be taught how to deal with abusive behavior from
   a. strangers.
   b. friends of the family.
   c. relatives.
   d. all of the above.

9. With regard to husband and wives, English Common Law
   a. tries to be fair.
   b. views women as the husband's property.
   c. gives the wife authority over the children.
   d. presents severe penalties for wife abuse.

10. The author implies that wife beating is most common among the
    a. rich.
    b. poor.
    c. middle class.
    d. foreign born.

Questions for Analysis and Application

1. How do you think sexism affects violence in the family?

2. How do you think that shelters for battered and abused women and children can reduce violence in the family?

VOCABULARY IN CONTEXT
Fill-in
Write the best word from this list in the blank in each sentence below:

dysfunctional   implicit   legitimate   prevalence

1. The _____ of racism in the United States is indisputable.

2. Psychologists often call families in which the children have severe emotional problems _____ .

3. When her neighbor's dog kept her awake with its barking night after night, she felt she had a _____ complaint.

4. In good friendships there is an _____ understanding that a friend will be available when the other person is in need.

SKILLS EXERCISE: OUTLINING

For explanation
see pp. 296–297

Fill in the missing parts of the following outline. You may look back at the reading selection.

Violence in the Family

I. Incidence of violence in the family

    A. Violent crimes have increased.

    B. Wife abuse decreased approximately 27 percent between 1975 and 1985.

    C. _____

        1. 25 percent in family
        2. More among friends and acquaintances

    D. _____

    E. One-third of female murder victims were killed by husbands or boyfriends.

    F. Patterned and normal among family members

II. _____

    A. Nine out of ten parents admit to using physical force to punish children.

    B. _____

    C. _____

        1. Seventy-four percent of 3- to 4-year-olds
        2. Diminishes to 36 percent at 15–17

    D. _____

        1. Husband beating almost as common
        2. Victims usually women

I. Problems

   A. Privacy of family — not open to social science or law enforcement

   B. Cultural attitudes cloud prevalence and seriousness

      1. _____

      2. _____

      3. Right of husband to beat wife — most bystanders won't interfere when a man attacks a woman.

   C. Legal issues

      1. _____

      2. Man is king in his castle.

   D. _____

      1. Shelters for battered and abused women and children — some indication they reduce family violence

      2. _____

   E. Reasons for wife beating

      1. Some suffering from psychological disorders
      2. Some from violent families of origin
      3. Many chronically unemployed and poorly educated
      4. Other factors

         a. _____

         b. _____

         c. _____

SKILLS EXERCISE:
TEXTBOOK GRAPHICS

Look at Figure 1 in this article and answer the following questions.

a. How many wives per thousand beat their husbands in 1985?

_____

b. Did wife beating increase or decrease between 1975 and 1985?

_____

Look at Figure 2 and answer the following questions.

a. How many couples per thousand were involved in pushing, grab-
bing, and shoving a spouse in 1985? _____

b. How many couples per thousand were involved in throwing
something at a spouse in 1975? _____

28

Introduction to Computers

SKILLS EXERCISE:
SURVEY

Survey the following article by reading the author's name, the title, and the headings. This should take no longer than thirty seconds. After your survey, and without looking back at the article, write three questions that you think will be answered by reading it.

1. _____

2. _____

3. _____

Now read the article. Write your starting time here: _____

28

Introduction to Computers

Karl J. Smith

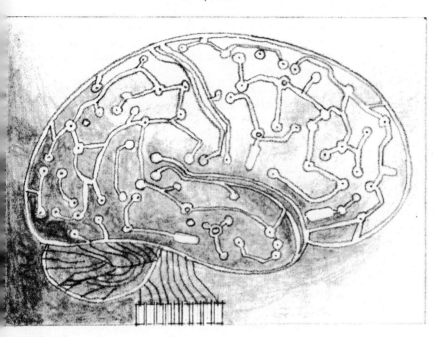

T
HE BIGGEST SURPRISE OF OUR TIME has been the impact of the personal computer on everyone's life. No one foresaw that the use of computers would jump the boundaries of the scientific and engineering communities and create a revolution in our way of life in the last half of the 20th century. No one expected to see a computer sitting on a desk, much less on desks in every type of business, large or small, and even in our homes. Today no one is ready to face the world without some knowledge of computers. What has created this change in our lives is not only the advances in technology that have made computers small and affordable, but the tremendous imagination shown in developing ways to use them.

EARLY COMPUTING DEVICES

Many people still think of computers in the way they were portrayed in the 1950s — as giant brains full of wires, chips, and integrated circuits with the potential for turning us into second-class citizens. It is astounding that computers, which influence our lives to a considerable extent every day, can remain misunderstood by the majority of our population. Even people who venture into one of the new computer stores for information may feel intimidated and overwhelmed by all the new terminology.

To function intelligently in our society, we need to understand how and why computers influence our lives. Every educated person should know something about computers and, if possible, have some experience with one. As computers diligently carry out assigned and generally tedious tasks, people are free to do creative thinking. It is mathematics, not computation, that is fascinating. Prolonged computations lead to weariness, errors, and a distaste for arithmetic. It is not surprising that we have developed devices to perform our calculations.

The first "device" for arithmetic computations is finger counting. It has the advantages of low cost and instant availability. You are familiar with addition and subtractions on your fingers, but here is a method of multiplication by nine. Place both hands as shown in the left drawing.

      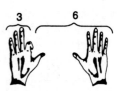

To multiply 4 × 9, simply bend the fourth finger from the left as shown at the right, above.

The answer is read as 36, the bent finger serving to distinguish between the first and second digits in the answer.

What about a two-digit number times 9? There is a procedure, provided the tens digit is smaller than the ones digit. For example, to multiply 36 × 9, separate the third and fourth fingers from the left (as shown), since 36 has 3 tens.

Next bend the sixth finger from the left, since 36 as 6 units. Now the answer can be read directly from the fingers. The answer is 324.

Numbers can also be represented by stones, slip knots, or beads on a string. These devices eventually evolved into the abacus. Abacuses were used thousands of years ago and are still used. In the hands of an expert, they rival even mechanical (but not electronic) calculators in speed. An abacus consists of rods containing sliding beads, four or five in the lower section and one or two in the upper. One in the upper equals five in the lower, and two in the upper equal one in the lower section of the next higher denomination. The abacus is useful today both for figuring business transactions and for teaching mathematics to youngsters. One can actually "see" the "carry" in addition and the "borrow" in subtraction.

FIRST CALCULATING MACHINES

The 17th century saw the beginnings of modern calculating machines. John Napier invented a device in 1624 that was similar to a multiplication table with movable parts, but the first real step was taken in 1642 by Blaise Pascal.

When Pascal was 19, he began to develop a machine that was supposed to add long columns of figures. The machine was essentially like those of today. He built several versions, and, since all were unreliable, he considered his project a failure. However, with the machine he introduced basic principles that are used in modern mathematical calculators.

The next advance in calculating devices came from Germany in about 1672. The great mathematician Gottfried Leibniz studied Pascal's calculators, made improvements on them, and drew up plans for a mechanical calculator. In 1695 a machine was actually built, but the resulting calculator was also unreliable

In the 18th century, an eccentric Englishman, Charles Babbage (1792–1871), developed a grandiose calculating machine called a "difference engine." It had thousands of gears, ratchets, and counters.

Four years later Babbage had still not built his difference engine, but he had designed a much more complicated machine — one capable of accuracy to 20 decimal places. However, it could not be completed since the technical knowledge to build it was not far enough advanced. This machine, the "Analytic Engine," was the forerunner of modern computers. In fact, International Business Machines Corporation has built an Analytic Engine based completely on Babbage's design. It uses, of course, modern technology — and it works perfectly.

In a paper on Babbage's analytic engine, Ada Byron, also known as Lady Lovelace, proposed using binary numbers. This system has become the basis for modern computers. Babbage's Analytic Engine was all mechanical. Modern calculating machines are powered electrically and can perform additions, subtractions, multiplications, and divisions. For raising to a power or taking roots, the device used for many years was a slide rule, which was also invented by Napier. The answers given by a slide rule are only approximate and do not have the precision that is often required. Electronic pocket calculators, which perform all these operations quickly and accurately, represent the latest advance in calculators.

FIRST COMPUTERS

The devices discussed thus far in this section would all be classified as calculators. With some of the new programmable calculators, the distinction between a calculator and a computer is less clear than it was in the past. Stimulated by the need to make ballistics calculations and to break secret codes during World War II, esearchers made great advances in calculating machines. During the late 1930s and early 1940s John Vincent Atanasoff, a physics professor at Iowa State, and his graduate student Clifford E. Berry built an electronic digital computer. However, the first working electronic computers were invented by J. Presper Eckert and John W. Mauchly at the University of Pennsylvania. All computers now in use derive from the original work they did between 1942 and 1946. They built the first fully electronic digital computer called ENIAC (Electronic Numerical Integrator and Calculator). The ENIAC filled a space 30 × 50 feet, weighed 30 tons, had 18,000 vacuum tubes, cost $487,000 to build, and used enough electricity to operate three 150-kilowatt radio stations. Vacuum tubes generate a lot of heat and the room where computers were installed had to be kept in a carefully controlled atmosphere. Still, the tubes had a substantial failure rate, and in order to "program" the computer, many switches and wires had to be adjusted.

The UNIVAC I, built in 1951 by the builders of the ENIAC, became the first commercially available computer. Unlike the ENIAC, it could handle alphabetic data as well as numeric data. The invention of the transistor in 1947 and solid-state devices throughout the 1950s provided the technology for smaller, faster, more reliable machines. In 1958, Seymour Cray developed the first **supercomputer**, a computer that can handle at least 10 million instructions per second. It was used in major scientific research and military defense installations.

Throughout the 1960s and early 1970s, computers continued to become faster and more powerful. They became a part of the business world. The "user" often never saw the machines. A **job** would be submitted to be "batch-processed" by someone trained to run the computer. The notion of "time sharing" developed, so that the computer could handle more than one job, apparently at the same time, by switching quickly from one job to another. Using a computer at this time was often frustrating because an incomplete job would be returned because of an error and the user would have to resubmit the job. It often took days to complete the project.

The large computers, known as *mainframes*, were followed by the **minicomputers**. They took up less than 3 cubic feet of space, and no longer required a controlled atmosphere. These were still used by many people at the same time, though often directly through the use of terminals.

In 1976, Steven Jobs and Stephen Wozniak built the Apple, the first personal computer to be commercially successful. This computer proved extremely popular. Small businesses could afford to purchase these machines that, with a printer attached, took up only twice the space of a typewriter. Technology "buffs" could purchase their own computers. This computer was designed so that innovations that would improve or enlarge the scope of performance of the machine could be added on with relatively little difficulty. Owners could open up their machines and install new devices. This increased contact between the user and the machine produced an atmosphere of tremendous creativity and innovation. In many cases, individual owners brought their own machines to work to introduce their superiors to the potential usefulness of the personal computer.

In the fast-moving technology of the computer world, the invention of language to describe it changes as fast as teenage slang. Today we have battery-powered laptops, weighing about ten pounds, which are more powerful than the huge ENIAC. In 1989 a pocket computer weighing only pound was introduced. The most recent trend has been to link together several personal computers so that they can share software and different users can easily access the same documents. These are called LANS, or local area networks.

USES FOR A COMPUTER

The machine, or computer itself, is referred to as **hardware**. A personal computer might sell for under $1,000. Many extras, called **peripherals**, can increase the price by several thousand dollars.

Communication with computers is becoming more and more sophisticated. When a computer is purchased it comes with several programs that allow the user to communicate with the computer. Programs that allow the user to carry out particular tasks on a computer are referred to as **software**.

The business world has welcomed the advances made possible by the use of personal computers and the powerful programs, known as **software packages**, that enable the computer to do many diverse tasks. The most important computer applications are word processing, data-base managers, and spreadsheets.

Today, computers are used for a variety of purposes. **Data processing** involves large collections of data on which relatively few calculations need to be made. For example, a credit card company could use the system to keep track of the balances of its customers' accounts. **Information retrieval** involves locating and displaying material from a description of its content. For example, a police department may want information about a suspect or a realtor may want listings that meet the criteria of a client. **Pattern recognition** is the identification and classification of shapes, forms, or relationships. For example, a chess player will examine the chessboard carefully to determine a good next move. Finally, a computer can be used for **simulation** of a real situation. For example, a prototype of a new spacecraft can be tested under various circumstances to determine its limitations. The computer carries out these tasks by accepting information, performing mathematical and logical operations with the information, and then supplying the results of the operations as new information.

By using a **modem**, installed internally or attached as a peripheral, and a program called a **communications package**, a computer can transfer information to and from other computers directly or over a phone line. If you send software or data from your computer to another, this is called **uploading**. If you get software or data from another computer, this is called **downloading**. A person or company may set up a computer specifically to be accessed by modem. The phone number is then made available to a private list of people or to the public. Some companies specialize in making data bases available commercially. There is a charge to use these services based on the time you are connected, or the time you are **online**. Networks have been designed specifically to enable people to send messages to each other via computer. Such networks, known as **electronic mail** or

E-mail, have become commonplace among large universities or companies. They are even available commercially to the public. Individuals or groups set up computers accessible by modem in order to share information about a common interest. These are called **bulletin boards**. Often, though not always, these are free and the only charge to the user is the cost of the telephone call.

Most companies and bulletin boards require a **password** or special procedures in order to be able to go online with their computers. A major problem for certain computer installations has been to make sure that it is impossible for the wrong person to get into their computer. There have been many instances where people have "broken into" computers just like a safecracker breaks into a safe. A few of these people have been caught and prosecuted. A security break of this nature can be very serious. By transferring funds in a bank computer, someone can steal money. By breaking into a military installation, a spy could steal secrets or commit sabotage. By breaking into a university's computers, grades or records could be changed. **Computer abuse** falls into two categories: illegal (as described above, but also including illegal copying of programs), or abuse caused by ignorance. Ignorance of computers leads to the assumption that the output data are always correct or that the use of a computer is beyond one's comprehension.

With the tremendous advances in computer technology, financial investors and analysts can simulate various possible outcomes and select strategies that best suit their goals. Designers and engineers use *computer-aided design*, known as CAD. Using computer graphics, sculptors can model their work on a computer that will rotate the image so that they can look at the proposed work from all sides. Computers have been used to help the handicapped with learning certain skills and by taking over certain functions. Computers can be used to "talk" by those without speech. For those without sight, there are artificial vision systems that translate a visual image to a tactile "image" that can be "seen" on the back of the blind person. A person who has never seen a candle burn can learn the shape and dynamic quality of a flame.

Along with the advances in computer technology came new courses, and even new departments in the colleges and universities. New specialties developed involving the design, use, and impact of computers on our society. The feats of the computer captured the imagination of some who believed that a computer could be designed to be as intelligent as a human mind. The field known as **artificial intelligence** was born. Many researchers worked on natural language translation with very high hopes initially, but the progress has been slow. Progress continues in *expert systems*, programs that involve sophisticated strategies of pushing the computer ever closer to human-like capabilities. The quest has produced powerful uses for computers.

What does the future hold? A design goal set by International Business Machines Corporation is to fit an entire computer, including all its memory, into a box 8 centimeters by 8 centimeters by 10 centimeters. That is less than half the volume of this book! Computers will no longer consist of transistors or other semiconductor components, but will instead consist of superconductors called Josephson-junction devices. This new generation of computers will shrink the time necessary to execute a single command from 50 nanoseconds (for present-day computers) to about 4 nanoseconds. A computer based on Josephson-junction switches could be as powerful as an IBM model 370/168 — a very powerful machine — yet fit into a cube 15 cm on a side! Apparently, IBM's design goal will be met not far in the future.

2600 words

Write your ending time here: ————————————————

Subtract your starting time: ————————————————

Total time: ————————————————————————

Check the Rate Chart in the back of the book to find out how many words per minute you have read and then record your score on the Progress Chart.

ANSWERS TO SURVEY QUESTIONS

Without looking back at the article, write the answers to your survey questions here:

1. _____

2. _____

3. _____

MAIN IDEA

Before going on to the Comprehension Check, and without looking back at the article, write a complete sentence stating the main idea of this article.

_____

_____

Your answer should be similar to the correct answer for question 2 in the Comprehension Check.

28

Introduction to Computers

Circle the letter before the best answer to each question below. Don't look back at the article.

Subject and Main Idea

1. The subject of the article is
   a. uses of computers.
   b. the impact of computers.
   c. types of computers.
   d. an orientation to computers.

2. The main idea is that
   a. familiarity with computers is important.
   b. the future of computers is exciting.
   c. computers take the drudgery out of mathematics.
   d. computers were invented in 1944.

Details

3. Computers have become consistently
   a. smaller.
   b. faster.
   c. cheaper.
   d. all of the above.

4. The first electronic digital computers used
   a. vacuum tubes.
   b. transistors.
   c. batteries.
   d. silicon chips.

5. The first successful personal computer was the
   a. IBM.
   b. Apple.
   c. Atari.
   d. Commodore.

421

6. Software includes
   a. the physical parts (mechanical, magnetic, electronic) of a computer.
   b. computer programs.
   c. peripherals.
   d. all of the above.

Inferences

7. If you want to look up a criminal's arrest record, you would use
   a. a modem.
   b. E-mail.
   c. information retrieval.
   d. data processing.

8. People unfamiliar with computers will
   a. not understand modern culture.
   b. not be able to support themselves.
   c. have to go into the liberal arts.
   d. do all of the above.

9. The history of computers suggests that creative geniuses regularly
   a. make a lot of money.
   b. experience failure.
   c. become famous during their lifetimes.
   d. die in poverty.

10. The author seems to find the future of computers
   a. frightening.
   b. exciting.
   c. depressing.
   d. boring.

QUESTIONS FOR ANALYSIS AND APPLICATION

1. Trace the development of computers from 1944 to the present.

2. Describe the changes anticipated in the new generation of computers.

VOCABULARY IN CONTEXT
Multiple Choice
Circle the letter before the best definition of each underlined word or phrase.

1. The prototype of the Lunar Landing Vehicle was tested at Edwards Air Force Base in California to see if it could withstand the rough terrain.
   a. copy   b. fuel   c. model   d. engine

2. If one counted diligently twenty-four hours a day, it would take 31,688 years to count to a trillion.
   a. industriously   b. continuously   c. slowly   d. quickly

3. Baby animals depend heavily on scent and on their tactile sense because their sight is so undeveloped.
   a. sense of touch   b. sense of smell   c. sense of sight
   d. sense of hearing

4. The monument at Mount Rushmore was a grandiose project.
   a. beautiful   b. impressive   c. expensive
   d. time-consuming

5. Corrections are so easy to make on a word processor that using an electric typewriter now seems tedious.
   a. simple   b. stupid   c. tiresome   d. inspiring

6. Many Hollywood actresses are eccentric in the way they dress.
   a. unconventional   b. classy   c. fashionable
   d. attractive

7. The terminology used in scientific journals is difficult for the average person to understand.
   a. dialect   b. ideas   c. subjects   d. vocabulary

8. The word sabotage comes from the practice of French peasants who damaged their employers' machinery by throwing their wooden shoes (sabots) into it.
   a. disappearance   b. destruction   c. creation
   d. rebuilding

9. Modern computers use binary number systems.
   a. single-digit   b. two-digit   c. multiple-digit
   d. nondigital

Fill-in

Write the best word from this list in the blank in each sentence below:

ballistics   denominations   modem   nanosecond

solid-state   digital   databases   simulation   ratchet

integrated circuits

10. U.S. coins come in only six _____ :
    silver dollar, half-dollar, quarter, dime, nickel, and penny.

11. A _____ allows you to transmit data to
    fellow computer users.

12. The _____ in video tape players made
    small portable units possible.

13. _____ tests can prove which gun a bullet
    was shot from.

14. Light travels one foot every _____ .

15. Many people fear that computer _____
    are becoming so extensive that no one will have any privacy in
    the future.

16. There are two kinds of computers: _____
    which work by counting, and analog which work by measuring.

17. If a TV commercial for camera film does not show an actual
    picture, it must be announced that what is shown is a

    _____ .

18. The strap that goes around a refrigerator when it is being moved
    on a dolly has a _____ so that it can be
    tightened easily and won't slip.

19. Most televisions today use _____ devices
    instead of tubes, which allow the televisions to last longer.

SKILLS EXERCISE: OUTLINING

For explanation
see pp. 296–297

Fill in the missing parts of the following outline, which is based on the reading selection.

Introduction to Computers

I. Impact of computers

II. _____

    A. _____

    B. Stones, slip knots, beads

    C. _____

III. _____

    A. _____

    B. _____

    C. _____

    D. _____

    E. Ada Byron proposed using binary numbers.

    F. Slide rule

    G. _____

IV. History of computers

    A. ENIAC 1942–46

        1. _____

        2. _____

        3. _____

        4. _____

        5. _____

        6. Carefully controlled atmosphere

    B. _____

C. Invention of transistors 1947 and solid-state devices
D. Super computer 1958
E. 1960s, early 1970s mainframes

   1. _____

   2. Part of business world

   3. Batch processing

   4. _____

   5. Frustrating handling of errors

F. _____

   1. Less than 3 cubic feet of space

   2. _____

G. Personal computers

   1. _____

   2. Affordable

   3. Small

   4. _____

   5. Battery powered laptops – 10 lbs.

   6. 1989 – pocket computer – 1 lb.

   7. _____

V. Uses

A. Parts

   1. _____

   2. Peripherals – extras

   3. _____

   4. Software packages for business

B. Uses for a computer

   1. _____

   2. _____

   3. _____

   4. _____

   5. Communication

      a. Modem and communication package to upload and download

      b. Commercial data bases

      c. _____

      d. _____

   6. Financial investors and analysts can choose strategies

   7. _____

   8. _____

   9. Help handicapped: talk, see

  10. New courses in artificial intelligence and expert systems

VI. The future

A. _____

B. Superconductors

C. _____

SKILLS EXERCISE:
STUDY MAPPING

For explanation
see pp. 297–299

Use the first three levels of the preceding outline in this chapter to fill in the blank spaces in the following study map.

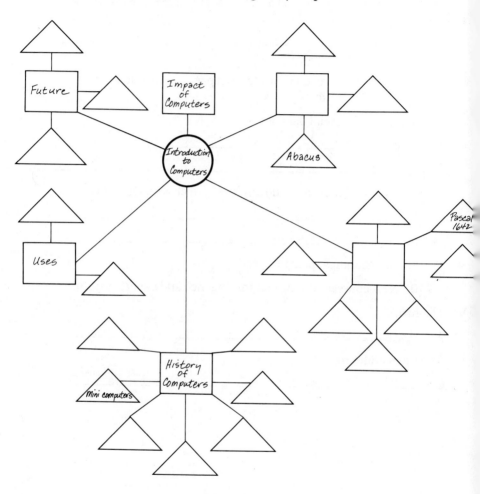

29

Listening Critically to Speeches

VOCABULARY PREVIEW

recounting (ri'kount'iŋ): telling in detail; narrating

venture (ven'chər): a risky undertaking, as in business

rivet (riv'it): to strongly hold one's attention

extraneous (ik strā'nē əs): irrelevant; coming from outside

arbitrary (är'bə trer'ē): based on one's preference or whim

dowdy (dou'dē): not neat or smart in dress

utterance (ut'ər əns): power or style of speaking

wary (war'ē): cautious

discerning (di surn'iŋ): having good judgment; discriminating

sarcastic (sär kas'tik): sneering; cutting; using ridicule

implications (im'plə kā'shənz): hints

mull over (mul' ō'vər): to think deeply about; consider carefully

paraphrasing (par'ə frāz'iŋ): rewording of meaning of something spoken
or written; putting in your own words

mnemonic (nē män'ik): an artificial technique to aid memory

fat, āpe, cär; ten, ēven; is, bīte; gō, hôrn, tōōl, look; oil, out; up, fur; chin, she; thin, then; zh,
leisure; ŋ, ring; ə for a in *ago;* ' as in *able* (ā'b'l)

SURVEY

Survey the following article by reading the author's name, the title, the headings, and the last sentence. This should take no longer than thirty seconds. After your survey, and without looking back at the article, write three questions that you think will be answered by reading it.

1. _____

2. _____

3. _____

Now read the article. Write your starting time here: _____

29

Listening Critically to Speeches

Rudolph F. Verderber

WHAT KIND OF LISTENER ARE YOU?

Perhaps you believe you are already a good listener. Although that may be true, most college students are not. In fact, studies indicate that college students listen at only about a 50 percent level of effectiveness. When a short delay occurs between when students listen and when they are tested, average listening efficiency drops to nearly 25 percent. For the past twenty years, Ralph Nichols, a leading authority on listening, has conducted numerous studies and has reported the research of others. All of his studies point to the same sad figures: 25 to 50 percent efficiency.[1] These low percentages are especially important when we realize that up to half of our daily communication time is spent listening.[2]

WHAT CAN YOU DO TO IMPROVE?

Assuming that your listening efficiency is about average, what can you do about it? With determination, an average listener can almost double listening efficiency in a few months. In fact, by following a few simple steps, you will note immediate improvement in your listening.

Adopt a Positive Listening Attitude

The first step to improving your listening is to *adopt a positive listening attitude*. There's no reason why you cannot improve your listening *if you want to*. It's up to you to decide that listening is important and that you are going to do whatever it takes to listen better.

Recognize Differences in Listening Difficulty

The second step to improving your listening is to *recognize differences in listening difficulty*. Listening is similar to reading in that you should listen differently depending on the purpose and degree of difficulty of the material. Yet many people "listen" about the same regardless of purpose or material. Listening intensity differs depending on whether you are listening primarily for enjoyment, for understanding, or for evaluation.

431

Much of our listening is for pleasure or enjoyment. Listening t music on the car radio is one example of this kind of listening. We ar aware of the background sound – we find it soothing, relaxing, and ger erally pleasant. Much of our listening to conversation is for this purpose For instance, when Tom and Paul talk about the game they saw o television, their listening is for pleasure, and the details of the conve sation are likely to be soon forgotten. Unfortunately, many people ap proach all situations as if they were listening for pleasure. Yet how yo listen should change qualitatively when you listen to understand or fc evaluation.

Listening to understand is a more difficult challenge than listenin for pleasure. For this kind of listening you need to develop greater inten sity. Your classroom lectures provide a situation requiring this type c listening. Likewise, such informal situations as listening to direction (how to get to a restaurant), listening to instructions (how to shift int reverse in a foreign car), and listening to explanations (a recounting c the new dorm rules) also require listening to understand.

But by far the most demanding challenge is listening to evaluate Every day we are flooded with messages designed to influence our be havior. To function best in this context, we have to be able to recogniz the facts, weigh them, separate them from emotional appeals, and deter mine the validity of the conclusions presented.

Critical listening takes time, effort, and energy; and to be frank many of us are just not willing to work at it. Many Americans conside listening a passive venture; they have fallen into the habit of "watching" television or "listening" to the radio to relax. As a result of years o associating listening with relaxing, many have acquired or developec bad listening habits. Whereas listening for entertainment may be relax ing, listening for information or listening critically is work. You have tc recognize when it is appropriate to "go into high gear" in your listening and equally important, you have to know what it means to be in high gear!

Get Ready to Listen

The third step to improving your listening is to get yourself ready tc listen. Listening efficiency increases when the listener follows the ap parently elementary practice of really being ready to listen. Getting ready involves both physical and mental application.

What physical characteristics indicate that you are ready to work at listening? An outward sign is whether you look as if you are listening. Poor listeners often slouch in their chairs. Their eyes wander from place to place. They appear to be bored by what is going on. In contrast, good listeners sit upright – sometimes almost on the edge of their chairs. They rivet their eyes on the speaker. These physical signs of attention indicate alertness.

These recommendations may sound simplistic to you. But test them out for yourself. When I discuss listening in class, I precede short comprehension tests by saying, "For the next five minutes, I want you to listen as hard as you can. Then I'm going to give a test on what you heard." What happens when the class realizes it has an investment in what will take place? Students straighten up and turn their eyes to the front of the room; extraneous noises — coughing, clearing throats, rustling — drop to zero.

Getting ready to listen also means getting ready mentally. Mentally, you need to stop thinking about any of the thousands of miscellaneous thoughts that constantly pass through your mind; all your attention should be directed to what a person is saying. In effect, anyone who is talking with you is in competition with all the miscellaneous thoughts and feelings that you are having. Some of them may be more pleasant to tune into than what people are saying to you. Anticipation of an exciting evening; thoughts about a game, a test, or what's for dinner; and re-creating scenes from a memorable movie or television show may offer more attractive pleasures than listening to the speaker. Yet attention paid to such competing thoughts and feelings is one of the leading causes of poor listening.

Withhold Evaluation

A fourth step in improving your listening is to withhold evaluation. This recommendation means you should control both arbitrary judgments about a subject and emotional responses to content. It is a human reaction to listen attentively only to what we like or what we want to hear. Yet such an attitude is self-limiting and self-defeating. We listen to learn and to gather data for evaluation. Neither of these goals is possible if we refuse to listen to anything outside our immediate interests. For instance, if a classmate indicates that he or she will talk about the history of a union, you may say you are interested neither in history in general nor in unions in particular. If during the first sentence or two of the speech you find yourself saying, "I don't think I am going to be interested in this topic," you should remind yourself that judgment must follow, not precede, the presentation of information. Poor listeners make value judgments about the content after the first few words; good listeners suspend judgment of the value of the message until they have heard it. It is true that some speeches will not be very good. But you will not be able to make this judgment until the speaker has finished. Often you will find that even a poor speech will have a good idea or some good supporting details that you will want to remember.

You also need to control your emotional responses to the speaker' personality. We all wish that every speaker we had to listen to wa physically appealing, dynamic, and exciting. The fact is that a numbe of speakers you hear will be dowdy and, at times, boring. Poor listener let the way a speaker looks and sounds turn them off. Poor listener make snap value judgments about quality of material on the basis o physical appearance. So at the beginning of a speech, you must tel yourself that you will hear the speaker out regardless of how the speake looks or sounds.

In addition, you need to control your emotional responses to the words you hear. Are there any words or ideas that act as red flags for you Does the mere utterance of these words cause you to lose any desire to listen attentively? For instance, do you have a tendency to react emo tionally when people use any of these words?

racist	communist	gay
Jew	Arab	yuppie
abortion	AIDS	gun control
feminist	busing	welfare

Would any of these or similar words turn you off? Often poor listeners (and occasionally even good listeners) are given an emotional jolt when a speaker touches a nerve. At this point all you can do is to be wary. When the speaker trips the switch to your emotional reaction – let a warning light go on before you turn off. Instead of tuning out or getting ready to fight, work that much harder at being objective. Can you do it? If you can, you will improve your listening.

Listen for Ideas and Meaning

A fifth step to improving your listening is to listen for ideas and mean-ing. Some people mistakenly think that their listening is at its best when they can feed back the words or the details that were communicated. But good listening goes beyond that. Good listening means understand-ing the key ideas behind the words and details presented. Listening for key ideas is one of the easiest parts of listening to learn.

For now, keep in mind that most speeches will usually have two to five main points. Often a speaker will preview the main points in the introduction. Early in the speech the speaker may say something like, "Today I want to share with you the three causes of juvenile crime – poverty, permissiveness, and broken homes." At this point you know that the speech will have three points and you can look for them. If the speaker does not preview points, you must still listen for them.

As important as recognizing major and minor points is discerning the overall meaning, which requires a sensitivity to the message's verbal and nonverbal elements. For instance, when a person says, "Isn't it a beautiful day?" in a sarcastic tone when the rain is pouring down, we are likely to recognize the conflict between the words spoken and the tone of voice. Nonverbal signs such as sarcastic vocal tone, body action, and movement may tell us to disregard the normal meaning of the words. In addition to contradicting meaning, nonverbal cues may supplement or modify the meaning. When a person says, "I'm really angry," we measure the degree of anger by the nonverbal cues; when a person says, "I'm not sure how much we should give," we measure the extent of undecidedness by the nonverbal cues. Since a speaker's meaning sometimes is communicated unintentionally by nonverbal cues, we must be alert to all aspects of the message.

A good listener, therefore, absorbs all the speaker's meaning by being sensitive to voice tone, facial expression, and body action, as well as to the words themselves. Nonverbal cues may reveal a speaker's sincerity, depth of conviction, confidence, and true understanding and may have many subtle implications, regardless of the words the speaker uses.

Listen Actively

The final step to improve your listening is to listen actively. Research on learning indicates that listeners learn better and faster and make sounder judgments about what they hear when they are mentally and physically active. Active listening involves you in the process of determining meaning. Too often people think of the listening experience as a passive activity in which what they remember is largely a matter of chance. In reality, good listening is hard work that requires concentration and willingness to mull over and at times verbalize what is said. Good listening requires using mental energy. If you really listen to an entire fifty-minute lecture, for instance, when the lecture is over you will feel tired because you will have put as much energy into listening as the lecturer put into talking. Since you can think faster than any speaker can talk, you will have time to use several active listening skills. Active listening includes repeating, questioning, paraphrasing, and notetaking.

Repeating items of information helps you remember. For instance, when the speaker says, "The first major election reform bill was passed in England in 1832," the active listener might mentally repeat, "reform bill, England, 1832."

Good questioning helps you anticipate material. For instance, when a speaker says, "There are four steps to coding data," you will ask yourself, "What are the four steps?" If the speaker goes on to tell you the steps, asking the question will help you emphasize the steps. If the speaker doesn't give you the steps, asking the question focuses on information you need to get. After the speech is over you may have an opportunity to ask the question directly, or later you can look up the steps. Good questioning also helps you test the soundness of the material. For instance, when the speaker says, "Swimming is an activity that provides exercise for almost every muscle," active listeners might inwardly question the point, examining the supporting material offered.

Paraphrasing helps you check your understanding. A *paraphrase* is a statement of what the person's words meant to you. After a speaker has talked for a few minutes, you can say to yourself, "In other words, how the mixture is put together may be more important than the ingredients used." If this makes sense to you, then you can be confident that you have an understanding. If you cannot paraphrase, it is likely that something was missing from the explanation or you weren't listening carefully enough.

Using *mnemonic devices* will also help. A *mnemonic device* is any artificial technique used as a memory aid. Some of the most common rules for forming mnemonics are taking the first letters of items that you are trying to remember and forming a word. For example, if you were listening to a professor lecture on three types of speeches intended to entertain, to inform, and to persuade, a useful mnemonic for remembering the three purposes is PIE, standing for *p*ersuade, *i*nform, and *e*ntertain. When you are trying to remember some items in sequence, you can form a sentence with the words themselves or you can assign words using the first letters of the words in sequence to form some easy-to-remember statement. For instance, when you first studied music, you may have learned the notes of the scale in the following way: For the notes on the treble clef lines (E-G-B-D-F) you may have learned "every good boy does fine," and for the notes of the treble clef spaces (F-A-C-E) you may have remembered the word *face*.

Active listening can also mean taking notes. Whereas poor listeners fidget, doodle, or look about the room, good listeners often take notes on what the speaker is saying. Repeating, asking questions, and paraphrasing helps you take good notes. Most college students take notes in classes; yet the quality of their notes varies tremendously. Just sitting down with a pen or pencil and a piece of paper does not guarantee good notetaking. Likewise, leaving class with pages of writing is not evidence of good notetaking either.

What are good notes? Good notes are a brief outline of what the speaker has said including the overall idea, the main points of the message, and key developmental material. Good notes are not necessarily very long. In fact, many excellent lectures can be reduced to a short outline.

Suppose you were listening to a supervisor instruct candidates for a secretarial position about the duties of the job. The supervisor might say:

> As prospective employees you should be aware of a few details. Typing and distributing mail are the most important duties of this job. Now about the typing. Some people may give you a lot, but it may not have anything to do with department work. You will want to be careful about spending time on private work. Some people will be real sticklers about details. Make sure that you check details carefully before you type. And of course, some will give you work at the last minute and expect you to finish it.
>
> Mail comes twice a day — at 10 and 2. You will sort it and put it in the respective boxes. If there is any mail that doesn't belong here, bundle it and mark it for return to the main post office.
>
> Now let me take a minute to talk about your breaks. You get ten minutes in the morning and afternoon (take your break at about 10:30 and 2:30 — they're relatively quiet times). And of course, you get an hour for lunch. Although the time for lunch is flexible, you should probably leave for lunch by 12:15.

Notes

Typing and mail most important duties

1. Typing
   Be sure it relates to dept. work
   Check details
   Be wary of late work

2. Mail
   10 and 2
   Sort
   Bundle left over, return to post office

3. Breaks
   2–10:30 and 2:30 best
   Take lunch by 12:15

This short passage included a lot of specific detail. Yet the 193 words of explanation can be outlined in just 44 words. Since the speeches you hear will vary in detail, good notetaking may range from 10 percent to as high as 20 percent (the amount in our example). The point is not the number of words, but how accurately the notes reflect the sense of what the speaker said.

The better note taker you become, the better listener you will be.

2800 words

Reference Notes

1. Ralph Nichols and Leonard A. Stevens, *Are You Listening?* (New York: McGraw-Hill, 1957), pp. 5–6.

2. Paul Tony Rankin, The Measurement of the Ability to Understand Spoken Language," doctoral dissertation, University of Michigan, 1926, University Microfilm, 1952, Publ. No. 4352; cited by Nichols and Stevens, *Are You Listening?* p. 6.

Write your ending time here: _____

Subtract your starting time: _____

Total time: _____

Check the Rate Chart in the back of the book to find out how many words per minute you have read, and then record your score on the Progress Chart.

ANSWERS TO SURVEY QUESTIONS

Without looking back at the article, write the answers to your survey questions here:

1. _____

2. _____

3. _____

29

Listening Critically to Speeches

Subject and Main Idea

1. The subject of the article is
   a. listening.
   b. becoming a better listener.
   c. critical thinking.
   d. why listening is important.

2. The main idea is that people
   a. don't know what kind of listeners they are.
   b. can become better listeners.
   c. are poor listeners.
   d. listen to what they want to hear.

Details

3. College students spend most of their time
   a. speaking.
   b. writing.
   c. reading.
   d. listening.

4. You can almost double your listening efficiency in a
   a. few days.
   b. matter of months.
   c. year with determined effort.
   d. special course in listening.

5. The first step in improving your listening is to
   a. relax.
   b. get paper and pencil.
   c. adopt a positive listening attitude.
   d. listen actively.

6. Which is *not* part of listening actively?
   a. paraphrasing
   b. using mnemonics
   c. adopting a positive attitude
   d. asking questions

Inferences

7. People can
   a. talk as fast as they can think.
   b. think only as fast as they can talk.
   c. think faster than they can talk.
   d. talk faster than they can read.

8. Active listening
   a. comes naturally.
   b. is encouraged by TV watching.
   c. requires you to exclude irrelevant thoughts from your mind.
   d. means you don't have to take notes.

9. Good listeners
   a. nod their heads constantly to show that they are listening.
   b. can distinguish fact from opinion.
   c. should outline everything a speaker says.
   d. are able to repeat everything they hear.

10. Good listening is more difficult when
    a. you are tired.
    b. you are sensitive about the subject.
    c. you are bored.
    d. all of the above are true.

QUESTIONS FOR ANALYSIS AND APPLICATION

1. List the six steps in listening improvement.

2. Describe what is meant by *active listening.*

VOCABULARY IN CONTEXT
Multiple Choice
Circle the letter before the best definition of each underlined word.

1. Even a certified public accountant might have difficulty in understanding a lecture recounting the change in tax laws.
   a. telling   b. eliminating   c. numbering   d. opposing

2. When you make a venture on the commodities market, you can earn a lot of money one day only to lose it and more the next day.
   a. loan   b. start   c. undertaking   d. failure

3. When you are in an auto accident, you should write down as much information as you can. Even what seems extraneous information at the time could help prove you were not at fault.
   a. necessary   b. surprising   c. faulty   d. extra

4. Heavy women must be especially careful in selecting flattering clothes because their weight can make them look dowdy.
   a. beautiful   b. dirty   c. unfashionable   d. silly

5. Be wary when walking along dark, deserted streets at night.
   a. scared   b. aggressive   c. cautious   d. suspicious

6. According to dog and cat food commercials, pets have discerning tastes when it comes to choosing different brands of food.
   a. discriminating   b. poor   c. stupid   d. changeable

7. Before signing a contract, you should mull over your decision, thinking about the obvious and hidden costs.
   a. forget   b. avoid   c. quickly make
   d. consider carefully

Fill-In

Write the best word from this list in the blank in each sentence below.

arbitrary   utterance   sarcastic   implications

paraphrasing   mnemonic   riveted

8. The _____ of new tax laws may take years for the courts to interpret.

9. Until an _____ decision by the government in 1903 made Panama part of North America, it was part of South America.

10. Most new parents listen for the _____ of a single sound while their babies are sleeping.

11. A teacher should not make _____ remarks when students are asking questions.

12. FACE is the _____ taught by most piano teachers to help students remember the spaces in the treble clef.

13. _____ an author's words does not eliminate the need for a footnote in a research paper.

14. *Citizen Kane*, a movie by Orson Welles, has often been considered the best film ever made; the plot, photography, and acting

    keep an audience _____ to the action until the end.

**SKILLS EXERCISE:
OUTLINING**

*For explanation
see pp. 296–297*

Fill in the missing parts of the following outline which is based on the reading selection.

Listening Critically to Speeches

I. _____

  A. _____

  B. _____

II. _____

  A. _____

  B. Recognize differences in listening difficulty.

    1. _____

      a. _____

      b. _____

      c. _____

    2. _____

  C. _____

    1. _____

    2. _____

  D. _____

    1. _____

    2. _____

  E. Listen for ideas and meaning.

    1. _____

    2. _____

  F. _____

    1. _____

    2. _____

    3. _____

    4. _____

    5. _____

SKILLS EXERCISE:
SUMMARIZING

For explanatio.
see p. 299

Use the outline to write a brief summary of the article in sentence form.

30

A Science of Society

VOCABULARY PREVIEW

empirical (em pir'i k'l): relying or based solely on experiment and observation rather than theory [the *empirical* method]

buzzword (buz'wʉrd'): a word or phrase used by members of some in-group, having little or unclear meaning but sounding impressive to outsiders

median (mē'dē'ən): the middle number in a series

unabated (un'ə bāt'id): undiminished; not lessened

deployment (dē ploi'mənt): placement; usage

deterrent (di tʉr'ənt): hindrance; discouraging factor

arsenal (ar's'n əl): a place for making or storing weapons and other munitions

deficit (def'ə sit): the amount by which a sum of money is less than the required amount; an excess of expenditures over income

per capita (pər kap'ə tə): for each person

keystones (kē'stōnz): main parts or principles

deliberations (di lib'ə rā'shənz): considerations and discussions of alternatives before reaching a decision

pseudo (sōō'dō): pretended; counterfeit

sector (sek'tər): distinct part of society or of an economy or group

mandatory (man'də tôr'ē): required

activism (ak'tə vis'm): the policy of taking positive, direct action to achieve an end, esp. a political or social end

inconclusive (in'kən klōō'siv): not leading to a clear result or interpretation

fat, āpe, cär; ten, ēven; is, bīte; gō, hôrn, tōōl, look; oil, out; up, fʉr; chin, she; thin, *then*; zh, leisure; ŋ, ring; ə for *a* in *ago;* ' as in *able* (ā'b'l)

SKILLS EXERCISE:
SQ3R

For explanation
see pp. 291–296

A. *Survey.* Survey the following article by reading the author's name, the title, and the first sentence of every paragraph. This should take no longer than thirty seconds.

B. *Question.* Without looking back at the article, write three questions that you think will be answered by reading it.

1. _____

2. _____

3. _____

C. *Read.* Now read the article. Write your starting time here: _____

30

A Science of Society

Earl Babbie

SOCIOLOGY SHOULDN'T BE CONFUSED with social philosophy. It is not a point of view about the way things ought to be. Rather, sociology deals with the way things *are*. Moreover, sociology is more than just an *opinion* about the way things are.

Sociology is a science of social life. Like other sciences, sociology has a **logical/empirical** basis. This means that, to be accepted, assertions must (1) make sense and (2) correspond to the facts. In this sense, sociology can be characterized by a current buzzword: *critical thinking*. The simple fact is that most of us, most of the time, are uncritical in our thinking. Much of the time we simply believe what we read or hear. Or, when we disagree, we do so on the basis of ideological points of view and prejudices that are not very well thought out.

Suppose you were talking with a friend about the value of going to college. Your friend disagrees: "College is a waste of time. You should get a head start in the job market instead. Most of today's millionaires never went to college, and there are plenty of college graduates pumping gas or out of work altogether." That's the kind of thing people sometimes say and it can be convincing — especially if it's said with conviction. But does it stand up to logical and empirical testing?

Logically, it doesn't seem to make much sense. A college education would seem to give a person access to high-paying occupations not open to people with less education.

How does the assertion stack up empirically? Table 1 lists the median incomes of families headed by individuals of different educational levels as reported by the Census Bureau.

There isn't any scientific support for the assertion that education is a worthless financial investment — even though there are some individual exceptions to the rule.

It's important to recognize that human beings generally have opinions about everything. People you deal with every day have a tendency to express opinions about the way things are — and what they say isn't always so. Consequently, you need to protect yourself from false information. That's what critical thinking is all about, and sociology provides some powerful critical-thinking tools.

Table 1
Median Income by Educational Level

Educational level	Median income
Less than 8 years	$ 9,221
8 years	11,811
1–3 years high school	13,705
4 years high school	20,800
1–3 years college	24,606
4 years college or more	34,709

Source: US Bureau of the Census, *Statistical Abstract of the United States*, Washington, DC: US Government Printing Office, 1985, p. 443.

Let's look at the twin foundations of critical thinking and of science in more detail — seeing how they apply to sociology in particular. Let's start with the
determination of *facts*.

THE SEARCH FOR FACTS: RESEARCH

At his August 5, 1985, news conference, President Reagan noted the fortieth anniversary of the Hiroshima
bombing. An unabated nuclear arms race led to increasing popular demands for a freeze on the manufacture
and deployment of nuclear weapons. In defense of his
administration's military policies, the president suggested that our store of nuclear weapons, coupled with
the horrible example of Hiroshima, "is a deterrent that
kept us at peace for the longest stretch we've ever
known, 40 years of peace."

Regardless of how you feel about the nuclear arms
race — whether we should be in it and who's winning —
the argument that our nuclear arsenal has at least kept
us at peace is a convincing one. In my review of the
media and public comments following the news conference, people disagreed on whether the nuclear deterrent
was the reason for the forty years of peace. Yet to my
amazement, no one questioned the empirical accuracy
of the assertion. A simple historical review of the period
from 1945 to 1985 turned up the Korean War from 1950
to 1953 and the extensive and expensive war in Vietnam,
which claimed 47,318 American lives between 1959 and
1973. This has to have been the bloodiest forty years of
peace in our national history.

Much of what you read and hear simply doesn't
correspond to the empirical facts. Inaccuracy gets overlooked in the heat of rhetoric. For example, when the
newspaper *USA Today* focused its attention on the national budget deficit, they interviewed seven men and
women "in the street" to get their opinions. One of those
interviewed, Glen Cemer, a retired photographer from
Battle Creek, Michigan, responded as follows:

> One way to lower the deficit would be to reduce the
> amount of foreign aid we provide to other countries. It's
> not winning any friends for us. Let's use that money to
> lower the deficit.[1]

---

[1] *USA Today,* September 25, 1985, p. 10A.

This comment is often heard when people discuss ways to reduce the federal deficit. On the one side, some people, like Mr. Cemer, can point to instances of foreign aid being wasted in various ways and cases where countries we have aided later turned against us. On the other side, people who support foreign aid point to positive accomplishments. We also feel a moral urge to help others less fortunate than ourselves.

Regardless of how you happen to feel about foreign aid in general, it is possible to determine, empirically, whether reducing foreign aid would be an effective way of reducing the federal budget deficit. In 1983, the United States gave a total of $8.6 billion in economic (nonmilitary) aid to other countries. Our budget deficit that year was $195.4 billion. Cancelling our foreign aid program altogether, therefore, would have reduced the deficit by only 4 percent. Whereas the budget deficit is sometimes expressed on a per capita basis, cancelling foreign aid in 1983 would have reduced the 1983 debt of each American from $836.81 to $799.98. This is not much of a reduction.

One of the things I hope you'll gain from this introduction to critical thinking is an ability to balance what you read and hear in your day-to-day life against empirical evidence. That's one of the keystones of sociology.

Over the past 150 years, sociologists have developed a number of research methods to assist in determining the facts of social life. **Survey research**, for example, involves the use of questionnaires to collect information. Sometimes people fill out the questionnaires themselves. Other times interviewers read the questions and take down the answers. In recent years, telephone interviewing has become increasingly popular and effective. In particular, computers have been adapted to support the interviewing process: selecting telephone numbers at random, showing interviewers what questions to ask, and recording the answers given for immediate analysis.

Usually, surveys are conducted among samples of people. The samples are selected in such a way that a few hundred or thousand respondents can provide an accurate assessment of much larger populations. For example, a political poll among a properly selected sample of 1600 voters can provide an accurate estimate of how ll 90 million American voters feel: accurate within 2.5 percentage points. I know that may be hard to believe ut sociologists are putting the logic and techniques of urvey sampling to effective use every day.

Sometimes, laboratory **experiments** are a more effective method of getting at the facts of social life. This echnique is commonly used in the study of small group ynamics, for example. As a practical example, some ociologists have used this technique to study the dynamics of jury deliberations. Hiring subjects to serve as seudo-jurors, the researchers can then observe their ubjects argue their way to a verdict.

A ready resource for sociological analysis exists in he great masses of data regularly compiled by governmental agencies and various groups in the private sector. As in the example of education and income that we examined earlier, it's often possible to find appropriate answers without the time and expense of conducting a survey, experiment, or comparable research project. Even in this situation, however, you need to exercise critical thinking, since the facts never really "speak for themselves." Here's an example.

When Ralph Nader published *Unsafe at Any Speed* n 1965, he launched a consumer rights movement that has touched most aspects of American life. In the realm of auto safety, numerous changes have occurred in the past twenty years. These include safer auto designs, mandatory seat belts, and reduced highway speed limits.

Although everyone is in favor of highway safety, the kinds of changes I've mentioned have been very controversial. Some people argue that the various changes have made driving safer; others disagree. This is a good place for empirical examination.

Let's see what has happened to the number of people killed on the nation's highways during this period of activity. Before we simply check on the *number* of people killed each year, we should recognize that our population—including the number of drivers—has grown each year. More people have been driving more cars more miles each year. To make a fair comparison, therefore, we need to take account of those increases.

Figure 1 indicates the number of traffic deaths pe 100 million miles driven each year from 1965 to 1984 This *rate* takes account of the increasing numbers o drivers, cars, and miles. It also gives us good grounds fo observing trends in highway deaths over the period i question.

As a general rule of thumb, it is usually a bad ide to evaluate any time-series data without seeing then within the context of a longer period of time. Althougl it certainly looks as though highway death rates hav been dropping since 1965, what was the trend like ear lier? Figure 2 answers that question.

What does this new graph show us? The most strik ing observation is that the highway death rate has bee decreasing pretty steadily since 1925, the first year sta tistics are available. In fact, the decrease from 1965 tc 1984 is dwarfed by the reductions prior to that.

The observed decline in highway deaths betweer 1965 and 1984, then, does not prove that the consume activism of that period was the cause. Do the data prove that the consumer activism had no effect? Not at all. We cannot assume from the data of 1925–1965 that the long-term decline in highway deaths would have contin- ued — without the speed laws, seat belts, etc.

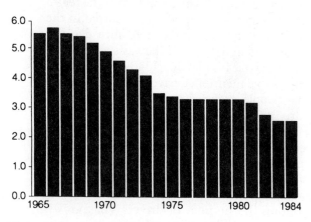

Figure 1. Highway deaths per 100 million miles driven: 1965–1984

Source: Data taken from US Bureau of the Census publications: *Statistical Abstract of the United Staes,* Washington, DC: US Government Printing Office, 1981, p. 622; 1982–1983, p. 615; 1984, p. 615; 1985, p. 599; and *Historical Statistics of the United States: Colonial Times to 1970,* Washington, DC: US Government Printing Office, 1975, pp. 719–720.

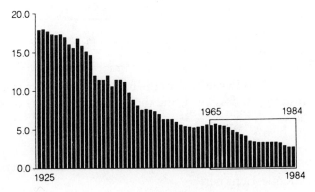

igure 2. Highway deaths per 100 million miles driven:
925–1984

urce: Data taken from US Bureau of the Census publications: *Statistical Abstract of the United
ates, Washington, DC: US Government Printing Office, 1981, p. 622; 1982–1983, p. 615; 1984, p. 615;
*85, p. 599; and *Historical Statistics of the United States: Colonial Times to 1970,* Washington, DC:
'S Government Printing Office, 1975, pp. 719–720.

There are legitimate reasons for suggesting that the
ong-term decline would not have continued. First, as
he death rate approaches zero, it begins to evidence a
loor-effect. It can never go below zero, and it's unlikely
hat it will ever even reach zero. There will probably be
*ome highway deaths as long as there are highways and
*rivers. It is quite possible that the highway death rate
vas about to level off at five to six per hundred million
niles driven.

Second, a closer inspection of the long-term graph
Figure 2) shows a small but steady increase in the death
ate from 1961 through 1964. Although that's too short
*a period to draw long-term conclusions from, it is cer-
ainly possible that the death rate was beginning to rise
gain.

If either of these possibilities was actually true, the
lata would suggest the consumer activism beginning
*round 1965 did, in fact, have an impact. At this point,
he data are inconclusive. I have pursued this example
or two reasons. First, I want to demonstrate that look-
*ng at the facts requires some sophistication and
*houghtfulness. Often, you need to look below the sur-
*ace to see what's going on.

Second, I want you to see that facts alone are seldom
*nough. Sociology is called logical/empirical because
*acts and reason go hand in hand. You need both.

1900 words

Write your ending time here: _____

Subtract your starting time: _____

Total time: _____

Check the Rate Chart in the back of the book to find how many words per minute you have read, and then record your score on the Progress Chart.

SQ3R

C. *Read.* Without looking back at the article, write the answers to your SQ3R questions here.

1. _____

2. _____

3. _____

Underline the main ideas and the supporting details in the article that you believe will be tested in the Comprehension Check.

Write in the *margin* short *notes* that will remind you of the main ideas and details you want to remember.

D. *Recite.* Now cover up the text of the article and use the marginal notes to test your memory of it. Check your underlining to see whether you forgot anything. Repeat this step until you are able to remember everything you underlined.

E. *Review.* This article is organized like a short textbook chapter. It is too short to break into sections, but if it were a long article, you might have had to divide it into sections. In that case, you would have done your major review immediately after you finished each section, again one week later, and then as often as needed to maintain your memory.

MAIN IDEA

Before going on to the Comprehension Check, and without looking back at the article, write one complete sentence stating the main idea of this article.

_____

_____

Your answer should be similar to the correct answer for question 2 in the Comprehension Check.

30

A Science of Society

Circle the letter before the best answer to each question below. Don't
look back at the article.

Subject and Main Idea
1. The subject of the article is
   a. sociology.
   b. social philosophy.
   c. critical thinking.
   d. social research.

2. The main idea of the article is that
   a. sociology generates a philosophy of social behavior.
   b. critical thinking is logical and empirical.
   c. sociology is a science of social life.
   d. research is a search for facts.

Details
3. Survey research always involves
   a. questionnaires.
   b. interviewers.
   c. telephones.
   d. computers.

4. The example concerning the effects of consumer activism on
   highways deaths is meant to show that
   a. it is not always simple to determine the facts.
   b. time-series data must be seen in the context of a longer time.
   c. some things can never be proven.
   d. consumer activism had no effect.

5. Experiments are generally performed
   a. in the streets.
   b. on the telephone.
   c. in the laboratory.
   d. in people's homes.

6. To draw valid conclusions from survey research,
    a. samples must be properly selected.
    b. computer data analysis is necessary.
    c. a whole population must be assessed.
    d. laboratory experiments may be required.

Inferences

7. In the article, the author uses the term *critical thinking* to refer to
    a. criticizing the quality of the writing we see.
    b. making valid inferences.
    c. making judgments about the author's qualifications.
    d. separating fact from opinion.

8. President Reagan probably stated that nuclear weapons caused 40 years of peace because he
    a. was unaware of the actual wars during the 40-year period.
    b. was distorting facts to get people to agree to the need for nuclear weapons.
    c. wanted his opponents to look bad.
    d. wanted to increase the budget deficit by additional spending on weapons.

9. The terms *logical* and *empirical* are approximately
    a. synonyms.
    b. antonyms.
    c. homonyms.
    d. acronyms.

10. The author implies that a concern with how a society should function is the job of the
    a. sociologist.
    b. social philosopher.
    c. consumer activist.
    d. researcher.

QUESTIONS FOR ANALYSIS AND APPLICATION

1. Look in a recent issue of a news magazine such as *Time* or *Newsweek*. Find three assertions that would probably fail an empirical test and explain why they would fail.

2. Describe a way to empirically test each of the following assertions:
    a. Senator X wants to freeze social security benefits.
    b. It's not a good idea to study with the radio on.
    c. Most Americans believe that Japanese cars are superior to American cars.

VOCABULARY IN CONTEXT
Multiple Choice
Circle the letter before the best definition of each underlined word.

1. The big decisions in life require a lot of deliberation.
   a. thought   b. preparedness   c. guesswork
   d. decisiveness

2. Having a valid driver's license is mandatory when driving a car.
   a. good idea   b. unnecessary   c. required   d. simple

3. When laboratory tests are inconclusive, a doctor will usually
   run more.
   a. frightening   b. unclear   c. poor   d. unsafe

4. China adopted a strict birth control policy because letting the
   population growth continue unabated would have led to disaster.
   a. lessened   b. uncontrolled   c. rewarded
   d. increasingly

5. It is controversial whether punishment is really a deterrent
   to crime.
   a. encouragement   b. discouragement   c. reward
   d. justification

6. The architecture of my house could be described as pseudo-
   Spanish.
   a. genuine   b. expensive   c. overdone   d. imitation

7. As of January 1, 1984, the Salt II limit on deployment of nuclear
   delivery vehicles was 2,250.
   a. placement   b. sending   c. building   d. elimination

Fill-in

Write the best word from this list in the blank in each sentence below:

sector   activism   deficit   per capita   buzzwords

median   empirical   keystones   arsenals

8. Common _____ used in business are
    interface, orchestrate, and *ASAP.*

9. _____ spending involves borrowing.

10. A _____ is one of three types of averages;
    the other two are the mean and the mode.

11. In the 1960s, Ralph Nader's _____
    concerning the dangers of driving compact cars led to new safety
    standards in the auto industry.

12. In 1980 the United States was fourteenth in

    _____ income, behind three Arab
    countries, nine West European countries, and Brunei.

13. The United States and Russia both have _____
    of nuclear weapons that could destroy the Earth several times.

14. The military _____ consumes up to
    15 percent of the gross national product of the major nations.

15. English and math skills are the _____
    of education.

16. Until people could conduct experiments from outer space, there

    was no _____ proof of Einstein's Theory
    of Relativity, $E = MC^2$.

SKILLS EXERCISE: SUMMARIZING

For explanation see p. 299

Use your marginal notes to write a brief summary of the article in sentence form.

SKILLS EXERCISE: TEXTBOOK GRAPHICS

1. Table 1 shows that in 1985
   a. the median gap in annual income between a high school graduate and a college graduate was nearly

      _____ .

   b. the difference in annual income between people who had some college and college graduates was more than

      _____ .

2. Figures 1 and 2 show that
   a. for each 100 million miles driven, highway deaths in 1975 were

      between _____ and _____ .

   b. the figure for 1925 was between _____ and _____ .

3. All the graphics in this article were obtained from

   _____ .

4. The same data can be presented in different graphic forms. The most common types of graphs are line, bar, and pie graphs. For example, the bar graph below is part of Figure 1 from the article with a line graph drawn over it. Note that the line graphs connects the midpoints of the bars.

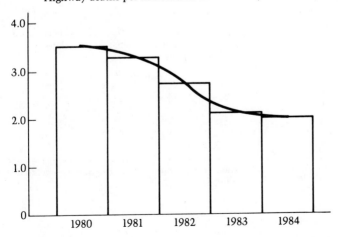

Highway deaths per 100 million miles driven, 1980–1984

Convert the information on the pie graph below to a line graph.

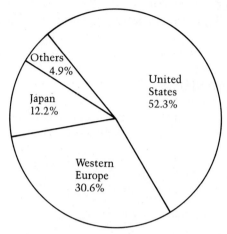

Market for computers installed worldwide, 1978

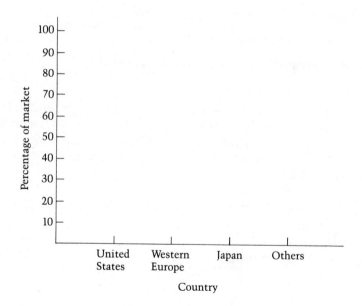

From information in Perry Edwards and Bruce Broadwell, *Data Processing: Computers in Action* (Belmont, Calif.: Wadsworth Publishing Co., 1979), p. 367.

RATE CHART

To find your reading rate, first look in the left-hand column of this chart to find the time it took you to read the article. Then look along that line until you come to the column headed by the number of words you read. Where the two lines cross, you will find a number indicating how many words per minute you have read. For example, if you read 1200 words in five minutes, you have read 240 WPM. Once you've found your score, enter it on the Progress Chart.

To find your reading rate for timings that do not appear on the chart, first compute your time in seconds. (Multiply the number of minutes by 60 and add the number of remaining seconds.) Then divide the number of words read by your time in seconds. Multiply the result by 60 to get back to minutes and seconds.

$$\text{WPM} = \frac{\text{Words read}}{\text{Time in seconds}} \times 60$$

Reading Time		Number of Words Read							
Min.	Sec.	900	1,000	1,050	1,150	1,200	1,450	1,600	1,700
	40	1,350	1,500	1,575					
	50	1,084	1,200	1,260	1,380	1,440			
1	00	900	1,000	1,050	1,150	1,200	1,450	1,371	1,457
1	10	769	855	897	983	1,026	1,243	1,200	1,275
1	20	677	752	789	865	902	1,090	1,066	1,133
1	30	600	667	700	767	800	967	958	1,020
1	40	539	599	629	689	719	868	800	850
1	50	492	546	574	628	656	792	687	729
2	00	450	500	525	575	600	725	599	638
2	10	415	461	484	530	553	668	533	567
2	20	386	429	451	494	515	622	480	510
2	30	360	400	420	460	480	580	436	464
2	40	337	375	393	431	449	543	400	425
2	50	318	353	371	406	424	512	370	392
3	00	300	333	350	383	400	483	343	364
3	20	270	300	315	345	360	435	320	340
3	40	245	272	286	313	327	395	300	319
4	00	225	250	263	287	300	322	267	283
4	30	200	222	233	256	267	322	267	283
5	00	180	200	210	230	240	290	246	268
5	30	164	189	191	209	218	264	229	243
6	00	150	167	175	192	200	242	213	227
7	00	129	143	150	164	171	207	200	212
8	00	113	125	131	144	150	181	188	200
9	00	100	111	117	128	133	161	177	189
10	00		100	105	115	120	145	160	170

Reading Time		Number of Words Read				
Min.	Sec.	1,900	2,200	2,600	2,700	2,800
1	40	1,138	1,320	1,560	1,620	1,680
2	00	950	1,100	1,300	1,350	1,400
2	20	815	943	1,114	1,157	1,200
2	40	712	825	975	1,012	1,050
3	00	633	733	867	900	933
3	20	571	660	780	810	840
3	40	518	600	709	736	764
4	00	475	550	650	675	700
4	20	439	508	600	623	646
4	40	407	471	557	579	600
5	00	380	440	520	540	560
5	20	356	413	487	506	525
5	40	335	388	459	476	560
6	00	317	367	433	450	467
6	30	292	338	400	415	431
7	00	271	314	371	386	400
7	30	253	293	347	360	373
8	00	237	275	325	338	350
8	30	224	259	306	318	329
9	00	211	245	289	300	311
10	00	190	220	260	270	280
11	00	173	200	236	245	255
12	00	158	183	217	225	233
13	00	146	169	200	208	215
14	00	136	157	186	193	200
15	00	127	147	173	180	187
16	00	119	137	162	169	175

OMPREHENSION CHART

◄ this chart, cross out the numbers of any questions you missed in the
omprehension Check. Your comprehension score is the total number
f questions you answered correctly. Remember to analyze your wrong
iswers so that you won't make the same mistakes in the future.

Article	Subject and Main Idea	Details	Inferences	Comprehension Score
Pretest	1 2	3 4 5 6	7 8 9 10	
1	1 2	3 4 5 6	7 8 9 10	
2	1 2	3 4 5 6	7 8 9 10	
3	1 2	3 4 5 6	7 8 9 10	
4	1 2	3 4 5 6	7 8 9 10	
5	1 2	3 4 5 6	7 8 9 10	
6	1 2	3 4 5 6	7 8 9 10	
7	1 2	3 4 5 6	7 8 9 10	
8	1 2	3 4 5 6	7 8 9 10	
9	1 2	3 4 5 6	7 8 9 10	
10	1 2	3 4 5 6	7 8 9 10	
11	1 2	3 4 5 6	7 8 9 10	
12	1 2	3 4 5 6	7 8 9 10	
13	1 2	3 4 5 6	7 8 9 10	
14	1 2	3 4 5 6	7 8 9 10	
15	1 2	3 4 5 6	7 8 9 10	
16	1 2	3 4 5 6	7 8 9 10	
17	1 2	3 4 5 6	7 8 9 10	
18	1 2	3 4 5 6	7 8 9 10	
19	1 2	3 4 5 6	7 8 9 10	
20	1 2	3 4 5 6	7 8 9 10	
21	1 2	3 4 5 6	7 8 9 10	
22	1 2	3 4 5 6	7 8 9 10	
23	1 2	3 4 5 6	7 8 9 10	
24	1 2	3 4 5 6	7 8 9 10	
25	1 2	3 4 5 6	7 8 9 10	
26	1 2	3 4 5 6	7 8 9 10	
27	1 2	3 4 5 6	7 8 9 10	
28	1 2	3 4 5 6	7 8 9 10	
29	1 2	3 4 5 6	7 8 9 10	
30	1 2	3 4 5 6	7 8 9 10	
Posttest	1 2	3 4 5 6	7 8 9 10	

PROGRESS CHART

At the bottom of the following chart, enter the date, your reading rate (in words per minute), and your comprehension score for each article you read. Then construct a graph by putting a dot in the square closes to your reading rate for each article. Make the graph by connecting the dots.

Your goal is to show improvement in rate with no loss in comprehension. A score of 80 percent comprehension is considered adequate for most purposes. However, even if you stay at the same reading rate for all 30 articles, you are still showing improvement. This is because the articles get harder in each section of the book. Don't worry if you see some dips as well as increases in your reading rate. Articles vary in difficulty because of the content, the vocabulary, your familiarity with the subject matter, and your level of interest. More difficult material should be read more slowly. However, if your reading rate appears to be dropping, you should discuss the problem with your instructor.

WPM

WPM	Prettest	1	2	3	4	5	6	7	8	9
1,000										
950										
925										
900										
850										
825										
800										
750										
725										
700										
675										
650										
625										
600										
575										
550										
525										
500										
475										
450										
425										
400										
375										
350										
325										
300										
275										
250										
225										
200										
175										
150										
125										
100										
Article	Prettest	1	2	3	4	5	6	7	8	9
Rate (WPM)										
Comprehension Score										
Date										

WPM

WPM											
1,000											
950											
925											
900											
850											
825											
800											
750											
725											
700											
675											
650											
625											
600											
575											
550											
525											
500											
475											
450											
425											
400											
375											
350											
325											
300											
275											
250											
225											
200											
175											
150											
125											
100											
Article	10	11	12	13	14	15	16	17	18	19	20
Rate (WPM)											
Comprehension Score											
Date											

WPM											
1,000											
950											
925											
900											
850											
825											
800											
750											
725											
700											
675											
650											
625											
600											
575											
550											
525											
500											
475											
450											
425											
400											
375											
350											
325											
300											
275											
250											
225											
200											
175											
150											
125											
100											
Article	21	22	23	24	25	26	27	28	29	30	Posttest
Rate (WPM)											
Comprehension Score											
Date											

Credits

Answers

Page 4. 1. *Raiders of the Lost Ark* 2. *The African Queen* 3. *The Bride of Frankenstein*

Page 5. 1. b 2. b 3. a

Page 6. 1. 2 2. 3b 3. 5

Page 7. Definition: to come to an end
Sentence: I had to move because my lease expired.

Page 8. 1. fus 2. vok 3. tract 4. or 5. pro 6. fus 7. mit 8. re
9. tract 10. sub

Page 9. 1. Comments 2. Fixed 3. Ghastly 4. At liberty (freed from a script) 5. Seeing
into

Page 18. 1. 5 2. Yes 3. No 4. Yes

Page 30. 1. a. Find the right answer. b. That's not logical. c. Follow
the rules. d. Be practical. e. Don't be foolish. f. Don't make
mistakes. g. That's not my area. h. I'm not creative. 2. No 3. Yes

Page 44. 1. Nonfiction 2. Seven 3. Yes

Page 58. 1. Teaches at UCLA 2. Quadriplegic student trying to join
Mr. Stussy's art class 3. He draws by holding the pencil in his teeth
4. An Oscar 5. He had died 6. Your answer should be similar to your answer to number 2 in the comprehension quiz.

Page 72. 1. The seven are the number 13, walking under ladders, getting out of bed on the
wrong side, spilling salt, breaking mirrors, meeting black cats, and whistling. 2.
Yes 3. Yes – cats

471